Designing Interactive Multimedia

Designing Interactive Multimedia

Arch C. Luther

BANTAM BOOKS
NEW YORK • TORONTO • LONDON • SYDNEY • AUCKLAND

DESIGNING INTERACTIVE MULTIMEDIA
A Bantam Book / October 1992

All rights reserved.
Copyright © 1992 by Multiscience Press, Inc.
Cover design by Edward Smith Design, Inc.

No part of this book may be reproduced or transmitted
in any form or by any means, electronic or mechanical,
including photocopying, recording, or by any information
storage and retrieval system, without permission in writing
from the publisher.
For information address: Bantam Books.

*Throughout the book, trade names and trademarks of some
companies and products have been used, and no such uses
are intended to convey endorsement of or other affiliations with the book.*

ISBN 0-553-09093-3
Library of Congress Catalog Card Number 92-73267

Published simultaneously in the United States and Canada

Bantam Books are published by Bantam Books, a division of Bantam Doubleday
Dell Publishing Group, Inc. Its trademark, consisting of the words "Bantam Books"
and the portrayal of a rooster, is Registered in U.S. Patent and Trademark Office
and in other countries. Marca Registrada, Bantam Books, Inc., 666 Fifth Avenue,
New York, New York 10103.

PRINTED IN THE UNITED STATES OF AMERICA

0 9 8 7 6 5 4 3 2 1

Contents

Preface xiii

Acknowledgments xvii

1 Introduction 1

What is Multimedia? 2
  Analog vs. Digital Multimedia 2
Interactivity 3
Creating Multimedia 4
Uses of Multimedia 5
  Multimedia for Business Presentations 5 • Multimedia for Training or Education 6 • Multimedia for Information Delivery or Exchange 8 • Multimedia for Sales and Merchandising 10 • Multimedia with Productivity Applications 10

2 Equipment and Software for Multimedia 13

Data Demands of Multimedia 14
Hardware for Multimedia 16
  The System CPU 17 • The System RAM 18 • The Video Display 19 • Audio System 21 • Mass Storage 21 • CD-ROM 22 • Coprocessors 24
The Multimedia PC 25
Special Multimedia Hardware 25
  DVI Technology 26 • Performance Parameters of DVI Technology 28
Additional Hardware for Authoring 30
Software for Multimedia 30
  Operating System Software 31 • Application Programs for Multimedia 36 • Distributing Applications 36 • Authoring Systems for Multimedia 37 • MEDIAscript OS/2 Desktop Edition 38
Multimedia Authoring Workstation 39

3 Objectives for Multimedia 41

Typical Multimedia Projects 42

Understanding the User 43

Multimedia for Selling 44

    Product Overview 44 • Answer Customers' Questions 45 • Specify the Exact Product 46 • Provide a Price Quotation 46 • Ask for the Order 46 • Order Entry 47

Multimedia for Teaching 47

    Getting the Student's Attention 47 • Presenting the Subject 48 • Student Questions and Answers 48 • Testing 49 • Student Record Keeping 49

Multimedia for Information Delivery 49

    Attract the User 50 • Teach How to Use the Application 50 • Making Information Available 51 • Closing Out the Session 52

Multimedia Used for Entertainment 52

The Content 53

Writing Down Objectives 54

Video Camcorder Selling Application 54

4 Multimedia Architectures 57

Building Blocks 57

    Presenting Activity 58 • Controlling Activity 59

Topology 59

    Linear Presentation 59 • A Data-Driven Engine 60 • Hierarchical Menus 63 • Information Retrieval 64 • Hypermedia 64 • Simulation 65

5 Multimedia Presentations 67

Interactivity in Presentations 67

    Canned Presentations 68 • Live Speaker Support Presentations 68 • End User Interactive Presentations 69

Steps of a Presentation 70

    Getting the User's Attention 70 • Setting the Mood 70 • Presenting the Material 71 • Answering Questions 73 • Concluding the Presentation 73

6 Using an Authoring Program 75

What Does an Authoring System Do? 76

Programming in Authoring Systems 77

Branching 78 • Variables 78 • Looping 79 • Conditions 79 • Nesting 80

Choosing an Authoring System 80

The MEDIAscript Multimedia Server 81

The MEDIAscript Authoring Interface 83

Asset File Management Considerations 83

MEDIAscript Projects 84

Starting the AUI 84

On-Line Help 85 • Opening a Project for Authoring 85 • MEDIAscript Script Window 87 • MEDIAscript Objects 89 • Features Common to All Object Dialogs 90 • MEDIAscript Capture Tools 103 • The MEDIAscript Organizer 103

Sample of an Authored Script 104

7 User Interfaces 107

Types of Multimedia User Interfaces 108

User Task Analysis 109

Consistency 110

Simplicity 110

Metaphors 111

User Control 111

The Television-Style Interface—Touch Screens 112

Selection Metaphors 113

Immediate Feedback 115

Windowing Environments 115

8 Designing an Application's Style 119

The Ingredients of Good Style 119

The Television Look or Style 120

The Computer Look or Style 121

Screen Design 121

How Much in One Screen? 122 • Screen Elements 123 • Dynamic Effects 137 • Layout of Screens 138

Elements of Aural Style 139

Style for a Business Presentation 140

Style for a Selling Application 142

Style in a Training Application 144

Style Maintenance 144

9 Multimedia Assets 147

Asset Files 147

Audio Assets 148

MIDI 148 • Audio Capture 149

The DVI .AVS File Format 150

Motion Video Assets 150

Image Assets 152

Animation Assets 154

Macromind Director 154 • Autodesk Animator 155 • MEDIAscript OS/2 155

Graphics and Text Assets 155

Data Assets 156

Using the Assets 157

Data Usage 158 • Time Schedule 158 • Existing Assets 159 • Asset-Making Facilities and Skills 160 • Special Needs of the Application 160 • Available Funds 160

10 Producing Your Own Audio 163

Equipment for Audio Capture and Processing 163

Basics of Audio Production 164

Achieving Audio-Video Synchronization 166

Equipment Setup 167

Audio Production Tips 169

Setting Audio Levels 169 • Microphone Technique 170 • Editing Technique 172 • Mixing Technique 173

Digital Audio Capture 175

11 Producing Your Own Still Images 179

DVI Images 179
  DVI Image Files 181
File Format Conversion 182
Image Compression 183
Equipment for Digitizing Images 183
  Capture with a Video Camera 184 • Doing the Capture 187 • Capturing Live Scenes 189
Image Processing 190
Image Scanners 191
Images from Paint Programs 191
  Text and Graphics 191

12 Producing Your Own Motion Video 193

Characteristics of Motion Video 193
Motion Video Compression 194
Video Production 196
Video Postproduction 196
Planning for Video 197
The Shoot 199
Using RTV Compression 200
Using PLV Compression 202
  Digital Postproduction 202

13 Animation 205

Frame Animation 205
Cel Animation 208
Animation with Graphics 209
Animated Transitions 211

14 Completing an Application 213

The Planning Process 214
Creating the Pets Application 216

x *Designing Interactive Multimedia*

Who Will Use the Application? 216 • A Treatment for the Pets Application 216 • Data List for Pets 217 • Flowchart for Pets 218 • Style Design of the Pets Application 219 • User Interface Design for Pets 220 • Authoring Approach for the Pets Application 220 • Design of the Screens for Pets 223 • Design of Presentations for Pets 225 • Estimating for Development of the Pets Application 226 • Creating the Main Script for Pets 227 • Creating the Species Script for the Pets Application 233 • Creating the Audio/Image Presentation Script for Pets 236 • Creating the Text/Image Presentation Script for Pets 238

Planning for the Camcorder Application 239

Users for the Camcorder Application 239 • Treatment for the Camcorder Application 239 • List of Data for the Camcorder Application 239 • Flowchart for the Camcorder Application 239 • Style for the Camcorder Application 241 • User Interface for the Camcorder Application 241 • Authoring Approach for the Camcorder Application 241 • Data List for the Camcorder Application 242 • Screen Designs for Camcorder Application 242 • Presentation Design for Camcorder Application 242 • Estimate for the Camcorder Application 244• Features Engine Script for the Camcorder Application 245 • The Specifications Presentation 248

The Soldering Training Application 249

Users of the Soldering Application 249 • Treatment for the Soldering Application 250 • Data List for the Soldering Application 251 • Flowchart for the Soldering Application 251 • Style for the Soldering Application 252 • User Interface for the Soldering Application 252 • Authoring Approach for the Soldering Application 253 • Data List for the Soldering Application 253 • Screen Design for the Soldering Application 253 • Presentation Designs for the Soldering Application 254 • Estimate for the Soldering Application 254

Distributing your Application 255

Floppy Disk Distribution 255 • Hard Disk Distribution 255 • CD-ROM Distribution 256 • Writeable Optical Distribution 257 • Digital Tape Distribution 257 • Distribution by Computer Network 258

15 Where Do We Go from Here? 261

Ingredients of a Forecast 262

The Need for Volume 262 • Standards 263 • IC Chip Technology 264 • PC Manufacturing 265 • Add-in Boards 265 • Operating

System Software 266 • Software Developers and Publishers 266 • New Businesses 267 • The Television Industry 268 • Television Broadcasting 270 • Audio Production and the Music Industry 271 • Uses of Multimedia 272

Now for the Forecast 272

Appendix A: Multimedia Hardware 275

Appendix B: Multimedia Software 289

Glossary 293

Bibliography 309

Index 313

Preface

"The personal computer will never be the same."

That remark was made in 1987 by a computer executive upon seeing DVI Technology video and audio playing from an IBM PC/AT at the David Sarnoff Research Center in Princeton, NJ. In the five years since, that capability has moved from the research laboratory into the mainstream of the personal computer industry. It has been joined by other technologies for audio, video, and animation. Today, all of this is called *multimedia*, and it promises soon to be common on desktops, in schools, and in homes around the world.

Multimedia is exciting when you see it in applications for training, information delivery, sales, entertainment, or education; but the *real* excitement comes when you learn to create your own multimedia to enhance your work. That is now possible, and you don't have to be a technical expert—this book will teach you how to do it all.

I assume that readers of this book have seen or read enough about multimedia to have an interest in learning how to use it in their work, but I do not assume any other knowledge of multimedia. I also expect that the reader is a computer user who is familiar with computer terminology and knows how to run various application programs.

I do not expect the reader to know much about formal programming, but any of that kind of knowledge is not going to hurt. Building a multimedia application cannot avoid some of the concepts of programming—flow charts, loops, variables, or condition statements. These have to show up, regardless of how powerful an environment you have. But when these concepts are first encountered in the book, they are explained to accommodate nonprogrammer readers.

As the momentum of multimedia is building, many different new products are being introduced. By itself, this would confuse the market and probably limit the growth; but all the new products are accompanied by a concerted industry effort to develop standards that will assure that all the products can work together in systems. The completion and universal adoption of the standards is crucial if the rate of growth is to be maintained.

The current proliferation of multimedia products makes it very dificult to write a book like this one—there's no way that I can cover all of the different approaches to everything. Therefore, I decided at the outset that I wouldn't try. When it comes to hardware and software, I discuss some of the fundamental considerations in choosing an approach, and then I use only one approach for my examples.

The choice of which hardware and software to focus on was easy for me—I used the ones that I think are best and that I know the most about, which just happen to be hardware and software in whose development I participated (DVI Technology hardware and MEDIAscript software). However, you will find that most of the presentation in the book is general, and that it will apply to hardware or software other than the ones used by my examples.

One of the challenges of multimedia development is that there are so many different disciplines involved in a project. In large organizations that develop multimedia applications, this is handled by having one or more experts for each discipline. A multimedia project team may include:

- a project manager,
- audio engineers,
- video engineers,
- computer engineers,
- producers,
- directors,
- graphic artists,
- instructional designers,
- script writers,
- programmers,
- publishers, and
- probably others.

This is not the kind of project this book is about. Here, I expect my readers to be doing all of the above things themselves. I fully accept the challenge to teach you how to handle all these disciplines. This breadth of skill is one of the excitements of multimedia.

If, however, you are a participant in an organization doing large multimedia projects, this book is still for you. It will give you a taste of all the parts of a project, not just the part that you do. It should increase your understanding of the overall task.

The book is organized as follows:

- Chapter 1 introduces you to multimedia and what it can do.
- Chapter 2 is an overview of hardware and software products for multimedia. This is further supported by Appendices A and B.

- Chapter 3 covers top-level planning of a multimedia application.
- Chapters 4 and 5 discuss planning and architectures in more detail.
- Chapter 6 is an introduction to multimedia authoring and describes MEDIAscript OS/2 in detail.
- Chapters 7 and 8 discuss the design issues of user interfaces and style.
- Chapter 9 introduces you to multimedia assets—audio, video, images, and data.
- Chapters 10, 11, and 12 discuss in detail the production of assets.
- Chapter 13 discusses animation.
- Chapter 14 covers the overall assembly of an application and discusses three examples in detail.
- In Chapter 15, I wave my hands in the air about the exciting future of multimedia.

Each of the disciplines involved in multimedia has its own jargon. To make you look like an expert in all of these disciplines, you must know the jargon and what it means. To help you become familiar with the terminology, whenever a new term is introduced for the first time, it is italicized, and a definition follows. All of these items are also listed in a Glossary (Appendix C). The Glossary entries are stand-alone definitions, which sometimes go beyond the definitions in the text.

I have always been disturbed by the need to use compound personal pronouns such as he/she or her/his to recognize both genders, since the English language doesn't provide anything simpler for this. In this book, I have adopted a simpler approach that I hope won't disturb any of you. In odd-numbered chapters, the personal pronouns are male, and in even-numbered chapters they are female. So, if you are upset with my use of personal pronouns, just read on to the next chapter.

It has been almost ten years since I jumped into what we now call multimedia computing. During that time, my interest and excitement has steadily increased. As you read this book, I hope you will get a taste of my excitement and begin feeling it yourself. I sincerely believe that working with multimedia is the most rewarding thing you can do with a personal computer.

Arch C. Luther
July 1992

Acknowledgments

The successful completion of a book project involves the interest and work of many people in addition to the author. This book is no exception. I would like to acknowledge the support of the following people: Tom Vreeland, John Scolio, and Kirk Marple at Network Technology Corporation; Alan Rose of Intertext Publications; Kim Fryer at Bantam Professional Books; Jay Silber of Jay Silber Productions; and Mike Palmer at American Management Systems, Inc.

In addition, the following companies provided photographs or other material that are important additions to the book: Howtek Corporation, Intel Corporation, Panasonic Company (who provided materials used in the Camcorder application, which was developed by me solely as an example for this book), and Yamaha Corporation.

Finally, the whole project would not have been finished without the constant help of Kayle Luther (my daughter), who handled all of the details of drawings, formatting, and printing of the manuscript. She worked with me full-time throughout the project and her support was essential.

1

Introduction

medium—an intervening thing through which a force acts or an effect is produced; any means, agency, or instrumentality; specif., a means of communication.
Webster's New World Dictionary, 1988

Communication is so pervasive in human existence that we seldom give thought to the means or "medium" of communication that we may be utilizing or experiencing at any moment. From face-to-face personal interaction, to reading books, listening to stereo, looking at photographs, talking on the telephone, watching television, going to the movies, working at our computers—we just do what is required without considering that each of these is a different means of communication—a different medium. Our daily lives are really multimedia experiences.

Each communication medium has its own set of characteristics and limitations. For example, face-to-face communication is effective as long as the communicators can actually be face-to-face; if one party is in California and the other is in New York, face-to-face just won't work. In that case we can use the telephone, which works well as long as it is not important to see the other party. Another example: Photography is valuable to show how a distant environment looks, but it does nothing to show us how that environment sounds, smells, or feels. Sometimes there's no substitute for being there.

Motion pictures and television provide moving pictures and sound; the combination significantly increases the effectiveness with which a distant environment is conveyed. When these media are used well and artistically, they can have tremendous impact on our emotions. In the sense that these systems utilize two media (moving pictures and sound) they are multimedia systems.

WHAT IS MULTIMEDIA?

The word *multimedia* has been used to mean a lot of different things. It was first associated with presentations that used more than one medium, such as 35mm slides and audio, or slides and moving picture film. In computers, the first "multimedia" systems combined only text and graphics. All current personal computers are multimedia systems under that definition! Since then, the capability of computers and the definition of multimedia have both been steadily broadening.

In this book, we broaden that definition even more—we expect that a multimedia system is capable of all the usual computer presentation types (text, graphics, animation, etc.) *plus* recorded real audio, full-screen motion video of real scenes, and photographic-quality still images. Such a multimedia system can do all the things you normally expect to see on television, while being a computer at the same time and displaying computer objects on the same screen. Anything less than that is not a complete multimedia system.

Analog vs. Digital Multimedia

Our definition of a multimedia computer recognizes that a computer is inherently a *digital* device and that multimedia peripherals also should be digital. Many multimedia hardware devices that have been connected to computers, such as audio systems, television receivers, video cameras, laser video disc players, and motion picture film, are *analog* devices, which means that they respond to continuous ranges of values for color, intensity, volume, etc. Because of their analog nature, they can never be fully integrated into the computer system itself; they will always be separate hardware and cannot benefit from the digital storage and processing capabilities of the computer.

In contrast, a digital computer is designed to work with discrete values of things, and while this is unnatural in nature (everything there is analog), it makes possible the electronic processing and mass storage required in a computer. Recent developments have produced low-cost digital versions of all the analog devices mentioned above, and one can now build an *all-digital* multimedia system. In this book we focus on *digital* multimedia devices and systems.

Computer multimedia is the combination of digital audio, digital still images, digital video, and all the other digital information that a computer can display or present so well: graphics, animation, data, and text. Having everything digital offers major advantages:

- All materials can be stored and distributed on standard computer media such as floppy disks, hard disks, digital tape, CD-ROM, computer networks, etc.
- The computer's digital processing power can be used to manipulate any part of the multimedia presentation.
- Digital multimedia components can plug right inside of the computer, so you have one box that does everything, without any external components or wires.
- Digital multimedia hardware will eventually be built into most PC systems.
- Everything about digital multimedia is programmable, so you can have it any way you like through software.

INTERACTIVITY

The other main ingredient of multimedia is *interactivity*, which means that the user is in control—what the user sees and hears is the result of choices and decisions he has made. The ultimate example of this is a video game. The player is presented with exciting visual and aural stimuli and must respond aggressively to continue the game. Here interactivity is the major appeal; the video and sound presentations exist to support the interactivity. Although our children would surely dispute the statement, there are many potentially more meaningful uses for interactivity between a user and a multimedia computer.

An interactive experience that we are all familiar with is driving an automobile, where the driver is in control. There usually is not a computer involved, at least not visible to us, but the interactivity with the visual, aural, and physical environment is complete.

There are also situations that are not interactive—a roller coaster, for example. The experience may be extreme, but the most we can hope for is that the car remains on the track and that we remain in the car. We have no control. A similar situation, but more comfortable, is flying in a commercial airliner. Again, we have no control—there is no interactivity.

The point is, interactivity requires control. We always feel comfortable when we are in control, and an environment of control makes us more receptive to new information and new situations. Also, interactivity and control makes the application more fun. An important requirement for multimedia is that it must create an interactive environment in which the user *will* be in control and *will* be comfortable with it. This element of multimedia is called the *user interface*, which is the subject of Chapter 6.

Therefore, the ingredients of multimedia as defined here are:

- a computer with all its usual capabilities,
- recorded digital audio capability,
- recorded digital video capability,
- digital still image capability, and
- interactivity.

CREATING MULTIMEDIA

Multimedia applications or projects are created by assembling the ingredients listed above in a way that suits the particular task at hand, whether it is training, entertainment, information delivery, or education. This process is called *authoring*, and it can be done by a large team of experts, or it can be done by a single person. Of course, a large team can create a larger and more sophisticated application and certainly do it quicker than a single person, but there are numerous multimedia needs that a single individual can readily handle alone. Those kinds of applications are the focus of this book.

Most multimedia applications up to now have been created by teams of experts; this is because so many different skills are required and because the hardware and software are expensive and difficult to master and use. That situation is now changing with the availability of lower-cost hardware and with software that simplifies the tasks of authoring. Therefore, there now is a need for a book like this that teaches all the different skills in one place and presents them at a level suitable for individual non-expert authors. This will greatly broaden the use of multimedia.

Someone who is going to tackle a multimedia application all by himself has to know about a lot of different skills that traditionally have been performed by experts. These include:

- audio production and postproduction
- video production and postproduction
- computer programming
- artistic design
- graphic art
- scriptwriting
- image processing
- user interface design
- multimedia architecture

and probably many others associated with the specific end use of the application. Of course, one person is not going to know as much about each of these subjects as a team of experts, but it is perfectly reasonable for you to know enough to do a credible job in all of these areas in your own multimedia. Read on!

USES OF MULTIMEDIA

There are many uses for multimedia that have already been exploited, and many more will appear as the community of multimedia users and authors grows. Here are some examples of multimedia applications, with discussion of how they apply to the individual-author environment we are discussing here.

Multimedia for Business Presentations

Multimedia is ideal for providing visual support to a live speaker presenting information before audiences of any size. The ease of creating exciting visuals with multimedia and the flexibility of presenting them will make business presentations become a major market for multimedia systems and software. Since the live speaker is providing most of the sound, there is not much use for the audio capability of multimedia in this application, but it is there when it is necessary to play prerecorded audio during a presentation.

Business presentations today are dominated by the use of overhead transparencies and 35mm film slides. Although computers are used widely for creation of both slides and overheads, these media have limitations, as shown by Table 1.1.

This writer has had a lot of experience doing high-end multimedia presentations for business executives who had previously used 35mm slides for their visuals. These people quickly learned of the flexibility of multimedia, which led them to deliberately pay less attention to their presentation until the last minute—often at the site of the meeting on the evening before the talk. At that time, the speech writer and I would meet with the executive and finalize the presentation, using a store of material that we had prepared ahead of time. The result was that I often had to work through much of the night to make changes in the material, but I was always able to complete the visuals in time. The executives really appreciated this, and it was a great saver of their time. This same advantage applies when the executive is doing his own multimedia, but of course the executive alone will not be able to do anything as elaborate or professional as when he has professional speech writers and presentation people.

	Overheads	35mm Slides	Multimedia
Creation	Design on computer, requires color printing	Design on computer, requires photolab	Design on computer
Changes	Requires reprint of transparency	Requires going back to photolab	Change on computer
Time needed to create or change	Hours	Days	Minutes
Presentation style	Unprofessional	Professional but limited flexibility	Professional
Audio	No	No	Yes
Video	No	No	Yes

Table 1.1 Characteristics of traditional presentation media

The interactivity of multimedia is valuable in a business presentation to cause things to happen on cue during the speech, and it can also be used to select backup material to display during question or discussion sessions following a formal speech.

Multimedia for Training or Education

The basic principle of education or training is that the student *sees* the subject more effectively than when the student only reads or hears about the subject. When the student actually *works* with the subject (interacts with it), it is even more effective for learning. With an interactive multimedia environment, learning by seeing and doing is a reality. A further advantage of using an interactive computer for training is that it is a one-on-one environment—one student and one computer. The student works by himself and at his own speed. Training can also be done at the student's convenience—any time of day or night. The result is more effective, lower-cost training.

Interactive training by a computer is not a new thing—it has been used widely for more than a decade under the name of computer-based training (CBT). The techniques for CBT have been highly developed and proven in thousands of applications. In fact, CBT has been the spawning ground for multimedia. CBT systems that could deliver real audio and video have been built using a collection of different types of hardware to accomplish what we can do today with a single computer system. These early multimedia systems typically used a computer with a laser video disc player for still and motion images, audio equipment for audio, and special computer boards to overlay computer text and graphics over the images. This collection of hardware was required because the video and audio were *analog* devices, while the computer is a *digital* device. The two technologies do not mix easily. Today's multimedia systems are more integrated, compact, and less expensive because the audio and video are now also digital, and all of the information is stored, processed, and controlled by one computer.

An example of a multimedia training application is the Dash 8 program developed by Jay Silber Productions, Inc., of Collegeville, PA, for FlightSafety International. This program is used for part of the training for certification of airline pilots who are checking out on the DeHavilland Dash 8 commuter aircraft. Figure 1.1 shows some screens from this program. The pilot is presented with a menu of subjects that he will have to complete to qualify for the aircraft. Each of the major subsystems of the aircraft is included. Training modules for each subject are presented, and in most cases a simulated control panel is shown on which the pilot operates the controls and sees the resulting actions in the other instruments and displays of the panel. Paths are available at all times so the pilot can exit the current module back to the menus, or the current module can be repeated or reviewed. The computer also keeps track of the progress of each student and can verify that each module has been completed successfully. The system also includes a linked text database that provides the student access to the FlightSafety training manuals, the manufacturer's operating manual, and the FAA Approved Flight Manual. This application was authored in DVI Technology, with MEDIAscript DOS Edition software. It was done by a team of people at Jay Silber Productions, Inc. Because of the large amount of data and the number of special simulations, this application is much too large for a single author. However, the techniques employed are applicable to smaller, single-author projects.

The Dash 8 application is in operation at a number of sites around the world. Because of the need for this kind of application to be constantly updated with new information or directives, a modem network is used

8   *Designing Interactive Multimedia*

Figure 1.1 Dash 8 pilot training application. Screens courtesy of Jay Silber Productions, Inc./FlightSafety International.

for regular updating of all sites by telephone. This is an important advantage of digital multimedia—updates can be accomplished using any of the many forms of digital communication.

Multimedia for Information Delivery or Exchange

You have probably seen computer-based information kiosks located in airports, shopping malls, or government buildings. These public-access systems present and gather a wide range of valuable information by interacting with their users. Most of these systems today are based on a combination of analog and digital equipment as described above for CBT systems; and although they certainly work, they pose many problems of design, cost, logistics, and reliability. Future public-access kiosks will enjoy rapidly expanding use by taking advantage of all-digital multimedia.

An example of a modern multimedia information kiosk is found in the Cellular Information Center (CIC), developed by the American Management Systems, Inc. (AMS) Multimedia Lab, Arlington, VA. (AMS is a leader in helping clients strengthen performance through the creative application of information technology.) The CIC utilizes interactive

Introduction 9

Figure 1.2 CIC information kiosk. Screens provided by American Management Systems, Inc.

multimedia to create a user-friendly interface to an otherwise complex computer system; it helps its users understand cellular telecommunications and available options for utilizing this convenient form of portable communication. Figure 1.2 shows some CIC screens.

To the user, the CIC appears to be an easy-to-use intelligent television, an illusion heightened by its touch screen input and the use of photographic images for control buttons. Behind the scenes, however, is another story—the CIC is actually an interface to certain portions of AMS's Mobile 2000™, a large-scale mainframe-based customer service and accounting application for cellular service providers. A typical Mobile 2000 installation may serve hundreds of extensively trained, highly skilled users, and process business data accounting for hundreds of millions of dollars in cellular service revenues. Through the user-friendly CIC front end, a cellular firm's existing or potential customers (including the untrained general public) can easily and safely interact with this sophisticated system.

Implemented using DVI Technology and authored with MEDIAscript OS/2 Desktop Edition, the CIC project has shown that the all-digital approach provides many benefits for information exchange applications.

Once a kiosk is deployed, perhaps in a shopping center, all data exchanges and updates are done using a cellular modem data link. Based on usage statistics gathered in real time, new information and interface options can be downloaded and tested, without requiring a technician's visit to the shopping center to swap video discs or CD-ROMs.

Multimedia for Sales and Merchandising

The same capability that is used for information delivery can also be placed at a point-of-sale (POS) to provide the information needed by a consumer who is considering a purchase. The characteristics and options of the product are described in the presentation, the user may ask questions and get answers, and pricing of the exact product desired by the customer can be calculated. Once the customer is satisfied with the product choice and its pricing, an order can be processed, payment method selected, and the delivery of the product can be authorized. In principle, no human salesperson needs to be involved. This method of sale is particularly suited to products that the customer does not need to "try on" or test.

An ideal POS application of digital multimedia is the marketing of recorded video tapes (movies). An information kiosk contains a database of the movies available, and also has brief video clips or trailers for each one. The customer can select tapes he is interested in by a variety of means, including search of the database by subject, actor or director's name, class of movie, or many other methods. Once the selection has been narrowed down, the customer can look at the trailers for the chosen movies, and when he has made final selections, the movies can be either rented or bought. Again, the kiosk can handle the ordering transaction, and the delivery of the product is authorized. The creation of the structure for this kind of application could be a single-author project, but the implementation of the full database of video clips and text data for the movie library would require several supporting people.

Multimedia with Productivity Applications

The principal use of computers in business is to run *productivity* applications—word processors, spreadsheets, databases, or planning applications. There are many opportunities in which multimedia capability would be valuable in these applications. For example, let's say that you have just prepared a spreadsheet that is a report of the sales for your department last month. Now you have to write a letter which explains the spreadsheet to the higher management of the company. Instead of doing that, simply pick up a microphone and record your comments with multimedia. Then hook this audio clip up to one of the cells of the spreadsheet; when that cell is clicked, the audio will play and explain your spreadsheet. This is possible today even with applications not designed for multimedia. It is done through a technique known as *interprocess communication*, which is a feature of the latest computer operating systems.

A special class of training in which multimedia has important advantages is on-line help or tutorials, which are provided with most major computer applications today. These systems are largely text-based, although the use of rich *hypertext* is becoming more common. In a hypertext environment, the user can click on a word or phrase and immediately go into deeper and more detailed information about the subject selected. However, these systems will become even richer when multimedia is used to add audio and video help in the same hypertext fashion (so it becomes hyper*media*).

While the text database of an on-line help system may contain all the information a user will ever need, it is difficult to present it in a friendly way, especially to a user who is not an experienced computer user. With multimedia, the cold text can be replaced by a warm human voice (audio) in most places, and where it will help, the presentation can also include motion video and sound or animations to explain confusing concepts. The result is that the user perceives the entire application to be more friendly and easier to learn and operate.

CHAPTER SUMMARY

Multimedia is a computer with real audio, real motion video, and real images. It is all-digital, requires interactivity, and is already used. Multimedia also has a future and is fun. And *everyone* in business should know how to use it.

2

Equipment and Software for Multimedia

The number of devices on an integrated circuit chip will double every two years.

The above statement is attributed to Gordon Moore of Intel Corporation and is known in the semiconductor industry as Moore's law. It articulates the reason for the continued cost reduction of electronic functionality that has occurred over the last 25 years. This progression is a result of constant industry efforts to pack semiconductor devices tighter and tighter and recognizes that the technological limits have been and will continue to be pushed back.

Moore's law has taken us from the early calculators through the first personal desktop computers to the mainframe power boxes that sit on our desks today. In spite of inflation, prices of computing devices have continuously gone down. And believe it or not, this trend is expected to continue past the year 2000! A state-of-the art integrated circuit today has 1,000,000 devices on it. In the year 2000, an integrated circuit may contain as many as 100,000,000 devices. The entire existence of the personal computer industry is a result of this progression; without this cost reduction, we could not afford to have such power on our desktops, nor would it fit there.

This steady downward trend of computing cost is also what has made digital multimedia possible. Multimedia poses great demands for computing power, and today's machines have just barely come up to the task; however, in only a few years, PCs will do multimedia in a breeze. Even though multimedia today may seem to be slightly impractical, that situation will rapidly change over the next few years, and it is not too soon for us to get on the bandwagon. What we do today will cost half as much in two years, a quarter as much in four years, etc. But much of the cost reduction will not be directed to making systems cheaper—it will go toward making them more powerful at the same or slightly lower cost. So don't give up on multimedia because of today's cost or performance limitations.

As defined in Chapter 1, multimedia is not new, it is just becoming more practical, more reliable, and lower in cost. The same can be said for the hardware required by multimedia; most of it is standard personal computer equipment, although it usually pushes the technical limits of what is currently available. This applies to PCs, hard drives, displays, etc. In those categories, the faster it is, the more storage it has, and (to a certain extent) the higher resolution it has, the better it is for multimedia. But the market for these items is rapidly growing, which will lead to volume-related price reductions (above and beyond Moore's law, by the way).

This chapter covers the considerations of hardware and software in detail, but without getting too technical. The material is intended primarily for non-technical readers; it will bring you on board so you can understand some of the technical aspects of multimedia. If you want more technical information than this, please consult either the appendices at the back of this book, manufacturers' literature, or user manuals.

DATA DEMANDS OF MULTIMEDIA

Before discussing the many varieties of hardware, we need to establish a baseline of things to look for in a PC system intended for multimedia use. What makes multimedia so demanding?

The demands largely come from the needs of dynamic video presentation. Every computer has a video display, but a multimedia computer really puts the video display through its paces with rapidly changing complex images. This means that the system must be able to rapidly retrieve video display information from mass storage, process it, and pass it to the video display subsystem for presentation. Sometimes this has to happen as fast as 30 times a second to create an adequate representation of smooth, fast motion. Higher video display quality (higher resolution, higher number of colors) makes this requirement even more demanding. Further, video data files can get so large that they become impractical without the use of *video compression*, which uses computer processing to remove redundancy from video images, thereby drastically reducing the data requirements. This adds substantially to the processing load. As described later in this chapter, these issues ultimately lead to using special hardware for multimedia video display.

To assign a few numbers to the needs of multimedia video display: A VGA display screen (VGA is the most commonly used computer screen format today) has 640 pixels (pixels are individual points of color in the image) across the screen and 480 lines of pixels from top to bottom of the screen. That is a total of 307,200 pixels for one image. The horizontal and vertical pixel counts (640×480) determine the *resolution* of the display sytem, which is its ability to display fine details in the image. To turn this number into a quantity of data, we must specify the number of different colors that could be displayed by each pixel. For example, a 16-color display (which is also the most commonly used format but does not make a very realistic picture), uses 4 bits of data for each pixel, or 1 byte of data for each two pixels. Thus, one screen of 16-color VGA uses 153,600 bytes of data (640 × 480/2).

A more realistic color image that begins to look like a photograph (which is what we want for multimedia) requires at least 32,768 colors or more. This takes 2 bytes of data for each pixel (16 bits per pixel, which actually will deliver 65,536 colors if all 16 bits are used for color data). Such an image at VGA resolution will occupy four times as much storage as above—614,400 bytes. An even better color system uses 24 bits per pixel, or 921,600 bytes for one image. A 24-bit system can display 16,777,216 colors, which is enough to accurately represent any natural image or photograph.

To produce smooth motion video using computer images, we have to display new images at least 15 times per second (30 times a second is even better). For the 16-bit VGA format image described above, 15 images per second works out to 9.2 megabytes of data *per second*, or an unbelievable 553 megabytes per minute! Those numbers are way beyond the capability of personal computers today and for some time to come. So you cannot actually do motion video simply by displaying a series of images retrieved from disk; instead, you have to use some of the many tricks that have been developed to reduce the data requirements so that a PC can handle motion video.

Without explaining how it is done (we'll come to that later), for the following discussion of systems, think in terms of a motion video data rate of about 10 megabytes per minute, and individual still images requiring around 50,000 bytes each. These are the numbers that the best image and motion video compression systems today can support.

The above discussion is for the picture only; it does not include the audio. We will begin discussing audio by using the numbers from the Compact Disc (CD) digital audio system used for home audio systems. CD audio has a data rate of 150,000 bytes per second, or 9 megabytes per minute—almost the same as indicated above for compressed motion video! Using that kind of audio with digital video would double the data rate!

Fortunately, the CD audio system is very conservatively designed, and it does not use any compression at all. It is possible to substantially reduce digital audio data rates by designing a less conservative system, possibly trading off a little audio quality and using some compression techniques. Depending on the audio quality desired, figure that you may need up to an additional 1 megabyte per minute for each channel of audio.

HARDWARE FOR MULTIMEDIA

There are numerous families of personal computers on the market, including the IBM-compatible machines, the Apple Macintosh family, Sun workstations, the Commodore Amiga, the NeXt computers, and others. All of these are suited to multimedia when they are equipped with enough power and storage. However, this book cannot possibly treat all the variations of the different systems. For that reason, specific examples here will involve only one family of systems—the IBM-compatible PCs, which include the IBM PS/2 family and all the systems that have been designed to be compatible with the IBM PC/AT and similar equipment. All of these machines use the Intel x86 family of microprocessors. Although much of the material in this book is general enough to apply to all families of machines, the specific details may apply only to the IBM-compatible computers. Therefore, when the acronym PC is used in this book, it means an IBM-compatible personal computer only.

Because of the tremendous range of equipment available on the market, the selection of a PC for any application is a complex task. That becomes doubly so for multimedia because multimedia is so demanding. In order to put some structure into the subject, Figure 2.1 shows the typical components of a PC.

The heart of the system is the main microprocessor chip, also called the Central Processing Unit (CPU). It is connected to a *system bus* to which all other units are also connected. The system bus is a standardized set of connections for hooking up all of the modules of a PC system. Since everything is parallel on the system bus, any unit can talk to any other unit, but only one path can be active at a time, under control of the CPU. Usually the system bus is physically located on the PC's motherboard. Some units such as memory and keyboard interface are wired directly on the motherboard, but plug-in sockets are provided for bus connections for other units, which tend to be optional. This has led to a large market for plug-in or add-in modules for PC systems, offering many options.

Equipment and Software 17

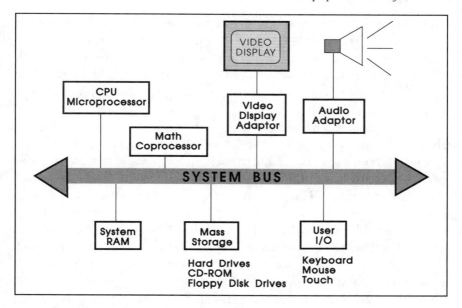

Figure 2.1 Diagram of PC bus and peripherals.

However, there is a trend to putting more of the common units on the motherboard; for example, many new computers have a VGA display adaptor and hard drive controller built on the motherboard. This reduces the system cost, but it also reduces flexibility.

This basic computer architecture is extremely flexible, but as explained above, only one unit on the bus can operate at a time. The same thing applies to the CPU—it does only one thing at a time. However, the CPU and the bus operate at millions of cycles per second, which makes most activities appear to occur instantly and simultaneously, even though they actually are happening in sequence. For example, the PC may seem to be making sounds and updating the video display at the same time; in fact, it is doing them sequentially at a rapid rate.

The System CPU

The CPU chip determines the character and speed of the entire machine. In the machines we are considering in this book, the CPU is a member of the Intel x86 family—for example, a 386 or a 486. The system provides a *clock frequency* for the chip, which drives it at a particular speed. For example, a 20 Mhz 386 PC runs its CPU chip at 20 Megahertz (a unit of speed: It means 20 *million cycles per second*). There is another measure of

CPU speed that is a *million instructions per second* or MIPS; this is not the same as clock frequency—it is typically lower because many CPU instructions take more than one clock cycle to complete. Intel has recently introduced a *clock doubler* version of the 486 CPU chip. The clock rate is doubled inside of the chip, so the chip actually runs faster than the clock rate would indicate.

A multimedia system will benefit from the fastest CPU you can get. You should consider nothing less than a 386 microprocessor at the highest clock speed you can afford. Note that a higher clock speed causes the cost of many other parts of the machine to go up, such as the memory and the bus components. This is because everything has to run faster to keep up with a fast CPU.

Another CPU option offered by Intel is the "SX" version of the 386 and 486 CPUs. These chips have a 16-bit external data path compared to a 32-bit data path for the standard "DX" versions. The 16-bit data path makes the motherboard and the memory less expensive, so an SX computer costs less than a DX computer. SX computers are also a little slower for the same chip clock speed. However, they are completely software compatible. Although multimedia software runs fine on SX computers, in the interest of getting all the speed you can, get a DX computer if at all possible.

The System RAM

The system random access memory (RAM) is probably the next most important part of the PC. It provides storage for temporary data and programs used by the CPU; the more system RAM the better. Most 386 and higher systems will support at least 16 megabytes (Mb) of RAM, and many will take even more. For multimedia use, have at least 8 Mb of RAM in a system that will be doing authoring, and not less than 6 Mb for a system that will only be used as a presenter. Both cases will benefit from more RAM than these numbers.

RAM is one area where cost is following Moore's law exactly; there is not much in a RAM memory except the integrated circuit chips themselves. Thus, RAM costs will continue to fall every year. At this writing, RAM chips contain either 1 megabit or 4 megabits of memory in each device, but 16 megabit devices are already in the pipeline, and people are talking about 64 megabit devices under development. The next eight years of Moore's law are already visible!

The Video Display

Video displays in all PCs use a *memory-mapped* approach in which a region of memory stores a list of all the pixel values to be displayed on the screen. To create the display, the video display adaptor reads through this memory at a rapid rate and converts the pixel values to signals that drive the display device itself. This process requires a massive amount of memory activity to move data out for refresh of the screen, typically at rates of 60 to 70 complete screens per second to prevent flicker of the display.

For instance, a 16-color VGA display at 640×480 resolution, refreshed 60 times a second, accesses 9.22 million bytes/second. The system bus could not handle this rate even if it did nothing else. Therefore, video display adaptors always include their own memory for storing the screen information, and they have separate circuits for refreshing the monitor from the screen memory without making any use of the system bus. Of course, the system bus is still used when the CPU has to update the information to be displayed.

VGA is not the only video display standard today. There are several higher resolution standards available such as super VGA, XGA, and others. Higher than 640×480 pixels is important when displays larger than 14" are going to be used on the desktop. On a 14" display at a normal desktop viewing distance of about 18", you cannot distinguish more than 640 pixels across anyway. However, if you are going to use a 16" or 19" display at this viewing distance, then you would benefit from having more pixels, such as an XGA display of 1024×768.

There is a tradeoff to higher resolutions, however, because having more pixels inherently means having more data, and that means greater storage and memory requirements, and slower operation—everything else being equal. Therefore, do not automatically go for the highest resolution available unless it is going to truly add something to your application. If you design your application with the display resolution in mind, almost any need can be adequately met with a 640×480 target resolution.

Another important specification of a video display is the number of colors that can be displayed. This is directly related to the number of bits of data allocated for each pixel (called bits per pixel or bpp), as shown by Table 2.1.

Most computers today only support 4 or 8 bits per pixel color displays. Although some of these machines are called multimedia PCs, they do not deserve that name in this book because 256 colors is woefully inadequate for reproducing real images or real video.

Bits Per Pixel	Number of Colors
1	2
4	16
8	256
16	65,536
24	16,777,216

Table 2.1 Number of colors displayed based on bpp range

Most video displays for 8 bpp use what is called the *color lookup table* or *color palette* approach to provide additional flexibility for choosing the specific 256 colors that will be available for the pixels. The palette is a table stored in the video display adaptor, which contains 18-bit or even 24-bit descriptions of the 256 different colors that can be represented by the 256 values of an 8-bit pixel. When each pixel is displayed, its value is used as an index into the palette, reading out the 24-bit color that is actually displayed. The advantage of this is that you can define the palette in order to have the 256 "best" colors for reproducing the current image. In principle, you can change the palette for every image.

However, in addition to the fact that 256 colors is not nearly enough to reproduce smoothly shaded scenes from real life, the palette approach has other disadvantages. You must do processing when capturing images into the computer to create its custom palette and store it with the image. This is at best an approximation, because a natural image is going to have tens of thousands of colors, which have to be squeezed down to only 256. But the real difficulty is that there is only one palette for the entire screen, so it can contain the values for only one image at a time. Therefore, it is impossible to build a screen containing more than one image. If you want to use two images, you have to process them ahead of time and build a custom palette that has the best approximation of the colors of both images. This flies in the face of interactivity. A palette display adaptor does not meet our requirements for a multimedia display.

The display of realistic images requires at least 16 bits per pixel. Sixteen bits per pixel systems have either 32,768 or 65,536 colors, depending on their use of the highest bit. Either of these will reproduce most natural scenes excellently, although you can occasionally see some trouble on scenes that have very smooth shaded colors, such as a closeup of a baby's face. To completely avoid this effect, which is called *contouring*, you have to go to 24 bpp. In this book, we consider 16 bpp to be good enough for multimedia. (In Chapter 11, we will talk about a system that is called 9 bpp, but you will find out that this is just a name for a system that actually behaves like a 24-bit color system.)

Audio System

The audio or sound capability of a typical computer consists of a small internal speaker driven by a 1-bit output from the computer. By rapidly switching this output, an amazing variety of sounds can be produced. However, the sounds are artificial, and such a sound system is incapable of anything close to real, natural audio. The situation is the same as for video. We need more bits to reproduce natural audio.

We can record natural audio digitally by *sampling* the analog audio. Sampling is a technique that repeatedly converts the value of an analog wave to a digital number. This is also called *analog to digital conversion* (ADC) or *digitizing*. For good audio quality, the *sampling rate*, or how fast we take new samples, must be 20,000 samples per second or higher. The accuracy of each sample, expressed in number of bits per sample, should be 14 to 16 bits for high-fidelity audio. When digital audio is played back, the reverse process (digital to analog conversion—DAC) is performed. A multimedia system needs this digital audio capability.

Another audio capability, which applies to the production of music, is called MIDI (Musical Instrument Digital Interface). MIDI is a digital communication standard developed by the musical instrument industry for transmitting commands between keyboards or other music controllers and sound producing units such as music synthesizers. MIDI commands, since they are digital, can be stored by a computer and then played back into one or more MIDI instruments to recreate the music at a later time. Some multimedia systems use synthesizer add-ons to create music this way. Depending on the ability and quality of the synthesizer(s) used, MIDI is capable of producing full orchestral music.

Mass Storage

Mass storage passes all of its data through the system bus to load into system RAM or the screen display RAM on the video display adaptor. The speed of mass storage devices is determined by the rate at which they can read from their storage medium. This operation also typically requires a lot of CPU involvement, and net data rates are much lower than either system bus speed or raw storage device read speed. For example, hard disk maximum data rates are around 500,000 bytes/second while a contiguous block of data is being read from the medium (so that there are no seeks involved). When the actions of the operating system and the system bus are included, it often becomes difficult to maintain an average hard disk data rate of more than about 150,000 bytes/second for any length of time.

In addition to having the fastest PC you can afford and 6–8 Mb or more of RAM, you need mass storage, because multimedia assets take a lot of storage. Motion video can require up to 10 Mb per minute, and individual still images from photographs are in the range of 50–100 Kb each. These numbers add up, and a 100 Mb hard disk is small for multimedia. You should carefully consider your needs for storage of multimedia assets before deciding about the hard disk size you want to order. Later chapters discuss the various multimedia data types and will help you in this decision.

CD-ROM

The Compact Disc Read Only Memory (CD-ROM) is an important storage medium for multimedia. Based on the hardware originally developed for digital audio players, the CD-ROM provides up to 680 Mb of storage in a single compact 12-cm disc; because of the digital audio heritage, CD-ROM hardware is inexpensive. However, it is a read-only medium, which means that once a CD-ROM has been produced, the data on it cannot be changed. This is both an advantage and a disadvantage: The data is permanent and cannot be easily corrupted, but you cannot add new data to the CD-ROM. Since many uses of a PC system require storage of new data, a CD-ROM drive alone does not serve all the mass storage needs of a typical multimedia system. In spite of the disadvantage, CD-ROM is still an important and low-cost medium for distribution of large amounts of data.

The CD-ROM achieves its large data capacity by using optical technology for the storage method. There are other storage devices on the market that use similar optical technology in a form that can be written as well as read, so new data can be added, and in some devices, old data can even be changed. The most common of these devices is the Write Once Read Many (WORM) drive, in which you can write to the disc once at any given location, but you can read it as many times as you like. With a WORM drive, you have to move to a new location on the disc to record new material; you cannot rerecord data. This is a useful feature when an audit trail of changes needs to be kept, and WORM drives are often used for archiving data. WORM systems are still quite expensive compared to magnetic hard drives, and a single standard has not been achieved by the several manufacturers of drives.

One version of WORM technology that should have important applications is the CD-WORM drive. This drive records on a disc that can be played back on any CD-ROM drive. This will be valuable for fast turn-around distribution of applications or data to a small community of users, a situation where conventional mastered and pressed CDs are not practical.

There are also rerecordable optical drives on the market, which operate almost the same as magnetic hard drives in that previously recorded data can be written over in order to make changes. They are, not surprisingly, more expensive than magnetic hard drives or WORM drives. This part of the digital optical recording field is still undergoing development and improvement—it is too early for hardware standards to be set.

All optical drives suffer from a slower seek time (the time to find a particular piece of data and begin reading it) than magnetic hard drives. This results from the need for an optical drive to read a data track before it can be sure what track it is on, whereas a magnetic drive knows its track location by simple mechanical positioning. The result is that magnetic drives today have 10 or more times faster seek times than optical drives. Seek time is important to multimedia applications because it contributes to the delay that may occur between the user making a choice and that choice beginning to appear on the screen.

Magnetic drive seek times are in the range of 12 to 25 milliseconds, which is usually negligible in an application. However, CD-ROM seek times can be one-half second or more, which becomes a factor that cannot be ignored in application design. (Often a particular multimedia activity can require several seeks before it is completed.) On the other hand, it would be dangerous to assume that the comparison will stay that way—competitive situations have a habit of changing once the market becomes large enough to support the developments needed to make improvements.

The creation of a CD-ROM requires a *mastering* process during which a disc master is made, from which multiple copies are replicated by an inexpensive pressing process. The pressing is like the technique that was used to make vinyl audio records. Mastering and replication require very expensive equipment and skilled personnel. Such a facility may cost millions of dollars; therefore, several companies offer mastering as a service. You send data to them and they perform all the steps of mastering and replication, returning finished discs in a week or so. The process typically has a one-time charge of approximately $1,500 to create a master, and then it costs $2 – $3 per disc, depending on quantity.

Before you can send data to a mastering vendor, you must do a step called *premastering* in which you arrange and format the data so that it can be efficiently accessed from the CD-ROM. One of the objectives of premastering is to optimize for the slow seek time of the CD-ROM drive.

Because of the expense and time cycle involved in CD-ROM production, most individual desktop authors probably will not be placing their multimedia presentations or applications on CD-ROM. Distribution of the smaller projects produced by individuals will usually be handled by use of floppy disks, hard disks, digital tape, or computer networks. The exact choice of medium will be based on:

- the size of your application,
- how many copies you need to distribute,
- how much time you have to accomplish distribution, and
- what you can afford.

This is something that must be thought through in planning multimedia. The tradeoffs involved in planning for distribution will be discussed further in Chapter 14.

Coprocessors

Certain tasks in a PC system occur repeatedly and can be speeded up by providing dedicated hardware instead of running the task entirely in software. The extra hardware is usually in the form of special integrated circuit chips designed for the purpose; they are referred to as *coprocessor* chips.

The most common coprocessor is one used in machines that run math-intensive programs—a math coprocessor. Math coprocessors are used for computer-aided design (CAD) applications, spreadsheet applications, and graphics modeling applications. Since coprocessors are IC chips—the same as the system CPU—features that begin in coprocessors will very likely become integrated into future CPU chips as Moore's law makes it possible and the volume of use makes it economical. This has already happened with the math coprocessor that is integrated into the 486DX CPU.

For multimedia, there are special needs that can be served by coprocessors—particularly associated with the video display, animation, audio, and video processing. These are covered in more detail below when we discuss technologies for multimedia.

THE MULTIMEDIA PC

Since multimedia computing requires both new hardware and software, there is a "chicken and egg" problem in starting its growth in the marketplace. Hardware has to exist in quantity before software developers will invest in special software. But you cannot sell special hardware without good software for the new features. Various approaches are being taken in the industry to get past this bottleneck.

One approach was to write a specification for a "multimedia PC," which defines a minimum level of capability in a PC intended for multimedia. The objective is to more quickly establish a base of systems for which multimedia software developers can write. It also can be a way to offer packaged systems that "contain everything you need for multimedia" at a special price. This is good for the early growth of the multimedia market, but it may be dangerous in the long run because it could limit the market to the level of performance that is available today, and it will make the move to the improved systems, which will come next year and beyond, more difficult.

A better approach is to view the multimedia hardware market as a moving target, which is going to improve over time because it needs to. Each multimedia software offering should specify its own requirements for a minimum system and, as much as possible, the software should be designed to take advantage of hardware performance beyond the minimum. In this way, we will not be held back by today's hardware performance, and software vendors can get as aggressive as they dare in terms of utilizing advanced hardware capabilities. Many vendors are already taking this approach, offering multimedia PCs or MPCs, which are special only in that a CD-ROM drive and some kind of sound card are bundled with a 386 or 486 PC.

SPECIAL MULTIMEDIA HARDWARE

The discussion so far has covered the standard computer components you must use for multimedia. However, standard computer display adaptors and sound systems do not support high-quality audio and realistic video capability. For these you need special add-in boards, often one for audio and one for video. There are also a few products that do both audio and video on the same board. Unfortunately, there is not much standardization of audio and video hardware, and each product requires its own proprietary software drivers and sometimes special

26 *Designing Interactive Multimedia*

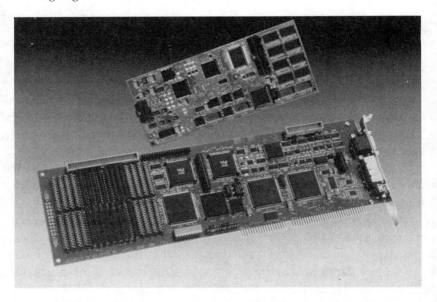

Figure 2.2 The ActionMedia II DVI board with capture board. Photo courtesy of Intel Corporation.

higher-level software as well. An objective of the MCI software discussed below is to provide a generic interface to a variety of boards.

We won't cover all the different multimedia hardware here, but you will find a lot of it described in Appendix A at the end of the book. For the rest of this book we will be referring to DVI Technology®, a product that combines both audio and video into a single add-in board.

DVI Technology

DVI Technology is available in the ActionMedia II™ family of boards from Intel Corporation and IBM Corporation, and is the only single board multimedia product that delivers high-quality stereo digital audio, full-screen digital motion video, and high-quality still images—all fully integrated with the other capabilities of the PC in which it resides. (See Figure 2.2.) Many system suppliers have plans to integrate DVI components onto the motherboards of future personal computers, so DVI capabilities will soon be widely available at low cost.

The ActionMedia II card contains a two-chip video coprocessor with its own separate RAM memory so that motion video decompression and display can operate completely in parallel with the system CPU. The DVI video display is capable of up to 24 bpp color, and it is integrated with the normal VGA or XGA display of the PC in a way that allows both to be used

Equipment and Software 27

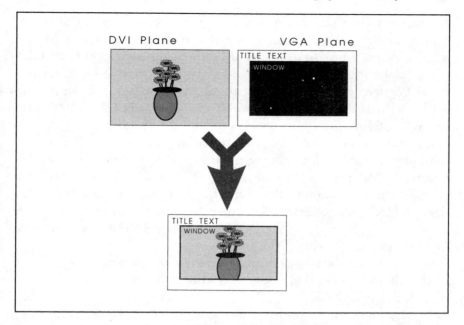

Figure 2.3 The ActionMedia II card combines two video planes. Black areas of the VGA plane are transparent and show the DVI plane.

at the same time, with the VGA display overlaying the DVI display on the same monitor. This is called a *two-plane* approach and it proves to be an extremely flexible technique, which allows the user to simultaneously see the results of two concurrent processes—one displaying in the DVI plane, and one displaying in the VGA (or XGA) plane. Figure 2.3 shows how this works.

A separate audio coprocessor chip with 16-bit digital audio outputs allows high-quality audio to be played concurrently.

The ActionMedia II card also has an optional add-on module that provides video and audio capture capability. This is a necessity for an authoring system. It allows you to input audio and/or video into the computer in real time, compress them, and store the resulting data. This simplifies significantly the process of creating the asset files for an application.

For the highest possible video compression quality, Intel also offers an off-line video compression process called Production Level Video (PLV). To use PLV, you create your video on analog video tape, send the tapes to Intel or another PLV compression house, and they will return (for a fee) digital tapes in a few days containing PLV files of your video.

But why do we need DVI Technology? Why can't we simply put the right software into our PC and do the same things? Why do we need special hardware? The answer is that most PCs do not have the ability to output quality audio and video, regardless of where it came from; the audio channel is usually designed just for making beep sounds, and the video display usually has too few colors to reproduce realistic images or video. We need different hardware to solve both of these problems. This is exactly the reason most PCs provide for add-in cards. (There are many different add-in cards on the market for audio and video.)

But there is another important reason to have even more special hardware: The data requirements of quality video and audio exceed the capabilities of the best PCs by 20 to 100 times, and the processing capability needed to apply video and audio compression to overcome that data problem also exceeds PC capability by more than 100 times. These discrepancies are simply too large for us to wait for Moore's law to catch up—it could take 10 years!

A number of software-only motion video compression systems are already on the market (Microsoft's AVI, IBM's Photomotion and Ultimotion, and Apple QuickTime). But, even with the fastest CPUs available today, they need to compromise resolution, number of colors, data rate, or frame rate. Because of their simplicity, software-only compressed video systems will find a market, but they will not compete head-to-head with video coprocessor systems which can deliver full-screen, full-color, 30 frames/second motion video at CD-ROM data rates.

By embracing the separate hardware now, we get onto the multimedia bandwagon, so the trend predicted by Moore's law will not only improve our PC performance in the future, it will also improve the audio and video performance, because that too is based on IC chips. The multimedia coprocessors available today someday will be built directly into future PCs, but with software compatibility for today's add-in cards. Therefore, a smooth transition to fully integrated hardware should be possible in the future.

Performance Parameters of DVI Technology

First, let's look at the performance capabilities of DVI audio. The ActionMedia II card has a programmable audio coprocessor that is interfaced to high-quality stereo audio output channels. The DVI system software that runs on the coprocessor provides a selection of audio channel configurations, both mono and stereo, with various compression and decompression parameters. The performance ranges from 32,000 bits per second mono audio at about AM radio quality up to 256,000 bits per second FM stereo quality. The selection is made through software. With software, you also can control channel volume levels and stereo mix.

To understand the video performance of DVI, we should explain more about the two-plane architecture mentioned earlier. With ActionMedia II, you essentially have two video display adaptors, each with its own display memory, but both display outputs are connected to the same monitor through some special logic. The VGA or XGA adaptor is always displayed directly on the monitor. This is the VGA plane. But the DVI plane is "behind" that display, and it will show through and be seen whenever VGA plane pixels are made black. Thus, a rectangular DVI image is displayed by putting the image into the DVI plane's memory, and then making a black rectangle at the same relative location in the VGA plane.

DVI still images can be displayed at two screen resolutions: 512×480 pixels and 256×240 pixels. (The numbers given are for a VGA display, and change slightly with an XGA display.) These resolution numbers are for the full-screen pixel counts for the DVI plane. Note that these numbers are different from the VGA or XGA planes, which is not a problem because the hardware combination of the two planes does not depend on pixel counts. Resolutions of 512×480 pixels deliver an image quality equivalent to television broadcast studio quality. Through software, the image resolution can be changed; and scaling or cropping of images, windowing, or dynamic transitions of images can be achieved.

DVI motion video is normally displayed at 256×240 pixels and 30 frames per second, which can be configured either for full-screen display or as quarter-screen display. In either case, the video can be dynamically combined with still images on the same screen or in the same window. Motion video can also be scaled to fit into a smaller window, under user control; and it can be paused, played at different speeds, or single-stepped—all under software control.

With the ActionMedia II capture module, audio, still images, and motion video can be captured, compressed on the fly, and saved to hard disk in real time. There are software choices for compression algorithms (techniques) that provide a range of performance for different applications. These algorithm choices include all the existing industry standards, and will be expanded as future standards are set. The internals of DVI Technology are all programmable, which provides the maximum flexibility for maintaining compatibility with future developments.

The video output from the ActionMedia II card normally is integrated with a VGA display as described above. However, there are other choices: It can be directed to a separate monitor for a two-display workstation, or it can be delivered in NTSC or PAL television formats for recording on videotape or displaying on a standard television display.

DVI Technology is the most complete, most flexible, and most expandable multimedia technology available today.

ADDITIONAL HARDWARE FOR AUTHORING

If you are assembling a system for authoring multimedia, you will need other equipment for the input of audio and video into the computer. Audio and video is generated with analog video and audio equipment, the same as used for television. Depending on the quality levels at which you need to work, you can use home video and audio equipment such as camcorders, VCRs, or cassette recorders. However, if you need the highest quality, you will want to use professional audio and video equipment, which, of course, is substantially more expensive.

Using a home-quality video camera or camcorder for capturing motion video is usually satisfactory for motion video that will be displayed at less than full screen; however, for the best possible motion video at full screen, you should use professional or broadcast-quality video cameras and recording equipment.

In the case of still images, a home-quality video camera is usually not satisfactory—these cameras have lower resolution, which will show up as fuzziness in still images. To capture still images of the highest quality, it is best to use a professional RGB camera, with a connection to an RGB-input video board in the computer. An alternative, when you already have your images in the form of hard copy or photographs, is to use a device called a *color scanner* (see Figure 2.4), which can scan color photographs directly into the digital format of the computer. Color scanners provide the best possible still image quality.

In addition to the input equipment mentioned above, you also need equipment for converting the analog audio and video to digital data in the computer. This capability is available via PC plug-in boards, and there are many different boards on the market, including the ActionMedia II capture adaptor mentioned earlier. Because there is not a single standard for digital audio and video, the different manufacturers of boards have a variety of data formats. Depending on the choices you make in this area, you also may need to add file conversion utilities to your software portfolio. (Equipment for audio and video capture will be discussed further in Chapters 10, 11, and 12 on audio, image, and video assets.)

SOFTWARE FOR MULTIMEDIA

You can do *anything* in software. That sweeping statement is, in fact, true. However, simply *doing* something does not necessarily mean that it is satisfactory. Multimedia software must do its tasks in ways that provide acceptable image, audio, and video quality; the audio and video must play

Figure 2.4 A typical color scanner, the Howtek Personal Color Scanner. Photo courtesy of Howtek Corporation.

smoothly without interruptions or distortions. The software must respond effectively to the user's interaction, and it must provide a degree of flexibility that will encompass all the different presentation metaphors that are required to cover a wide range of applications. Sometimes the demands of such capable software exceed the power of even the most advanced PC hardware. In that case, additional hardware assists are needed to achieve an adequate result. DVI Technology is an example of a hardware assist that solves the above problems.

For the purpose of this discussion, we will break the subject of multimedia software into three parts:

1. Operating systems—the underlying software, which gives applications access to the computer's resources.
2. Application programs—software that produces a complete multimedia environment to a user for a specific purpose.
3. Authoring software—software that allows an author to create application programs and collect all the necessary multimedia assets.

Figure 2.5 shows a block diagram of a typical PC software system. This diagram will be used in the following discussion.

Operating System Software

An operating system is software that manages the use of the computer's resources. It typically includes a file system for handling floppy disk and

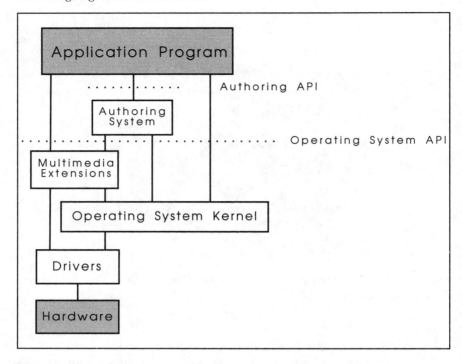

Figure 2.5 PC software system diagram, showing levels of software.

hard disk storage, and I/O for keyboard and video display. The operating system includes an *application programming interface* (API) so that application writers can access the system resources from their programs. The API is standardized so that it remains the same regardless of what hardware may lie below.

In order to provide that hardware independence, operating systems are normally divided into a *kernel*, which provides all the basic functionality of the API, and a set of *drivers*, which mate specific hardware to the kernel. Thus, to adapt an operating system to new hardware, it is only necessary to provide new drivers for that hardware. The kernel does not have to be changed.

However, sometimes new hardware adds features that require changes to the API. In that case, it is common to provide *extensions* to the operating system. An extension is a separate software module that modifies or enhances the API to accommodate the new features. It may have to have access to the driver level as shown in Figure 2.5. For example, when the CD-ROM was introduced, it required the addition of extensions to existing operating systems.

Typical PC operating systems are MS-DOS and OS/2. Both of these are *single-user* operating systems; that is, they support one user interacting with one PC. (A multiple-user system has a number of users sharing one computer; each user has her own keyboard and display terminal.) Note that the widely used Microsoft Windows is not technically an operating system; it is an extension module that runs on top of MS-DOS.

Before we had real-time audio or video capability in a computer, a single-user operating system had nothing else to do while waiting for disk I/O. Therefore, it was common for single-user operating systems such as MS-DOS to simply tie up all the bus cycles during mass storage accesses. This caused all other CPU processing to stop during disk accesses, and it is unacceptable in a multimedia system. It means that the CPU cannot be processing audio or video data for presentation at the same time that data is being read from storage. Various software strategies have been developed to get around this problem in MS-DOS systems, but the real answer is what is called a true *multitasking* operating system such as OS/2. In OS/2, with properly constructed application programs, the system resources (CPU, bus, storage, etc.) are never tied up completely by one application or one task within an application.

Multimedia applications make heavy demands on an operating system because of the large amounts of data that must be handled and the time-critical nature of that data. When the sound system needs more sound data, the operating system must deliver data immediately, or the sound will be interrupted. Multimedia requires that the operating system provide a strategy for concurrently supplying data and CPU cycles to a number of parallel activities. This capability is called multitasking and it is not available in many operating systems. In a non-multitasking system, a multimedia application must set up its own multitasking within the application in order to provide the necessary concurrency. This can be made to work up to a point, but it breaks down if there is any other software present in the machine that the application does not know about, such as a communications server, or any kind of TSR (terminate-and-stay-resident) program.

The best approach is to build multitasking into the operating system itself. OS/2 is an example of such a system. It manages the needs of all applications, which makes it possible to run multimedia along with other applications that may or may not be multimedia applications. For example, under OS/2 you can run a spreadsheet program and set it up so that certain cells of the spreadsheet will open a new window and play motion video when they are clicked on by the user. This can be done even though the spreadsheet program was designed without any regard for multimedia, and the user can still interact with the spreadsheet while video is playing.

The spreadsheet with video is achieved by using a multimedia *server* application, which runs concurrently and responds to command messages sent to it by the spreadsheet (or any other application). The person who creates the spreadsheet simply programs the video cells to send the appropriate commands to the multimedia server to obtain whatever action is desired. The "sending" of these commands is done by using one of the *interprocess communication* protocols available in the multitasking operating system. In the case above, it might be done via the *Dynamic Data Exchange* (DDE) protocol in OS/2. Note that a non-multitasking operating system does not need and does not have interprocess communication, because there can't be more than one process at a time anyway.

Although it runs on top of MS-DOS, which is not a multitasking operating system, Microsoft Windows 3.x provides some of the functionality of a multitasking system, including interprocess communication; but it is ultimately limited by the underlying MS-DOS. Windows 3.x does not provide a strong enough foundation for a sophisticated digital multimedia system such as ActionMedia II; it will support only the simplest multimedia functions and features. Microsoft is developing a new generation of Windows (the NT version) that provides full multitasking from the ground up and no longer requires the use of MS-DOS. This will be a boost to multimedia applications for Windows, which will then be fully competitive with OS/2 multimedia.

Both OS/2 Version 2.0 and Windows NT support the concurrent running of OS/2, Windows, and DOS applications—each in a separate window. They also provide for interprocess communication to operate among all concurrent applications regardless of their type. This means, for example, that an OS/2 multimedia server could provide multimedia's services to a Windows application running under OS/2. In such an environment, any application that supports interprocess communication can be enabled for multimedia.

Multitasking is just the first step in implementing an operating system for multimedia. Multimedia adds its own new kinds of resources that have to be managed, and it is a possibility that the operating system should manage them also. The need for this is shown by industry efforts to provide extensions to existing operating systems for certain multimedia needs. For example, there is an extension for MS-DOS called MSCDEX that extends that operating system to support CD-ROM drives. An extension is needed because CD-ROM is hardware that operates differently, but still should be accessible through the main operating system's file system. You would like to access files from a CD disc in exactly the same way that you access floppy or hard disks. Thus, it is necessary and desirable to "extend" an operating system to support CD-ROM.

Microsoft has also introduced a *Multimedia Extension* for Windows 3.x. Included in this is the *Media Control Interface* (MCI), which has been endorsed by a consortium of companies. MCI is a generalized API interface that theoretically allows multimedia applications to seamlessly (so far as the end user is concerned) include a variety of hardware and software from different vendors. It is important to have an architecture that will allow any authoring or application software to work with any hardware because there are so many possibilities for what multimedia can eventually do. It is unlikely that any one software/hardware combination will include all of the effects anyone might possibly want. If everyone implements the MCI interface for their hardware, users will be able to select the hardware with the features they want—and separately choose the authoring software they like. MCI will ensure that all combinations will work.

MCI is accomplished by providing a means in the operating system to send text commands to a peripheral device. With MCI, each specialized multimedia device responds to a set of text commands, using a control language. The operating system simply contains a capability to pass such text commands directly to the device driver without any translation. Each device has to have its own driver program that hooks it up to the MCI port of the operating system, and also hooks up the means to supply the data other than commands. MCI also provides another kind of interface, which is a standardized function-call interface for use with a language such as C. The function-call interface can provide more flexibility than the text-based interface. MCI is another way of achieving the same interprocess communication described above using DDE in OS/2. The same as DDE, it is a general capability that can work with any system and any hardware. MCI does have to be written into the operating system, however. This has been done for Windows 3.1 and OS/2 2.0.

A question still remains about how far to go in standardizing this approach. For example, should there be a standard language for MCI commands? That would make the MCI command interface independent of the particular hardware being used, but it also might limit some new hardware which contained new capabilities that the existing language never thought of. The correct approach is to standardize the language in such a way that it can be extended upwardly as new capabilities come forth. However, the operating system's interface should not be made aware of the language, because building the language in would make it much more difficult to make extensions in the future.

At this time the CD-ROM drive is a reasonably well-standardized piece of hardware, and that is an important motivator to building it into the operating system. However, there are other kinds of hardware on the market that are not so well standardized, but still they need to be accessed by the systems that use them. Examples of this are the several varieties of sound (digital audio) boards that are available. In such cases it is much harder to decide what should be included as an operating system extension, and what should remain as a dedicated "driver" to be supplied by the manufacturer of the board. In my view, none of these proprietary boards should be part of an operating system specification.

Although it does not apply to the PC family we are covering here, the Apple QuickTime system for Macintosh computers is a good example of an operating system multimedia extension. QuickTime provides the real-time multitasking capability needed to handle audio and video playback and it defines new data types for audio and video, which are fully supported by the same Macintosh operating system features that support earlier data types (cut, copy, paste, drag and drop, etc.). At the same time, QuickTime has left the door open for various compression techniques and other processes that applications can develop for themselves.

Application Programs for Multimedia

Multimedia application programs can exist as single executable files, or they can consist of a command file along with a *runtime* or *server* executable module. In almost all cases, the *assets* (audio, video, and images) required by the application will be in separate files from the executable and command files. Only the simplest of multimedia applications could fit entirely in one reasonably sized file.

Distributing Applications

Because of the data size of multimedia assets, distribution of a major multimedia application is not a simple problem. There may be hundreds of megabytes of data, and distribution by normal floppy disks is impractical. The best solution available today is CD-ROM, where up to 680 Mb of data can be distributed on one disc. CD-ROM is also a low-cost medium, costing only a few dollars each in quantities of 1,000 or so. However, you have to go through the mastering process to produce a CD, which entails sending your data to a mastering center, paying a fee (currently less than $1,500), and then waiting a week or so for the result. But this really is the best choice if you have more than a few copies to distribute.

For small numbers of copies, you can also distribute on WORM or optical-eraseable media, or with one of the several archival digital tape systems that are available. However, these require everyone to have the same special equipment. WORM is not suitable for large-scale distribution because of the cost of the equipment and the medium, and the amount of time and labor involved in individually recording each copy. Several companies are producing desktop WORM recorders that create disks at a cost of $75–$100 each, in a format that can be played by a standard CD-ROM drive. There will be more of these drives in the future, and their prices will come down.

For internal distribution in your company, a computer network is an ideal distribution medium for multimedia. Although there have been numerous demonstrations of multimedia audio and video being played from a server on a network, this places a heavy demand on the network's data handling capacity. When multimedia is to be played repeatedly (and possibly simultaneously) by a number of users, it is probably a better strategy to copy the multimedia application to the user's local hard drive and then play it from there. This way, the network's resources are tied up only once for each user, and the timing of that can be controlled to occur when the heavy load can be tolerated by other users.

Authoring Systems for Multimedia

Multimedia application programs can be created by writing in a general-purpose programming language such as C, or they can be created with very little programming by using an *authoring* program. The end result is the same, except that with an authoring system you may pay a small price in performance or flexibility compared to the nuts and bolts C programmed approach. However, the ease of creation and speed of completion with an authoring system far surpasses anything you can achieve in C. This makes any small tradeoff worth it for almost all applications.

As with everything else discussed in this section, there are a variety of multimedia authoring systems available. Some authoring systems work with an easy-to-use programming language tailored for multimedia, and others have a "point-and-click" authoring approach, from which you simply choose items for your application with a mouse. An authoring system designer faces a tradeoff between a very easy-to-use system, which may have limitations in flexibility, and an extremely flexible language-based approach that requires some programming skill to master its advanced features.

Most systems have favored the easy-to-use consideration, which is usually implemented with a point-and-click author interface. However, you can never completely get away from using the keyboard, and you will always have an advantage if you understand programming philosophy, but point-and-click authoring systems are the wave of the future.

There are over a hundred authoring system products, so we will not even try to cover them all in this book; rather, we will teach you about authoring systems in a broader context. Most of the material here will apply to whatever authoring system you use. Where we need to reference a real authoring system, we will use the MEDIAscript OS/2 Desktop Edition authoring system from Network Technology Corporation. MEDIAscript is a complete system for advanced multimedia including DVI Technology and OS/2 Presentation Manager authoring, with audio, video, and image capture tools built in; and it is a point-and-click environment that retains most of the flexibility of language-based authoring. MEDIAscript OS/2 provides several levels of authoring, from a simple template-based approach up to very flexible icon-based scripting, which can even be used to write custom templates for use by the other approach. A list of other authoring system vendors is given in Appendix B.

MEDIAscript OS/2 Desktop Edition

The name indicates that MEDIAscript OS/2 is designed for the OS/2 operating system. This choice is simply because OS/2 is currently the best PC operating system to fully support the concurrency needed to run multimedia along with multiple other applications in a multitasking environment. Network Technology Corporation also has a widely used MEDIAscript product for MS-DOS. MEDIAscript DOS is a language-based system and has a command-line interface instead of a point-and-click interface. It has extensive capabilities for creation and manipulation of DVI images, including DVI text and graphics. A MEDIAscript product for Windows is also planned; it will support the Windows NT version.

MEDIAscript OS/2 is based on a Multimedia Server (MMS), which provides easy access to all multimedia facilities through a command-driven interface. The MMS is a stand-alone program that is used for running authored applications. For authoring, a separate author interface program called the AUI runs concurrently with the MMS. MMS commands are grouped into files, which are called *scripts* or *projects*. The MMS is installed on the OS/2 desktop, and remains as a minimized icon ready to run multimedia items whenever it receives a script. In an authoring environment, the AUI runs separately, but it is linked to the MMS via DDE. Thus, you can create multimedia scripts in the AUI and immediately run them (or any part of them) on the MMS, which is always ready to go.

The AUI has a full set of tools for capturing audio, video, or still images, and including them in your scripts. You can also perform limited graphic drawing with the AUI, saving the resulting drawing commands in the script being authored. The AUI also supports programming constructs for looping, variables, arrays, and tables, which make possible more sophisticated presentations or effects, database applications, and more. An author can use as much of this capability as she is ready for; if only simple selections are made, then a default type of presentation will occur. You can build elaborate structures without getting into any programming concepts, but with programming you can make the result more sophisticated in almost any way you desire.

The AUI also provides an approach from which you build your multimedia projects by using templates or samples. A special window holds a variety of samples that you can use singly or in combination for your work. In most cases, you simply copy a sample into your project and then open it to customize filenames and other parameters, and you immediately have a version of the sample that suits your application. Further, the details of the samples are always accessible, and (if you know enough) you can modify them any way you like.

There is another MEDIAscript OS/2 authoring product called the Professional Edition (PE), which provides advanced features for professional application designers who are writing applications for commercial use. The PE also supports direct access to the MEDIAscript internal language, which provides the ultimate flexibility for designing the most sophisticated applications. (Further discussion of authoring software and a full description of the MEDIAscript OS/2 Desktop Edition is given in Chapter 6.)

MULTIMEDIA AUTHORING WORKSTATION

From the foregoing discussion you can see that there are many choices to make in setting up the hardware and software for multimedia delivery or authoring. While we are not going to make specific equipment recommendations here, a concrete example will surely help you to understand how it all goes together. Therefore, the following is an example of an equipment setup. It is one used by the author and it is neither the best nor the worst, but it has been used to develop most of the example applications in this book. Figure 2.6 is a photograph of the equipment setup, and the list below gives the actual equipment included:

- PC: IBM PS/2 Model 80—300 Mb hard drive, 10 Mb RAM, DVI ActionMedia II delivery card, DVI ActionMedia II capture adaptor
- Display: IBM 8514 14" VGA Monitor
- Camcorder: Panasonic PV-41—Tripod, VCR
- Video Switcher: Radio Shack 15-1956A

Figure 2.6 The author's multimedia workstation.

- Audio—4-track cassette recorder and mixer: Yamaha MT-120, microphone, CD player
- Software List—Operating System: OS/2 Version 2.0, Multimedia Authoring: MEDIAscript OS/2 Desktop Edition

Note that this example workstation uses consumer-grade video equipment. As discussed earlier in this chapter, that does not always provide the best possible performance, particularly for still images. This is simply a tradeoff in favor of price.

CHAPTER SUMMARY

All the equipment you need to set up a desktop multimedia system is currently available. Select the highest performance PC system you can afford, with a 20 MHz 386DX system being the minimum. It should have at least 8 Mb of RAM. The system should have as much hard disk storage as you can afford—200 Mb or more. DVI Technology is the recommended multimedia hardware; it gives you everything you need on a single card. You will also need an authoring software package such as MEDIAscript Desktop Edition.

3

Objectives for Multimedia

There is no point in carrying the ball until you learn where the goal is.
anonymous

In this chapter we discuss the setting of objectives for a multimedia project. It begins with knowing the task that you want to accomplish, and then thinking about what multimedia might do for the task. In order to do that, we consider four different kinds of tasks, break them down into steps, and then look at how multimedia might apply to each step. The four tasks are:

- selling,
- teaching,
- informing, and
- entertaining.

Once we see how to use multimedia for each step of a task, we discuss how to decide the actual content, its presentation, and where to get it.

Much of the early planning of a multimedia project boils down to simple application of common sense. You need to think broadly about what you want to do, who your users or your customers are, and what material you will be using. Out of that you can crystallize your objectives, as we will do at the end of this chapter for a hypothetical application. The material in this chapter is not intended to be a "cookbook" of planning, rather it will just help you see how to do your own thinking and planning.

TYPICAL MULTIMEDIA PROJECTS

To begin with, it is assumed that you have some kind of project in mind and that you think multimedia is an effective way to accomplish the project. To give you an idea of the sort of things that fit that description, the following is a "shopping list" of tasks to stimulate your thinking toward the kinds of tasks to which multimedia is suited. Some of the items obviously are too big to be completed in a reasonable time by a single person working at his desktop; but even in those cases, a single person can be responsible for the overall planning at this level. Other items may appear a little farfetched right now, but as multimedia systems come down in cost and are more widely used, they will become perfectly reasonable.

- *Help travelers find their way around an airport*—build an interactive kiosk for a large international airport that travelers will use to locate facilities and services available in the airport.
- *Assist in the sale of automobiles*—build a system that customers can use to get answers to their questions and to explore the various models and options that are available.
- *Museum exhibit about an archaeological site in Egypt*—present audio, video, images, and sketches from an archaeological site in a way that enables a visitor to interactively explore the information and learn about any of the things that interest him.
- *Teach someone how to program a VCR*—introduce a new VCR with advanced features for recording television programs and provide an interactive tutorial to the consumer on how to use the VCR.
- *Make a game based on video collected during a crime investigation*—assemble video and photographs from a "real" crime investigation into a game format from which the user can conduct his own investigation to solve the crime.
- *Sell travel vacations*—present advertising materials about travel packages or cruises to help a client select travel for a vacation.
- *Create a multimedia newsletter about activities in your school*—make a weekly newsletter available to the members of your computer class about current activities in the school.
- *Build an interactive index of your home videos*—organize your home videos so that they can be explored interactively and selected items played in full.
- *Make a presentation to convince your boss about a new project*—present a great idea for a new project and put together a "killer" presentation about it.

- *Provide a database of information on handling hazardous materials*—show videos of procedures for handling hazardous materials based on selection of the material and the situation.
- *Make an interactive database that runs on the central computer of a yacht*—provide an interactive multimedia database about the features of the yacht, their operation, and general boating safety matters for a company that builds yachts.
- *Teach someone how to train and handle his dog*—present the techniques for training and handling pet dogs in various situations.
- *Present a proposal for a new building*—design an architectural firm's proposal for a new building and show plans, costs, data, and computer simulations of areas of the new building; present a video showing models that have been constructed for the building.
- *Make an interactive display of anatomical drawings*—create a system for a doctor's office that allows rapid display of any parts of the body at any level of detail.
- *Make a CD-ROM annual report for your company*—distribute an annual report on CD-ROM and include audio, video, and photographs along with financial and performance data.

The above list is just a teaser. Depending on who you are and what you do, you will have your own ideas. Keep those ideas in mind as you read the rest of this chapter and see what items fit into your plan.

Now we will look at each of the four types of tasks and examine the steps of the task and how multimedia may apply to each step. Note that in addition to studying the multimedia task to be accomplished, we also must know the characteristics of the intended users and tailor the application to suit them.

UNDERSTANDING THE USER

We usually think about groups of users in terms of their demographics: age, gender, education, income, marital status, etc. This also applies in planning your application: Clearly specify what you expect of your user(s)—you can't properly design your application without that information.

An important demographic question for multimedia applications is: How familiar is the user with computers? This will determine what kind of user interface you must provide, and whether or not you should let the user believe he is interacting with a computer.

When dealing with the general public, do not assume much about familiarity with computers. In fact, it is probably better if your application does not even look like a computer or computer screen. Many people are still afraid of computers and will not even go near them. In a public setting, it is better if your application looks like a television instead.

Specialized applications require particular knowledge or skill from the user. For example, if you are teaching airline pilots how to fly a new aircraft, you can reasonably assume that the user already knows how to fly something! In planning your application, carefully spell out any special skills or knowledge you expect from the user and make sure at the start of the application that the user has these skills.

Another important consideration about the user is: How much time does he have for this? The interface and operation of your application and the amount of material presented should be consistent with the user's time frame. For example, it would not make sense to begin a five-minute video about the beauties of the city when a traveller is just trying to find out how to get a bus to take him downtown!

Finally, make sure you know why a user might use your application. What does the user expect to get from the application? What are his objectives? Does the very nature of the application raise certain expectations in the user? Be sure that the actual performance of the application is consistent with the user's expectations. A good technique is to map out the tasks for which the user is responsible before setting objectives for the application itself. This is discussed further in Chapter 7.

MULTIMEDIA FOR SELLING

One way to understand a task is to break it down into smaller steps and then examine each step. The steps of selling are:

- presenting a product overview,
- answering customer questions,
- helping the customer select the one to buy,
- quoting prices,
- asking for the order, and
- entering the order.

Product Overview

Whether we are selling a product or service, we begin with some kind of overview of the product or service, which is intended to attract the potential customer's attention and make him receptive to the further steps of selling. This is somewhat akin to the purpose of a TV commercial and should be a glitzy presentation. Using motion video for this step is a natural. If motion video is not available, then it should be some kind of dynamic animation or other interesting means of presentation. The purpose is to draw the customer into further and more detailed steps of selling.

Answer Customers' Questions

Once we have attracted the customer to our product, the next step is to give the customer more information and encourage him to ask questions. Often it is a good idea to provide these two functions separately: Begin with a presentation of facts but set things up so that the customer knows he can interrupt at any point to ask questions. This is naturally accomplished by providing an interactive environment in which the customer can choose to be presented with information, to explore for it, or to specifically ask for something. All of this serves the purpose of getting the customer familiar enough with the product so that he is ready to specify exactly what variations of the product he might want to buy. We need to give the customer as much time as he likes in this stage, especially if the product is complex, like an automobile.

Using the computer to answer the customer's questions is particularly valuable because the process can be time-consuming and is not necessarily efficient use of a salesperson's time. Also, the presence of a salesperson may inhibit the customer and prevent all questions from being asked or cause the customer to lose interest. For the computer to be successful without a salesperson, however, this portion of the sales program must have very complete data, with good visuals, and it must be very well designed so that the customer is able to find the information and answers he needs. This portion usually can be done primarily with text, graphics, or photographs, and there may not be much need for video unless there are dynamics about the product that should be shown.

The materials for the question and answer section are usually available from the product literature and other promotional materials prepared for other forms of marketing. Of course, they will probably need reformatting for use in multimedia.

When interacting with a customer, it is preferable to use audio because a human voice providing information is much friendlier than the computer screen doing it. Even when the factual information is best shown on the screen, using a voice-over helps the customer remain at ease and continue to be interested.

Specify the Exact Product

When the customer appears to be ready, encourage him to try to choose the exact model and variation of the product he might be interested in buying. The Q & A screens should have a button for the customer to click when he is ready to choose a configuration. It is a positive indication when we succeed in getting the customer to click that button. The configuration selection process will use much of the same information that was provided in the previous section, although it will have to be more formally collected so that an exact product is specified. One approach is to open an additional window along with the Q & A screens in which the product selection is recorded. That way, the customer can work with both at the same time on the same screen.

Provide a Price Quotation

When the computer "senses" that the customer has completed a product selection, it can offer a price quotation for that product. You probably do not want to have the computer try to negotiate price with the customer; if price negotiation is part of the store's sales practices, the salesperson should take over at this point.

Once a price has been quoted, the customer may wish to explore other configurations of the product vs. price. Allow the quotation process to be iterated, or to quote prices on a range of configurations at once. Either way, the customer question process may continue, and it now should include price.

During this stage, there may be an advantage to running a glitzy video or animation to remind the customer about the overall qualities of the product. This might be the same as the original overview, or something different that takes into account that the customer now knows a lot more about the product. In order not to interrupt the question and answer process, this presentation could be set up to begin in a partial-screen window whenever the customer does not interact with the Q & A windows for a specific length of time. However, the Q & A windows should remain active during the presentation and may take over any time the customer touches them.

Ask for the Order

The final step of a sales presentation is to "ask for the order." A good salesperson instinctively knows when the customer is ready to consider such a question, but it may be more difficult for the computer to know this. One reasonable approach is to provide a button on the screen that the customer can click to place an order. This button could appear once the price quotation phase is entered.

Order Entry

If the customer says, "Yes, I'll buy," there remains only the mechanical process of booking the order. The product description is already in the computer, and we only need to get the customer's name and address, shipping information if needed, and method of payment. At this point the sale is completed.

You can see from the foregoing that there is a lot to think about when planning for a multimedia selling program. Exactly how to apply this will of course depend on the nature of your product and the way your business operates. You will find this task worthwhile because of the advantages of multimedia selling, which are:

- It saves time for your salespersons.
- The customer may be more at ease taking the computer's time to get answers to questions rather than talking to a person who probably has a lot of other things to do and might push too fast for a conclusion.
- Every customer will get the same story. This eliminates the chance for errors or discrimination.
- Selling is a valuable application for multimedia, and as costs come down and systems are more widespread, we will see it everywhere.

MULTIMEDIA FOR TEACHING

The steps of teaching used for this discussion are:

- getting the student's attention,
- presenting the subject,
- questions and answers,
- testing, and
- student records.

Getting the Student's Attention

In a classroom environment, something must be done to get the student's attention. This can be even more important in the multimedia situation in which the teaching terminal may be located on a factory floor or in a busy office where there are many distractions. The approach to this is similar to the Product Overview step of selling—a snappy presentation or video is used to draw the student into the subject. In the kiosk business, this is referred to as the "attract" stage of the presentation.

In addition to getting the student's attention, it is necessary to make him receptive to new material. This is somewhat more subtle, but nonetheless important. It is usually done by exposing a little of the new material, preferably a very interesting part, to try and turn on the student's inquisitiveness and make him want to know more.

Presenting the Subject

The usual approaches to delivering material in classroom teaching involve either the lecture approach, where a teacher presents the material, or the textbook approach, where the student reads the material from a book. Most courses use a combination of both methods. The equivalents in multimedia are the non-interactive presentation (lecture) and the interactive (textbook) approach. Since the interactivity of multimedia is so much better than a textbook, interactivity is the preferred approach.

A good method is to show the student something that begins a path through the material, and then let him explore the rest of that path by himself. Using drawings, images, or video to let the student see the subject is better than using just text, and it is better still when the subject can be simulated by the computer and the student can work directly with it. The purpose of this section of the teaching program is to expose the student to the subject in a way that enables him to understand its structure and details. It is better to set this up as a series of steps or exercises, which are not viewed as tests (tests come later).

Student Questions and Answers

In classroom teaching, the instructor normally conducts a free-form question and answer session or discussion. In the computer multimedia environment, a free-form discussion is impossible, so the computer needs some other method to know what the student has a question about. Part of this can be handled in the previous section if the exercises are designed so that the student knows whether he has mastered a particular module. When it is not mastered, the student is free to repeat it and find what might have been missed the first time.

A more difficult situation occurs when the student has worked with a module, but finally throws up his hands and says, "I just don't understand this." That means there is something in the presentation that has not gotten through to that particular student. It usually calls for the subject to be presented in a different way in order to get over whatever roadblock the student has. It is difficult for the computer to interact with the student the way an instructor would to find where the problem area is. Usually, you just have to offer alternate explanations of the subject, which the student can access when there is a problem. Fortunately, most subjects can be broken up into small enough pieces that this problem doesn't occur too often; but when there is a portion of the material that presents a lot of problems, try to add alternate presentations to it.

Testing

Methods of student testing with a computer have been highly developed in the CBT (Computer-Based Training) field. In fact, one of the main approaches of CBT is to use a test-only method, where the student takes tests repeatedly until he has figured out how to pass them and go on. The typical computer-based test is a multiple-choice type, or possibly a numerical value test since the computer is not good at interpreting free-form text answers from students. Except for presentation of the question itself by using images, audio, or video, multimedia does not add anything new or special to the problem of computer-based testing.

Student Record Keeping

Student records are kept by the computer, in the background if necessary, during any kind of training or education. Multimedia does not add anything for this capability. Some CBT authoring systems have extensive modules to support student records; however, most multimedia authoring systems are not that specific, and recordkeeping may have to be programmed using the language of the authoring system.

MULTIMEDIA FOR INFORMATION DELIVERY

Information delivery is distinguished from selling by the fact that there is no follow-up to get an order. Sometimes this line is rather thin, and an information application may really be a selling application, but we won't worry about that here. We will discuss information delivery applications in the context of providing information in a public place through an interactive kiosk system, usually with a touch screen interface. The steps of such an information delivery application are:

- attract the user,
- teach the user how to use the application,
- make the information available, and
- close out the session.

Attract the User

This is very similar to the first step of a selling application, and it was discussed extensively there. However, an information application may have a more difficult problem in that potential users may see the application kiosk and not realize what it can do for them. Therefore, the application may need to sell itself. This is especially true in a public situation where the general public is passing and has no idea what that kiosk is there for. As in the selling situation, a dynamic presentation or video of some sort is the best way to draw attention to a screen. It is *not* acceptable to use audio in the attract mode, especially in a public place such as a museum where there may be several different kiosks vying for attention. There is enough noise pollution in the world without interactive kiosks adding to it!

Teach How to Use the Application

In all applications the user must know how to use the application. We haven't discussed this in the other cases because for selling or teaching there usually is time for this before beginning the application. Also in those cases, the user may work with the application over and over, but of course the learning problem occurs only once.

In the case of an information kiosk, be aware that the user has never seen the kiosk before, and probably does not have a lot of time. Therefore, the learning problem is acute and must be solved quickly and efficiently or the user will give up and go on.

The first principle of solving the learning problem is to make the application *simple*. There will never be time to teach a complex application interface no matter how important it is. Begin by letting the user know that he must touch the screen to be recognized by the kiosk. Ordinarily, the attract screen will prominently display the message, "Touch me."

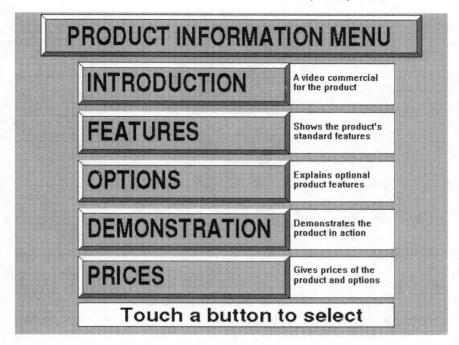

Figure 3.1 A simple, self-teaching menu screen.

Once the user has touched the screen, go into a combined teaching and menu mode. Usually a consumer will understand a screen divided into a small number of blocks (such as five or six), with each block identifying itself by text, and an additional text message that says, "Touch your selection." Figure 3.1 is an example of such a self-teaching menu. Once we have gotten the user to touch the menu, we are in the information presentation mode.

One strategy that solves the problem of attraction and lets the consumer know what the kiosk is for is to sequence between some attraction screens and one or more of the menu screens of the application. This sequencing should cycle every two or three seconds. The contents of the menus tell what is in the application, and the other screens simply create interest. Again, once the consumer touches the screen, the application will switch into the menu mode.

Making Information Available

Generally it is best to display information from only one menu or from a simple hierarchy of menus. Each level of menus should follow the rule of not too many selections, and everything should be clear and easy to understand. Once you have passed the first menu, it is best to use visual menus when they make sense. For example, showing the user a map on which he touches a location for more information makes sense and is a good approach. In such a case, however, there still should be a message on the map that says, "Touch a location."

Depending on the purpose of the kiosk, the information may consist of any of the metaphors of multimedia: data, text, drawings, audio, video, etc. In all cases, the screen should always contain touch buttons so the user can back up to the menus, move forward in the information, or abort entirely.

Closing Out the Session

When the user has finished finding the desired information, there may be some things you want to do to close out the session for him. The application could offer to print out the information or to follow up by making reservations, for example. This latter case is, of course, moving toward the selling arena, but it is perfectly reasonable if you want your application to do that.

If the user simply walks away, as indicated by the interaction stopping for a time, the application should automatically revert to the attract mode. A period of 30 seconds or so without interaction is usually reasonable for doing this, unless you are presenting information that has a longer reading time.

MULTIMEDIA USED FOR ENTERTAINMENT

Multimedia entertainment is difficult to break down into steps. It always will be interactive—simply playing a movie on the system does not fit our definition of multimedia.

Often, entertainment involves some kind of game scenario. In such a case, there is need for the user to know the "rules"; therefore, some opening screens must be devoted to that. A game scenario also usually involves keeping track of certain parameters, such as locations and scores, for which there will be a database structure associated with the game. The user moves in the database according to his interaction with the game.

An entertainment application usually does not need an attract mode, except in the situation where several games are competing with each other for the user's attention, as in a video arcade setting. However, if a game has a number of options from which the user can choose, you might want to have a "demo" mode that shows the user how the game looks with different choices.

THE CONTENT

At an early planning stage, you cannot expect to be able to map out the application content in detail. However, there are some general questions that should be answered and made part of the plan before you proceed. By content we mean the "information" in an information delivery application, the course material in a teaching application, and the product information in a selling application. In an entertainment application, the content is the support material for the game or entertainment scenario.

First, try to describe the content in general terms. For example, the material for an information kiosk in a shopping mall might consist of the following:

- names of all stores in the mall,
- locations of all stores and services,
- photographs or videos of locations,
- advertisements from the stores,
- special events in the mall, and
- community service announcements.

A list such as the above immediately lets you begin mapping out in more detail how big things are, how many of each element there might be, and how many different formats are necessary.

Once the content is listed, then figure out where to get it. How much of the information is already available, and how much will you have to create? For the material that already exists, how much modification will be required before you can place it in the application? Also, for existing material, are there any rights issues for which permission is required?

The previous details then lead to questions about the cost of the material, the amount of storage it will take in the application, and the amount of work necessary to collect, create, and adapt the material. Processing the material is normally the largest task in multimedia applications.

Many applications require that the material be kept up to date as the application is used over time. Again, once you know what the material is and where it comes from, you can begin planning strategies for maintaining the material after the application is in service.

54 *Designing Interactive Multimedia*

Figure 3.2 Proposed selling kiosk for camcorders.

WRITING DOWN OBJECTIVES

After you have gone through all of the considerations discussed in this chapter, you must then make decisions for your proposed application about what approaches you will take, and set them down on paper. This is called a *treatment* for the application. This will become your first description of the application you are planning. If you do this process well, much of the rest of the application development process will flow smoothly, and you will have a good idea of what lies ahead in the project.

As an example of a treatment for an application, the following is a description of the plan for an application that will sell a line of video camcorders. A sketch of the proposed selling kiosk is shown in Figure 3.2.

VIDEO CAMCORDER SELLING APPLICATION

The user for the camcorder application is expected to be an adult with some knowledge of home video, but not necessarily any knowledge of computers.

1. A new home camcorder product line will be sold through an interactive multimedia program to run on kiosks placed in audio/video stores and department store electronics departments. The line has

four products: from a leader item that provides the most value at a low price to a top-of-the-line product with outstanding new features, including electronic image processing of the captured video.

2. The selling kiosk has a touch screen display and will include a sample of the top-line camera, which the customer can operate during the application. The output of this camera appears in a quarter-screen window on the application screen. For quality examination, the camera window can be expanded to full screen. Any touch of the screen in the full-screen mode will return to the small window mode.

3. An attract video will be produced from the TV commercials that already exist for the product. These videos will require some re-editing for use in this way, but there will be no rights problems because the manufacturer already owns them.

4. Once a customer has touched the screen, we will present the product overview. This will be an audio plus still image presentation. It will show the four models of the cameras with closeup shots, and audio will briefly explain the features. This should be a maximum of one minute in length.

5. The product information section of the application will be based on existing product literature and still photos of the cameras and their controls. The architecture of this section will be a main menu from which to select one of the four cameras, and then a combination of menus and touch controls on pictures of the camera. A highlight of this section is that the customer can select a feature of the camera and audio explains to him how to demonstrate that feature on the live camera that is in the kiosk.

6. A button labeled "Ordering" opens a window of options from which to choose. As the customer selects options, the price of the current camera with the selected options is computed and displayed.

CHAPTER SUMMARY

This chapter covered the top-level planning considerations for a multimedia application. The steps of that planning are:
- Choose what your application is doing: selling, teaching, informing, or entertaining.
- Understand who your user is and what his demographics are.
- Plan what you will do at each step of the application.

- Figure out what the material for each step is, where it is going to come from, and what you may have to do to get it.
- Put it all down on paper.

4

Multimedia Architectures

In my experience, if you have to keep the lavatory door shut by extending your left leg, it's modern architecture.
  Nancy Banks-Smith: *Guardian*, February 1979

Computer applications are like buildings: They start with a structure and should be completed with a lot of adornment. In this chapter we will discuss the structure part. Later chapters will take up the adornments.

BUILDING BLOCKS

Just like a building's structure is made from concrete and steel, building blocks or ingredients are used for developing multimedia applications. An application is a computer program with structure at many levels—from the individual CPU instructions to the bit patterns within the instructions. It is not particularly useful for us to study those lower levels, just as it is not useful to examine the steel grains or atoms used to design a building. We can work at much higher levels of abstraction. However, there are many possible high-level representations for displaying a structure, so we must choose an appropriate high-level model for application structure.

The model we will use here is based on building blocks called *activities*. An activity is a collection of actions in series—one thing after another. Activities always have a single start point, but they can have multiple end points. The model for an application is built by hanging activities together

58 *Designing Interactive Multimedia*

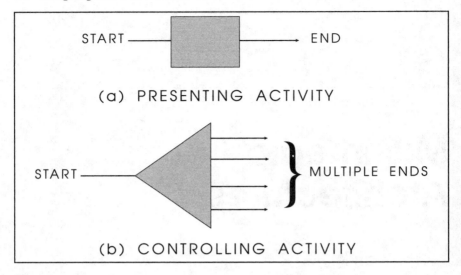

Figure 4.1 Application building blocks or activities: (a) Presenting activity: one start point, one end point. (b) Controlling activitiy: one start point, one or more end points, user input.

with logical connectors called *links*. To complete this model, we will define two kinds of activities:

- presenting activities and
- controlling activities.

Applications of great complexity can be built from networks of these activities. In this chapter we will examine these activities.

Presenting Activity

An extremely simple activity is one that does nothing more than display an image or play a video. A more elaborate activity might play a series of images, one after another. A further enhancement might begin playing audio at the start, and then show a series of images cued to specific points in the audio. All of these fit the definition of a presenting activity: one thing after another, as shown in Figure 4.1 (a). Running a series of presenting activities one after another is still a presenting activity. To deviate from that, obviously we have to move into structures that are not "one after another."

Controlling Activity

The simplest case from which we depart the "one after another" activity is a menu selection structure. Beginning with a menu screen, the user selects from a number of choices. Usually, the result of the selection is that another activity is run. At the end of that activity, the user is returned to the menu. The menu activity in this structure is not a presenting activity, it is a *controlling* activity.

A menu selector has one start point and multiple end points; it responds to user input to determine which end point to use. This is shown in Figure 4.1 (b).

Another kind of controlling activity has no input from the user; it responds to things that are happening to the system internally. For example, to make something happen at a particular frame number while video is playing, we would use a controlling activity that responds on a particular frame number. Of course, controlling activities can do both: respond to the user and respond to status in the same activity.

TOPOLOGY

This simple activity model can be used to demonstrate different types of application structures. We'll look at six classes:

- linear presentation,
- data-driven engine,
- hierarchical menu,
- information retrieval,
- hypermedia, and
- simulation.

Linear Presentation

A linear presentation has the same definition as a presenting activity—one thing after another. However, a useful presentation needs to have some control, so the most common structure has alternating presenting and controlling activities, as shown in Figure 4.2 (a). The reason for the controlling activities is to establish the timing of the presentation. For example, if the presentation will be used to support a live speaker, the controlling activities would probably be set up to receive cues from the speaker as she goes along. The cues could be in the form of keystrokes (any key). In that way, the presentation is synchronized with the speaker.

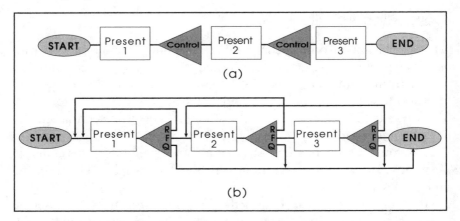

Figure 4.2 Structures for linear presentations: (a) Alternating presenting and controlling activities—no choices. (b) Same as (a), but each control point has the option to reverse or quit.

A more elaborate speaker-support presentation might have some other choices at each control point: the ability to go forward or backward in the presentation, or the option to simply quit the presentation. Hopefully these would not have to be used during the actual presentation to the final audience, but they will be invaluable for rehearsing it beforehand. An implementation of these options is shown in Figure 4.2 (b).

A Data-Driven Engine

Of course, even more elaborate options could be provided, but you can see that the structure is already getting complicated for something that is really doing a very simple task. One way to greatly simplify linear presentations is to use the *data-driven engine* approach. The idea is to make a program, called an *engine*, which reads instructions from a text file that specifies what happens at each step of the presentation. The text file has the items to present arranged in the desired sequence. Then, a single presenting activity is written to present whatever is specified, and a single controlling activity follows to await user commands about what to do next. For example, when showing a series of slides in a presentation, the sequence list would be just a list of the names of the slides to show.

Usually, the text file is set up to have one event per line. If the user chooses to go forward, we simply advance to the next line in the text file and repeat the presenting activity; if the user wants to back up, we back up to the previous line in the text file and repeat the presenting activity; if the user chooses to quit, we just quit. Figure 4.3 shows the structure of a linear presentation using the data-driven engine approach.

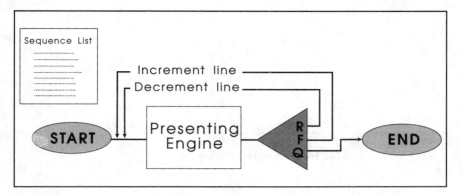

Figure 4.3 Structure for a linear presentation. This is an example of a data-driven engine.

The structure of a data-driven engine remains the same no matter how many items are presented—the controlling text file just gets longer with more items. If the author wants to change the order of the presentation, she simply rearranges the items in the text file. The presenting activity of the engine has the capability to read file names, and perhaps some other instructions from a text file; this is set up by programming with the authoring system. However, that programming has to be done only once, and then different presentations are created simply by making new text files.

The presentation by the engine can be made much more elaborate than just a slide show. By adding some instruction words to the text line for each item to present, we can gain control over the formatting of the item (whether it is a slide or a video) or the type of transition to use when the item is shown. This way, very sophisticated presentations can be created easily by writing simple text files. The text file becomes a very high-level language for writing presentations. An example of that is shown in Listing 4.1.

Listing 4.1 is set up so that each line of the control file contains three words. The engine program will take apart (parse) the control line and respond to each word. The first word specifies the type of activity, and the engine program interprets that word to tell whether to present audio, video, or an image. The second word of each line contains the file name of the item to present; the last word specifies whether to wait for the end of play in the case of audio or video, or the type of transition to use when showing an image.

The presentation produced by the control file in Listing 4.1 begins with the image **intro** and an audio message; the script waits for the audio to be finished. The engine program is set up to display a prompt to tell the

image	intro	h-wipe
audio	ending.avs	wait
image	trees	h-wipe
image	house	y-wipe
image	garden	bt
video	ending.avs	wait

Listing 4.1 Control file for data-driven engine

user that an action is required between each item. When the audio is done, and the user clicks the mouse or hits a key, the image **trees** is displayed using a horizontal wipe transition. On the next user action, the image **house** is shown, this time using a vertical wipe transition. Similarly, on another user action, the image **garden** is shown with a random-block transition (bt). On the last user action, the video **ending.avs** is played, and the script waits for it to finish.

This approach can be elaborated; for example, text could be displayed with each image either by adding another field to each line, or by adding a new activity type "text," which would display text without requiring any user action. The text activity might also be formatted to include some coordinate numbers for positioning the text on the screen. You could also specify colors for the text, perhaps add some graphics commands, etc. Soon, you have built your own multimedia language!

The MEDIAscript authoring system supports the authoring of data-driven engine scripts. It contains all the functionality needed to access control files, parse the control strings, and specify the indicated actions. The MEDIAscript OS/2 package offers a number of sample engine scripts that can be used as templates. Modifications may be made to these, or you can create additional engine formats by using the authoring features. The data-driven engine is an extremely powerful and flexible approach for multimedia presentations.

Some authoring programs have one or more data-driven engines built into their runtime modules. The authoring of an appropriate data file is supported in the authoring interface of the product. This makes the authoring of presentations extremely easy, but you are limited to only the presentation styles that are built in. The MEDIAscript OS/2 approach provides the same advantages, but the fact that the engine scripts are open and can be modified by a knowledgeable author greatly increases the flexibility.

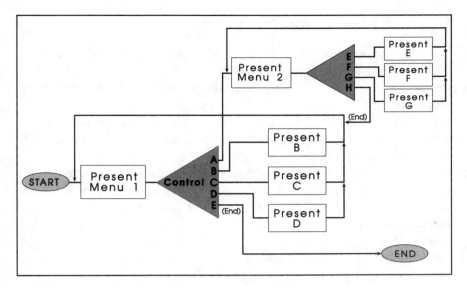

Figure 4.4 Structure for a hierarchical menu application

Hierarchical Menus

As shown in Figure 4.4, a menu is implemented by using a presenting activity to display the menu, and then a controlling activity to receive the user's selection. The result of the selection could go directly to another presenting activity or it might go to another level of menu. Figure 4.4 shows both possibilities. Notice that when a menu selection is completed, you return to the menu. Similarly, when you quit from menu 2, you return to the main menu. You have to go back to the main menu to end the application.

A menu setup like this can become very complicated quickly, especially if some of the possible activities appear on more than one menu. Again, this structure can be simplified by using the data-driven engine approach. One way to do that is to associate a text file with each menu, describing the menu items and the names of the presentations that they run when selected. A menu engine program can be written to display the menu from this file and then pass the name of the selected item to a single presentation engine program. Thus, the entire structure consists of just two engine programs—menu and presentation; and the complex application structure is actually held in a group of text files, which will be easy to build and maintain without any programming skill.

Information Retrieval

An information retrieval application deals with a multimedia database which can be a text database that has multimedia assets: text, audio, video, or images attached to the data items. For example, a multimedia encyclopedia would have the usual text information about each item, but it would also include photographs, audio clips, or even video segments about any of the entries. Flags or tag words in the database would identify the multimedia files that are connected to each text item.

The user is given various ways to enter the database and view it. Usually one way is to do a text search for particular items by use of keywords or names. The search takes place in the text part of the database using conventional text search software; but, when items are found, they are displayed along with their attached multimedia assets.

Usually you would begin with a menu structure from which the user chooses a viewing approach, and then selects or inputs the items to be searched in the form of a search pattern. The search pattern might be constructed by selecting items from an icon menu, but of course a text pattern is actually constructed in the program. The search activity would then be run, and the result of the search displayed as a list or a group of icons (assuming more than one item can be found). The user is then asked to select one or more items and specify what she wants to do with them.

This scenario involves a series of menus and input fields to receive the user's choices, followed by presenting activities to show the results; thus, it combines some of the structures already described. The only new item is the search activity, which is considered to be a special case of controlling activity. The searching and database access could be provided by a separate specialized program for that purpose, communicating with your multimedia program via DDE.

Hypermedia

In an information retrieval application, you may wish to allow the user to make selections directly on the data that has been retrieved in order to invoke further access. For example, if an image of a map has been retrieved, we would like the user to be able to click directly on the map in order to request more information about a location. This is hypermedia.

Implementing this map example means that somewhere in the database there is data that can be used to translate the position of the user's click into names or addresses for the associated information. The key is in setting up the multimedia database so that all the possible links are defined. This is a complex task, and it is seldom done in complete detail. What usually happens is that only the most important links are defined and, when an item is displayed, the positions on the screen that represent active (often called *hot*) links are somehow highlighted. The user knows that the highlighted items are defined links and chooses accordingly. Thus, in a block of text, you don't expect that there is a link behind every word.

A hypermedia system like this demands an engine approach, both for displaying and searching. It also usually requires writing special tool programs to create and format the database containing all the special link tags. The details of both of these are beyond the scope of this book. However, this is an important class of application, and there are specialized authoring programs available just for hypermedia.

Simulation

The final application type is one that simulates a real system, such as an aircraft cockpit or a truck cab. These applications typically are very specific and no generic structures apply. For example, a simulation of the electrical control panel in an aircraft cockpit would require very specific programming so that the displays and meters respond appropriately when the user changes switch settings on the panel. Although it is possible to make a structural diagram for that, it would be specific for only one simulation. Obviously, each simulation application must have its own structure.

Many applications will actually be a mixture of the types listed above. For example, an application may begin with a menu structure but, depending on the menu selection made, may follow with presentations, information retrieval, hypermedia, simulation, or even all of them. It is important that an authoring system be flexible enough to support such mixed types of applications.

CHAPTER SUMMARY

Multimedia applications are built by combining presenting and controlling activities. Typical generic application types are:

- linear presentation,
- data-driven engine,

- hierarchical menu,
- information retrieval,
- hypermedia, and
- simulation.

The data-driven engine approach is the most effective way to create complex applications with minimal programming. In this approach, generic modules are written so that the application is controlled by simple commands that these modules read from one or more text files. An engine program can be used for different applications of the same type without reprogramming simply by editing the control text files. Similarly, an application can be expanded to present more information simply by writing more text files for it.

5

Multimedia Presentations

A picture is worth a thousand words....

The statement above expresses the reason so many people who speak before an audience want to use pictures to illustrate their talks. With pictures, they can say more in less time, which is important because any speaker with something to say never has enough time. Thus, the efficiency of communication moves up several notches.

Because multimedia used creatively is an even more effective medium of communication than slides alone, it is natural that today's smartest public speakers are embracing multimedia. Presentations, whether for speaker support or for other purposes, probably make the most use of multimedia. Most multimedia applications do much of their work in the presentation mode; and the presentation is a building block of larger things.

This chapter details the interactivity of presentations, their structure, and how to design a presentation. For this chapter, a presentation is defined as any group of multimedia activities that run sequentially without branching. This does not preclude interactivity, however—we will see that there are still many opportunities—in fact, necessities—for interaction.

INTERACTIVITY IN PRESENTATIONS

Although non-interactive presentations do not fit our definition of multimedia, we include them here because they often exist in an application

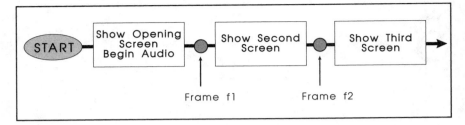

Figure 5.1 Example of a canned presentation. The presentation is controlled from an audio file.

that is interactive at a higher level. For example, the user may choose a menu item that then plays a canned, non-interactive presentation. At the end of this presentation, the application returns to the interactive menus.

Canned Presentations

Canned presentations have to contain controlling activities in order to establish timing. A common approach is to begin by playing an audio file. The audio then establishes the time line, and all other activities can be controlled by tying them to cue points (identified by frame numbers) of the audio file. A block diagram for this kind of presentation is shown in Figure 5.1.

It is also possible to run this kind of presentation from a data-driven engine program as discussed in Chapter 4. The control text file would begin with the first line giving the name of the audio file to play, and then each succeeding line would start with the frame number to cue on; the rest of the line would describe what to do on that cue.

The timing of a canned presentation can also be controlled by using delays. Most authoring systems provide for that, and it is the approach you have to use in any presentation that does not have an audio or a video file playing all the time to establish a time line.

Live Speaker Support Presentations

When a presentation is created for supporting a live speaker, the timing is uncertain, because it depends on how fast the speaker delivers the speech, as well as anything else that occurs to interrupt or divert the meeting. In such cases, it is best to set up the timing control interactively so that it can be determined by the speaker himself, or by an assistant. One simple approach is to make the presentation advance to the next step on any keystroke on the keyboard or on a mouse click. There are several controllers on the market that can be operated by the speaker from the podium using infrared or radio technology. Such controllers require a special interface to the computer, usually provided by means of an add-in board, or by using a serial port on the PC connected with an external box that holds the controller electronics.

Any of these control methods assume that the speech is planned well enough so that the speaker knows the order of the visuals and that he will be able to decide "on the fly" when to bring up the next item.

A problem with this "advance to next" type of control is that the speaker may accidentally move to the next item before he intended to, and there is no way to back up. Similarly, there may be a question from the audience that would best be answered by backing up to a previous screen. Both of these situations can be handled if the presentation is designed with a backup feature. This might be hooked to a particular key, such as the up-arrow or the backspace key (or both). Refer to Figure 4.2 (b), which showed a diagram for a script that does this. Similarly, another key such as Escape could be hooked up to abort the rest of the presentation. This is useful when the speaker has several presentation programs and wants to jump between them.

With an authoring system, you can construct any of these variations or even more elaborate ones. They can be designed as templates or engines so that you can easily put together different shows just by working with the content materials.

End User Interactive Presentations

When designing a presentation that an end user is going to view one-on-one interactively, you probably want to have a combination of the two types of control just described. The presentation is essentially canned, but you give the user some options to maybe back up, jump forward, or abort. Thus, the controlling activities respond to frame numbers when the user does nothing; but if the user makes a request, that takes precedence. (Of course, it doesn't have to be that way—design it to suit the situation.)

This type of control is probably best handled by giving the user a control panel on screen that he can click with the mouse. This works well in a windowed environment, where such controls can be placed in a different window from the one being used by the active presentation. The control window might be designed to be present during the entire application, and always provide the same options regardless of what activity is currently running. (We will soon see how important it is to provide a consistent interface to the user.)

STEPS OF A PRESENTATION

Designing the content of a presentation can be broken down into steps just as we did for selling, teaching, etc. The steps of a presentation are:

- getting the audience's attention,
- setting the mood,
- presenting the material,
- answering questions, and
- concluding.

Of course, these steps (and the discussion below) apply to any kind of presentation, whether it is multimedia or not. They deal with the environment of the presentation and are independent of the artistic or literary style of the presentation, which we will not cover here.

Getting the User's Attention

In a live meeting, the chairman often uses the gavel to get the audience's attention. In a one-on-one computer environment, we need to make sure that the user is watching and listening before starting the presentation. If the presentation is started because the user selected it, we can expect that we already have his attention; but, if it is invoked on a time cue or some other event that the user did not initiate, we should probably signal the user and possibly require an acknowledgment before starting.

Sound is a good way to get the user's attention. The presentation may begin with some sound that is not important to the material, but it serves as an attention getter. Then, after allowing enough time for the user to respond, we can continue with the actual material.

Setting the Mood

It is not enough to have someone's attention—we also need to be sure that he is going to be receptive to what we are about to say and that he will not just turn us off and miss the point. In live speeches, this is accomplished by opening with material that is intended to put the audience at ease with the speaker. Often this is in the form of humor. The same things will work with multimedia—you just need to make sure your opening approach fits the environment at hand.

If the presentation requires a major change in environment from the previous parts of the application, do this deliberately at the start of the presentation. You may want to completely change the screen, and cover up all of the previous material. This clearly tells the user that there is a change, and for the next part of the application, things are going to be different. To some extent, this is a style issue. We will address style and consistency in a later chapter, but it must be stated here that in the interest of making deliberate change clearly visible, there are style elements that should *not* be consistent.

Presenting the Material

This is the working part of the presentation, in which we present the material and, if there is a case to be made—make it. We won't try to cover all the variables of this part—again, there are all kinds of artistic and literary issues. However, we will discuss the proper use of the multimedia elements in a presentation.

1. First, it should be clear who is telling the story. All other multimedia elements should remain subordinate to the storyteller. With a live speaker, the speaker himself is usually the storyteller. Video or images on the screen and any sound from the system are clearly subordinate to the speaker. This relationship is usually easy to maintain.

2. In the case where there is no live speaker, defining the storyteller role is more difficult, but if you don't do this properly and consistently, your message may be distorted or lost. The simple parallel to the live speaker situation is to have an audio voice track that tells the story. This is a good approach, and one that the user will easily understand. Of course, this also works well when there is video along with the audio.

3. If you do not plan to have any audio, then you have to give some visual element the lead in telling the story. You might have an area of the screen (or a window) in which you dynamically display some text at the beginning of each step of the story. This would be a kind of header or preview of the subject coming up. Once that text has been displayed and the user reads it, he is then free to interact with other areas of the screen, which provide additional information about the subject that was introduced by the opening text. When the user is satisfied with this screen, he hits a "next" or "forward" button, which clears the screen and begins with new preview text. This way, the user remains in control, but the screen is telling the story.

4. Once you have chosen the storyteller, map out the story. If you are using an audio track or a live speaker, the natural way to map it out is to write a script for the speaker. However, you still need a way to show what the visual elements are and how they relate to the voice

72 *Designing Interactive Multimedia*

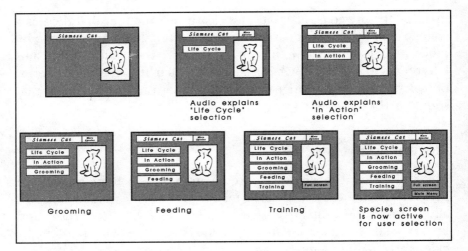

Figure 5.2 A storyboard for the cats presentation in the *Learn About Your Pet* **application.**

track. One way to do that is to write your script in a *two-column* format, where one column contains the text to be spoken, and the other column has notes about what happens visually. The visual notes are positioned relative to the text at the points where visual changes occur.

Another tool for this purpose is the *storyboard.* Figure 5.2 is a storyboard for a brief presentation about cats. This presentation is part of an application on the subject of pets; it is described in detail in Chapter 14. The cat presentation runs when the user chooses cats from the main menu, and it is the introduction to a submenu that offers more information about cats. The full application would have a similarly structured presentation for each of the other pets on the main menu.

The storyboard example shows that the cat presentation begins with a title and an image, then an audio voice-over introduces and explains the items on the submenu as it is built. It ends with the activation of the submenu for further user selection.

Large organizations have standards for how to write storyboards. When you are working alone, a formal standard is not necessary because you are just doing the storyboard for your own use, and you can develop your own notation to describe what you want to happen. What is important is that your storyboard should show step by step what happens on the screen, how one step transitions to the next, and what the audio track is doing at the same time. You can also add any other notes that you need to express what you want to happen. The example in Figure 5.2 shows this author's approach for that.

To coordinate the storyboard with the audio track, identify cue points in the audio track where each storyboard event occurs. After the audio has been recorded, these points will be converted into audio track frame numbers. The storyboard tells what you will have to author for each cue point.

Answering Questions

In a canned, non-interactive presentation, there is no opportunity for the user to ask questions. In this case, you have to foresee all questions and answer them in the basic material. If you forget an important question, the user will never know the answer, even if you know it.

An interactive environment does let the user "question" the subject, although there still is no way for the computer to answer a new, never-anticipated question. Therefore, you still have to foresee all possible questions. All you really can do is make sure that everything you know about the subject is on-line, and give the user ways to find whatever he is interested in. This is usually done by arranging the material into a menu structure or presenting it hypermedia style.

Ordinarily, this interactive environment should contain more information and more detail than that used in the formal body of the presentation. However, we can use a simpler method of presentation and depart from the style that was used in the main presentation. This is like going to the back of a flashy brochure and studying the specification sheets. Building the information database for this part can be a lot of work, and if we can simplify the style to make that easier, OK. It's more important to get all the information in the application than it is for it to be beautiful.

Concluding the Presentation

When the body of your presentation has been shown and questions have been answered, you probably want to provide a summary of conclusions or points made. In the case of a selling presentation, this is also the point at which you "ask for the order." The summary should be presented by the same storyteller element as used in the body, and with the same style. The purpose of this section is to help the user remember your points. If there are some dynamic things you can do to help that, now is the time. Next, if the presentation is part of a larger application, bring back the controls that will allow the user to navigate back to the main application.

CHAPTER SUMMARY

Multimedia presentations are the working part of multimedia applications. They are the place in which all the information is presented. They may be interactive or non-interactive. You should create a storyboard for the body of your presentation, and tie every event to an audio cue.

6

Using an Authoring Program

I love being a writer. What I can't stand is the paperwork.

Peter De Vries

Writers are authors, but in this book an author is much more than a writer. Most of the increase lies in the areas covered by an authoring program—and it's not paperwork! An authoring program is a tool for an author to create the structure of an application, to collect, create, and organize the content material, and to test the growing application.

In some books, the term *author* is used to mean *programmer*, referring to a person who does only the programming of an application. However, when there is only one person working at a desktop system and doing *all* of the tasks for an application, that person is called the author. Thus, our definition of author includes:

- application design,
- storyboarding,
- asset acquisition,
- programming,
- testing,
- distribution, or
- everything needed to create the application.

In a large project, there could easily be one or more specialists for each of these tasks. On the desktop, you, as the author, are doing it all.

If you are going to practice what this book teaches, you need to learn about authoring systems. A comprehensive authoring system is the principal tool for creating multimedia applications. This chapter defines what authoring systems do and how to choose one. Then, the MEDIAscript OS/2 Desktop authoring system, which was introduced in Chapter 2, is covered in detail. This description will give you a good picture of what MEDIAscript is like, what it does, and how applications look when created in MEDIAscript. In later chapters some actual application examples are presented in the MEDIAscript authoring notation.

WHAT DOES AN AUTHORING SYSTEM DO?

An authoring system helps you create an application. When a multimedia PC runs an application, a program tells the computer what to do. The program is usually in the form of one or more computer files, and the task of assembling an application is the task of creating the program files.

The contents of program files are computer instructions that the CPU will understand and execute to produce the application. For that reason they are called *executable* files. However, the author of an application will usually never see these instructions because she will work at a much different level. An authoring system presents the application to the author through an interface that is far easier to understand than the computer instructions.

Authoring can be done by skilled programmers working in a computer language such as C, BASIC, or Pascal. Those languages are all *higher level* than the actual computer instructions, meaning that they are less complex and less detailed. When a programmer finishes defining her program, she tells the computer to *compile* the program to the actual instructions. Only when that is done can the programmer test the program by actually running it. In this book, we are not interested in authoring by skilled programmers; rather, we are concerned with authoring with an *authoring system*, which makes it possible to author at a still higher level of abstraction without needing a lot of programming skill.

First and foremost, an authoring system gives the author a way to describe what goes into the application and what the application will do. This may be in the form of a special language that the author uses—somewhat like a programming language, but easier. Alternatively, the authoring system may use a graphical description of the application, which the author creates and manipulates with a mouse or other pointing device. Some authoring systems provide both approaches. In any case, the authoring system takes care of the task of converting (compiling) the authored description into a file containing the actual computer instructions. This process may be invisible to the author.

Some authoring systems use an *interpreter* instead of, or in addition to, a compiler to create the computer instructions to test the application. An interpreter reads the high-level program and sends instructions directly to the computer in real time. The advantage of an interpreter is that you are able to test your program as you go along, without waiting for a compiler to create an executable file. A disadvantage is that an interpreter may be a little slower than a compiled application. This can be important if the application contains looped activities which must run as fast as possible. Authoring systems based on interpreters usually have a strategy for getting around the interpreter slowness in places where the fastest execution is necessary.

Authoring systems can and do have other features, also called tools, particularly associated with the various *assets* needed—audio, video, image, and data files. These tools may perform audio, video, or image capture from live input signals; editing of those assets; management of asset files and directory structures; maintaining storyboards; and many other tasks. It is important that an authoring system include as many tools as possible.

PROGRAMMING IN AUTHORING SYSTEMS

Most authoring systems try to minimize the programming part of authoring by using a simplified language or a graphical interface. However, the need for some understanding of the concepts of programming cannot be removed entirely except in the simplest of cases. As soon as your application has interactivity using menu selections, or it requires textual input from the user, or it needs anything else that cannot be determined at the time of authoring, the programming concepts of *branching, variables, looping, conditions,* and *nesting* need to be understood. All authoring systems face this and they take different approaches to it; but beware, you will eventually get boxed in by a system that tries to hide programming concepts entirely.

Don't be intimidated by this admonition if you are not a programmer. The concepts needed are things that anyone can understand—you don't need a degree in computer science. Understanding these concepts will help you no matter what authoring system you are using, and we'll discuss each one here before continuing.

Branching

Whenever there is a decision point in your application, such as a menu selection by the user, you face a branching situation. This is because a computer program is simply a sequence of instructions that will be executed in order by the CPU. Thus, at a decision point where there are several choices for what should happen next, only one of those choices can be accommodated by continuing the sequence of instructions. All other choices are done by telling the CPU to jump (branch) to some other place in the instruction sequence at which the instructions for that choice begin. In most computer languages, this kind of action is handled by a GOTO command, and a *label* marker is placed in the program at the point to which you are going. This obviously leads to the concept of "going to" a point that is identified by a label. Authoring systems often may not show the actual GOTO command, but they use other ways of accomplishing the same result.

Variables

If your application needs to keep track of something that the user did so it can refer to it later, it will use one or more *variables*. Variables are simply places in memory where the application can temporarily store things. A variable always has a type so the computer can tell whether the variable is storing a number, a text string, a color, or many other types. Often variables are given names by which the author can address them; other times they are placed in *arrays*, which are groups of variables of the same type placed adjacent to each other in memory. Array variables are accessed by specifying an *index* number, which identifies which variable in the array you want. Array variables are convenient when you want to do a process on a whole group of variables; with arrays you can simply run the same process over and over incrementing the index number each time to move through the array. Most authoring systems provide for variables of several different types; they also provide various *functions*, which can be used with the variables. For example, numeric variables always will have available a set of *arithmetic functions* to perform normal arithmetic operations. Often the variable functions will be used by the author to write statements that look like algebra; actually, this is getting pretty close to programming.

Looping

The example in the previous paragraph of repeatedly running the same process for each variable of an array is a case of *looping*. Computer loops are used when you want to perform the same process or run the same block of instructions over and over. Setting up a loop involves three parts:

- establishing the initial conditions,
- establishing the condition for ending the loop, and
- the loop process itself.

The initial conditions are always set up before starting the loop; in the example above, initializing would be just to point the index number (a variable) at the first variable in the array. Similarly, the condition for ending the loop of the example would be to stop when the index number went beyond the last item of the array. This would normally be done by incrementing the index number at the end of the process and then testing the index against the number of array items. If the index is beyond the end of the array, the loop ends; otherwise, the process is performed again. There are also loop constructs used in programming languages that let you specify the ending condition before the loop starts; the instructions generated by the language then automatically take care of testing for the end condition—you do not have to specifically program for it. All of these possibilities occur in authoring systems; many approaches are used to simplify the setting up of loops, but in the end you have to understand what is going on in order to know when you need a loop in the first place.

Conditions

There are times when you will want your application to do something special when one or more variables reach particular values. This requires a *condition* statement. You specify a condition by using *comparison operators* such as = (equals), < (less than), > (greater than), != (not equal), and many others. Typical condition statements are:

```
xx < 10
yy = 123
str(0)="test"
(xx/yy) > 10
```

The first two just test numeric variables against constants, the third tests the contents of a string array against a string constant, and the last one performs division on two numeric variables before testing the result against a constant value. This looks like programming, and to an extent it is; authoring systems use different approaches as to how much of this they support, and to what extent they hide the details from you. Once you have the condition statement, the other part of the job is to act upon it. This is based on whether the result of evaluating the condition is TRUE or FALSE. If it is true, then a specified action will be performed; if the condition is FALSE, either nothing will be done, or in some systems you are able to specify an "else" action to be performed when the condition is FALSE.

Nesting

Any time you can specify a generalized group of actions to occur as the result of a condition (for example), it becomes possible to have another condition statement within the actions that occurred as the result of the first condition. This is called *nesting*, and it often will go on for many levels. Another case of nesting is in an environment in which you may divide your program into modules, and a module is capable of calling (running) another module. In this case, the second module is nested within the first one. Nesting ordinarily implies that the computer will remember the path it took to get to a particular nested item, and when that item ends the computer can back up to continue the previous item, etc. Most authoring systems support nesting, but they vary in the ways they hide it from you.

CHOOSING AN AUTHORING SYSTEM

We have already mentioned that there are over 100 authoring systems on the market. Choosing the right one for you can be quite a challenge. Fortunately, you can usually narrow the field substantially by considering the following issues:

- The authoring system must support your intended computer platform and multimedia hardware configuration. For example, if you are using DVI Technology, which is quite new, there are only a handful of systems to consider.
- If you lack programming skill, you probably want to exclude systems that use only a language-based interface. However, some systems that have a language also have a graphical point-and-click interface. This can give you the best of both worlds—as you become proficient with the graphical interface, you can begin learning the language which lies below and tap new levels of power for your applications.

- The various metaphors supported by the authoring system must include the things you will want to do in your applications. For example, if you want to include motion video in windows, make sure that your chosen authoring system can do that.
- The authoring system should match the scale of work you intend to do. Some authoring systems are intended for use by large organizations doing many projects. Such systems are more expensive and contain many features that are unnecessary for an individual user.
- Finally, the style of your authoring system should match your style— it's not going to be satisfactory to live with a system that does things in ways that you find awkward.

Thus, it is important for you to research the various systems that apply to your intended uses, and find opportunities to try out one or more of them before you make a final decision. Appendix B lists authoring systems which support DVI Technology. This may help you begin the search. Now we will turn our attention to MEDIAscript OS/2 and describe it in detail.

THE MEDIAscript MULTIMEDIA SERVER

The MEDIAscript architecture embodies *both* an authoring language and a graphical approach to authoring. It does this by using a multimedia authoring language as an interface to a special module called the MEDIAscript Multimedia Server (MMS), which interprets the language in real time and runs it on the multimedia PC. The Server is designed to be installed on your PC's OS/2 desktop (like a terminate-and-stay-resident program under DOS). It remains inactive until you send it some commands, and then it runs the commands to give you the requested multimedia service(s), after which it returns back to the inactive state, awaiting other commands.

The capabilities of the Server are:

- playback of DVI audio and motion video;
- display of DVI or Presentation Manager still images;
- creation of Presentation Manager windows;
- drawing Presentation Manager graphics and text;
- setting integer, string, rectangle, or color variables and data tables;
- collecting user input from mouse and keyboard;
- specifying program control features for building applications of any size and complexity;
- using DDE communication for control of other applications or control of the Server;

- support of serial I/O;
- support of file I/O;
- interfacing a printer;
- limited database functions; and
- audio/video editing.

The MEDIAscript Multimedia Language is an English-like language that provides high-level single commands for doing multimedia tasks such as playing audio, video, or showing images. It also includes lower-level features that give access to all of the capabilities of the host multimedia PC, and it has a large selection of computer variable constructs, mathematical functions, logical functions, and program-control constructs. Almost any type of application can be programmed with this language.

The MEDIAscript Language is also *device-independent*, meaning that it remains the same regardless of what multimedia hardware is in the PC. Differences in hardware are handled by making a Server that is tailored to the hardware you have. So, if in the future a competitor to DVI Technology comes out, a Server can be developed for it, and then all of the scripts you previously developed for DVI Technology should run on the new system as well.

Language commands to the Server are supplied in ASCII text files, called *scripts*. You activate the Server by giving it the name of a script to run. There are two ways to do that: You can enter it through a control panel on the Server, or you can send a DDE message with the name of a script to the Server. For a large application made of many scripts, one script is the starting point, and that script calls other scripts, and so on.

Because the Server accepts script names from DDE, you can invoke Server multimedia functions from any application that can use DDE. Applications such as Microsoft Excel or Asymetrix Toolbook can now integrate multimedia capabilities even though they were never designed for multimedia. Under OS/2 2.0, you can even do this from Windows applications. By simply writing a DDE macro in your Windows application, you can tell the MEDIAscript Server to open a window and play motion video (or do anything else that the Server is capable of)—completely under the control of your non-multimedia Windows application. The Server enables multimedia capability for your existing productivity applications!

THE MEDIAscript AUTHORING INTERFACE

The Server is an execution module for scripts or projects—it does no authoring functions. Although you can write scripts with any text editor, you need to know the language, and that is programming. Most people will want to use the second module of MEDIAscript OS/2 Desktop Edition, the Authoring Interface (AUI) module. The AUI is a second program module that runs independently of the Server; but when the AUI is invoked, it sets up a DDE communication channel to a Server, if one exists on the desktop. Working through this connection, the AUI and Server make an interactive, graphical authoring environment of unusual power and flexibility.

When you work in the AUI, your work is saved as script files which can be run directly by the Server without an AUI, or the scripts can be opened by the AUI for further authoring, testing, or modification.

The Server-AUI architecture has a number of advantages:

- Completed applications are run by the Server alone—there is no need to have the AUI module for this.
- During authoring, all execution of proposed scripts is performed by *exactly* the same module that will ultimately run the application. There is no possibility of things working differently during authoring and upon distribution.
- As already explained, the language interface is device-independent. New hardware is supported by updating the Server only. The AUI and any authored scripts do not have to change.
- More advanced authoring tools may be added to the system at any time; the Server is not affected by authoring improvements.

ASSET FILE MANAGEMENT CONSIDERATIONS

As stated repeatedly, multimedia assets (audio, video, images) can take up a lot of disk space. Furthermore, they are usually in individual files, which leads to a lot of files. The management of the asset files is a major concern, one that MEDIAscript provides for in both the Server and the AUI.

When you install the Server, you can specify a default directory structure for multimedia assets. Separate directories can be specified for script, audio, video, image, and other data files. Many people will want to keep their collections of these files together in specific directories; thus, they can tell the Server about their default directories.

However, when you are installing a large multimedia application on your machine you probably do not want its assets to get mixed in with your own. Thus, you need a way to change the default directories when an application runs. The AUI makes it possible to specify the directories to be used for each application you author. This is one of the features of a MEDIAscript *project.*

MEDIAscript PROJECTS

In the AUI, when you begin a new application, you open a new *project,* which is an AUI construct to manage all the parts of an application. A project creates two special files (which are actually scripts) that handle the overall management of the project when in the AUI and also when it is later run by the Server. These special files have filename extensions **.prj** and **.prs**, whereas all other scripts have the filename extension **.ms**. The project files keep track of all the scripts used by the application and how they will be run from one another.

The project files contain an asset directory structure that the Server will use when running the project. This directory structure may be authored specifically for each project. Thus, the asset filenames in the project's scripts do not need to have path names with them—the paths come from what was set up by the project. The project files also keep track of any variables that are used in the scripts of the project.

STARTING THE AUI

When you start the AUI, a number of windows normally appear, as shown in Figure 6.1. The window in the upper left corner is the Projects window, which shows all the projects that are available on your machine. You set this up by having one directory that holds all your **.prj** files. The AUI searches that directory to find the projects, and shows an icon for each project along with its name in the Projects window.

A second window, to the right in Figure 6.1, is called the Authoring Messages window. This shows debugging or error messages that come from the Server when you test your scripts. Also note at the lower right the icon for the MEDIAscript Server, which indicates that the Server is available for use by the AUI.

The AUI has a Configure option which lets you specify how these windows (and others) will appear when you start up. You can arrange your authoring screen the way you want it, setting window sizes and

Using an Authoring Program 85

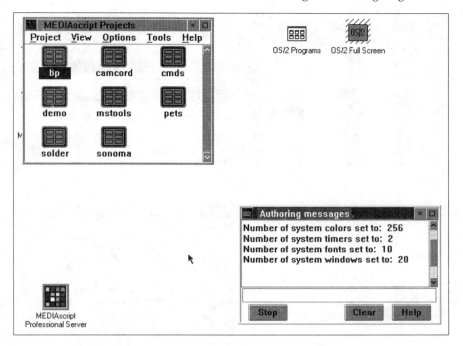

Figure 6.1 Opening screen of the AUI.

positions, and then tell the Configure option to save and restore it every time you start up.

On-Line Help

At all points in the AUI, an on-line Help system is available by hitting F1 on the keyboard. This opens the Help window, shown in Figure 6.2. The Help window provides *context-sensitive* help (the help subject displayed refers to what you were doing when you entered Help), along with hypertext links for you to navigate within Help. Most authoring dialogs also have a Help button that operates the same as the F1 key.

Opening a Project for Authoring

Select a project to work on by clicking on its icon in the Projects window. Then select Open from the Project menu of the menu bar, or double-click the project's icon. A new window will appear for that project, showing icons for all its scripts. This is a Project window, and is shown in Figure 6.3.

86 *Designing Interactive Multimedia*

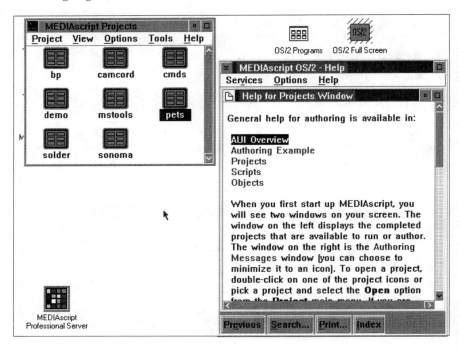

Figure 6.2 AUI on-line help.

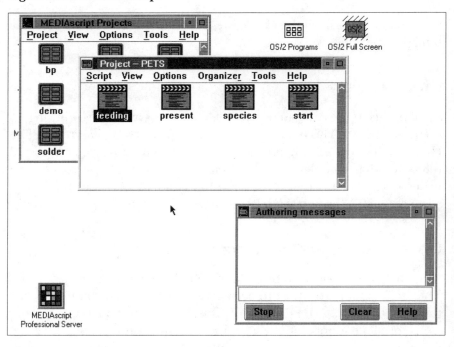

Figure 6.3 AUI screen showing contents of a project.

In the Project window, each script shows as an icon. In this case, the window is showing not a directory of the project, but all the scripts that are known by the project file. This means that you either must create the script in the project, or you must *Import* it into the project using the Import selection from the Script menu of the menu bar. (You cannot just copy a script into the project's directory—the script will not be listed in the project files and you will be unable to open it for authoring.)

MEDIAscript Script Window

The next level of the MEDIAscript authoring hierarchy is to open a script to see its contents, which are called *objects*; scripts are simply a list of objects. There are only 14 types of objects (described below), but this small number embraces all the multimedia constructs you need. Figure 6.4 shows a Script window that appears when you double-click on a script icon.

In the Script window, each line represents an object; the type is indicated by an icon, and some descriptive text follows to help the author understand what the object is doing. You can open multiple scripts at once for authoring, although the screen will quickly get filled with

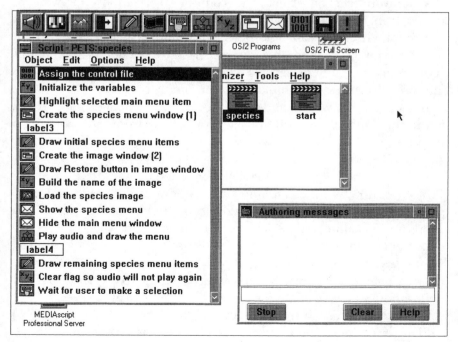

Figure 6.4 The AUI screen showing a Script window.

windows if you do very many. It is usually better to stick to one thing at a time unless you are specifically comparing or moving objects between scripts.

Notice in Figure 6.4 that there is a palette of icons at the top of the screen. This is the Object Palette and it appears whenever one or more Script windows is open. Use the Object Palette when building a new script or when adding new objects to an existing script.

Authoring of a new script consists of selecting New from the Script menu of the Project window. This causes an empty *unnamed* Script window to appear, along with the Object Palette, if it is not already on the screen. Double-click in the Object Palette to create objects to place in your new script.

When you double-click in the Object Palette, or you double-click an existing object in a script, an authoring dialog opens for that object. Fill in whatever options you need and click OK to complete the object and place it in your script. All objects have default behaviors, so you only need to enter items you wish to change from the defaults in the object dialogs. Objects that have mandatory entry, such as an image object that always requires a filename, will have their OK button disabled until you enter the mandatory information.

When you select an object or a group of objects in a script, you can choose from the Edit item of the menu bar to cut or copy the objects from the script. In either case, the objects go onto a special clipboard in MEDIAscript. From there they can be pasted to another location in this script or into a different script. This feature is important, as it simplifies authoring by the use of sample scripts or sample objects.

A special window is included in the AUI to facilitate sample-based authoring. Open this window by selecting Library from the Tools menu of either the Projects or Project windows. A Library window appears, as shown in Figure 6.5, containing an array of sample scripts.

A script in the Library window can be opened the same as a script in a Project window, but the resulting Script window is different. Figure 6.5 shows an open Library Script window to the right, but the objects in a Library script cannot be opened. All you can do here is select objects and copy them to the clipboard for pasting into scripts in your project. If you want to use a complete Library script, it is easiest to Import it into your project. That makes a copy of it in your project, which you can then freely edit without worrying about damaging the Library copy.

Over 25 Library scripts are provided with the first release of MEDIAscript, including a wide range of functions that are ready to go with minimal further authoring. You can also create your own samples by authoring them in a project, and then copying them into the Library

Using an Authoring Program 89

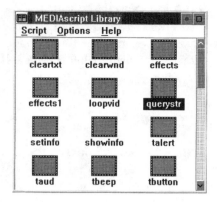 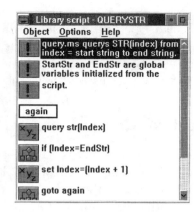

Figure 6.5 The Library window containing sample scripts. A sample script window is open to the right.

directory using OS/2. Your own samples will then appear in the Library window along with the standard ones.

MEDIAscript Objects

Figure 6.6 shows the Object Palette icons with the names of each object type. Certain objects have different uses; for example, the Window, Audio, Video, Image, Transition, Animation, Draw, and Alert objects are for use

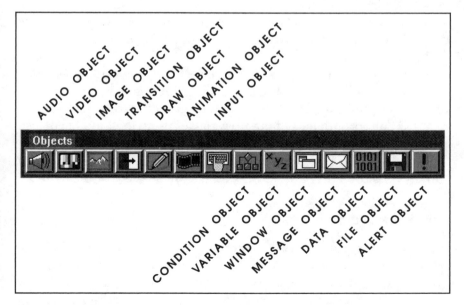

Figure 6.6 Object Palette and object names

in presenting activities. The Input, Condition, Variable, and Message objects are part of controlling activities; and the Data and File objects are collections of related commands for data processing and file management, respectively. Below, we will show the authoring dialog for each object type and discuss the features of the object.

Features Common to All Object Dialogs

All of the object dialogs have a little button marked "*" next to the OK button. This allows you to optionally author a line of comment text, which will be kept with the object. The comments appear next to the object's icon in the script listing of the Script window. If an object does not have any comment text, then the Script window displays some statistics about the object instead.

As you work with the authoring dialogs, you will notice that the coordinate numbers seem very large—they go up to 10240 × 7680. These numbers are the full-screen size in MEDIAscript *abstract coordinates*. Since an author may be dealing with many different coordinate systems between VGA, XGA, and DVI (which itself has several sets of numbers), MEDIAscript simplifies this by having only one coordinate system. The Server converts these numbers to whatever physical screen size is in use at runtime. Thus, you can author a script and use specific coordinates to position objects on the screen and it will look the same when running on either a VGA or an XGA screen. The large coordinate range, 10240 × 7680, was chosen so that conversion to most physical resolutions can be done without interpolation. In MEDIAscript OS/2, you have to get used to thinking about a screen that is 10240 units wide and 7680 units high!

In all the object dialog entry fields where an integer number is called for, you can always enter a MEDIAscript variable name or an expression of variables. Thus, you can have any parameter adjusted dynamically at runtime by appropriately setting up variables using the Variable object. Similarly, all object dialog entry fields that call for a text string (such as a filename) will also accept the name of a MEDIAscript string variable. At runtime, the contents of the string variable will be used for the name.

The Window Object

All visual information in a MEDIAscript application is presented in one or more windows. You must create a window before you can show images, graphics, or video. Windows basically exist on the VGA plane, but if they are filled with black, they become transparent and also display the DVI plane, which is behind the window (see Chapter 2). Windows may be

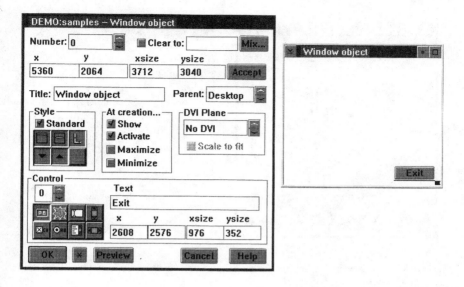

Figure 6.7 The Window object authoring dialog with the authored window shown to the right.

specified any size up to full-screen, and they may have borders and other attributes. The Window dialog, shown in Figure 6.7, is used to create an application's windows.

When you open the Window authoring dialog, the actual window being authored also appears on the screen—it is the smaller window shown at the right in Figure 6.7. The author has the choice to adjust either the sample window on-screen, or enter parameters into the authoring dialog. This procedure works for the window's overall dimensions and for the dimensions of any window controls that are desired in this window. In the authoring dialog you can choose the window's style, specify a window title, whether you want the window to appear immediately when it is created, and various other attributes.

You can also create any of eight types of window controls: pushbuttons, radio buttons, check boxes, hot spots, list boxes, entry fields, or scroll bars. The controls exist in the VGA plane, so they always appear on top of any DVI images or video. They also are automatically connected into the Input object for controlling purposes.

The Audio Object

The Audio object controls the playing of DVI compressed audio files. The Audio authoring dialog is shown in Figure 6.8. It requires you to specify a filename before an audio object will be created. You can type in the

92 *Designing Interactive Multimedia*

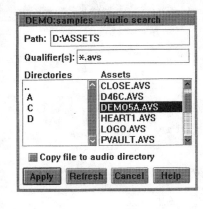

Figure 6.8 The Audio object authoring dialog with the Audio Search dialog to the right.

name if you know it, or explore your hard disk to find the file using the Find... button, which opens the "Audio search" dialog. When you have located the audio file you want, simply select it in the Find window; its name appears in the Audio dialog. This method of finding filenames is available everywhere in MEDIAscript that you need to enter filenames.

The Play button in the audio dialog can be used to preview the audio you have selected. When you select Play, a small control panel appears enabling you to play, pause, or stop the audio. This panel also displays frame numbers when the audio is paused, so you can use the player to find exact frame numbers if you need them.

The audio dialog also provides options to set the audio volume, specify when to play the audio, whether to play it more than once (loop), and set starting or ending frame numbers if you don't want to play the entire file. You can also access the Audio Capture tool from the Audio dialog, a process we'll discuss later.

The Video Object

The Video object controls the playing of DVI compressed video files. The Video authoring dialogs are shown in Figure 6.9. It also requires that you specify a filename before a video object is created. When a filename is entered, a Play button is activated so that you can preview the video. A separate window shows the video, and when you pause it, the current frame number is displayed.

Using an Authoring Program 93

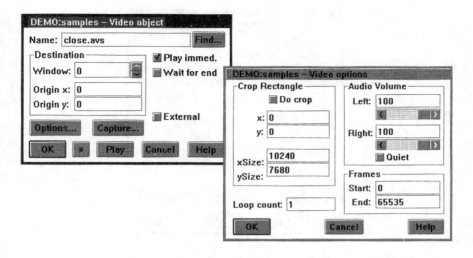

Figure 6.9 The Video object authoring dialogs with the Video Options dialog open on the right.

Other video authoring options control how the video is to be started, what window to play it in, how to position it in that window, whether to crop the video when playing it, start or ending frame numbers, looping, and audio volume. All of these have defaults, and they do not have to be filled in unless you want to change from the defaults. Since playing of video always requires a window, you must create a window in your script before playing video. However, you can create a window once and use it again and again for video, images, or graphics, or all at the same time.

The Image Object

The Image object controls the presentation of Presentation Manager or DVI still images. The Image authoring dialog is shown in Figure 6.10. This dialog requires you to specify a filename before an image object is created. When you have entered a filename, you can select the Preview button to open a separate window, which will show your image to make sure you have the correct one. An information window with the preview image shows the image's type and size.

Other options in the Image dialog let you specify the destination window for the image, positioning and cropping of the image, and whether you want to immediately transition the image. The image capture tool is also accessible from this dialog.

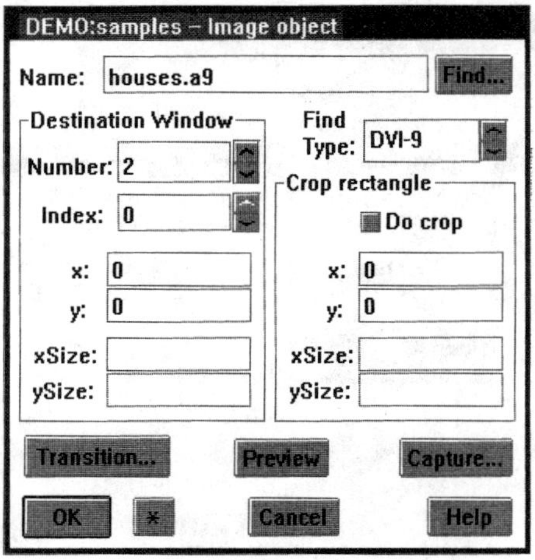

Figure 6.10 The Image object authoring dialog.

The Transition Object

The Transition object produces dynamic transitions between images. The Transition authoring dialog is shown in Figure 6.11.

The Transition object is used to move images from a source window to a destination window. Normally, the source window is invisible (you can specify this when you create the window), and the destination window is visible. To transition an image, both source and destination windows must

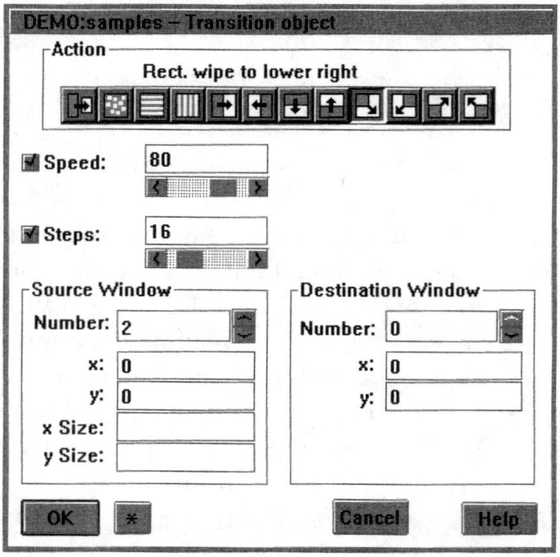

Figure 6.11 The Transition object authoring dialog.

first be created. Then load the image to the source window using an Image object. Finally, create the effect using the Transition object. Depending on the choice of transition type, you can cause the source image to appear instantly, to wipe into the destination window, to appear in random blocks, or to appear as a row of bands that fill in.

For a transition, you can specify which windows to use for source and destination, crop the source image, and specify position or size for the destination image.

The instantaneous transition, which is simply a copy, can also be used to build a screen from several images. You can also write a script that repeats a copy while incrementing its parameters, which you specified as MEDIAscript variables. This way you can create your own unique transition effects. Another feature of the instantaneous copy transition is that you can specify values for the brightness, contrast, color tint, or color saturation for the image. Thus, you can modify the appearance of an image at the same time that you copy it.

The Animation Object

The MEDIAscript Animation object facilitates the playing of *frame* animations. These are animations that are based on sequentially displaying frames from an array of images. Figure 6.12 shows how frame animation works, and it is explained further in Chapter 13.

The dialog for the Animation object is shown in Figure 6.13. The Animation object uses a window for its source. Often you will have the source frame array in an image, so you would create the source window invisible with a Window object, and then use an image object to place the source image into the window. You could also build the source array from

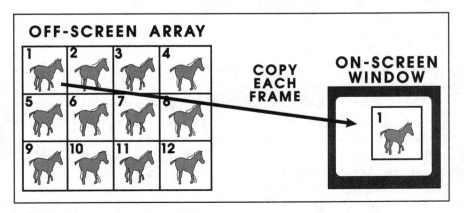

Figure 6.12 Frame animation concept.

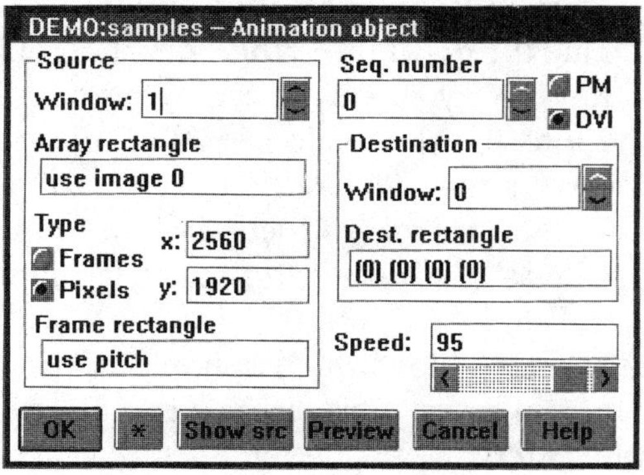

Figure 6.13 The Animation object authoring dialog.

several images, or even draw it. Then you would author the Animation object, which will perform the animation into another window that would normally be visible on the screen.

In the Animation dialog, you must specify either the number of frames in each direction in the source array, or the x and y sizes of one frame in pixels. If the source window and image exist in memory, you can use the Preview button to display the animation while you are authoring. The dialog also provides options to crop the source frame, to specify the position and size of the destination animation, and to set the speed of the animation. By specifying frame sizes properly, you can also create a moving panorama effect.

MEDIAscript can have multiple animations running concurrently; you specify each one by using different Sequence numbers. You can also have animations running in either the PM or the DVI plane. The limit to the number of animations is determined by system memory and speed.

The Draw Object

You can add graphics and text to a window by using the Draw object, whose dialogs are shown in Figure 6.14.

When you open a Draw object, a destination window showing the drawing opens along with the authoring dialog. Draw by selecting draw tools from the palette in the Draw dialog, choosing a color from the color palette, and then drawing with the mouse in the Destination window. Drawing is always in the Presentation Manager plane, not DVI, so you are restricted to the colors available in that plane. A color mixing window can also be opened with the Mix... button to create PM dithered colors.

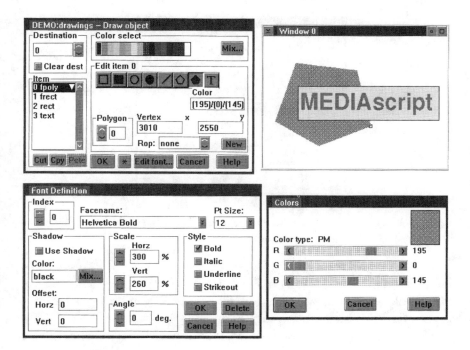

Figure 6.14 The Draw object authoring dialogs.

To draw text, click the Edit Font... button to select a font type, style, and size. Then enter the text into an entry field in the Draw dialog. The text is drawn by clicking the right mouse button, which causes the entire drawing to be refreshed. Your drawing is saved as a series of individual commands in the script. An abbreviated list of the commands appears in a list box at the left of the dialog, and it can be used for editing the list by cut, copy, or paste modifications. You can also move draw items from one Draw object to another using a special Draw clipboard.

The Alert Object

The Alert object lets you add comments to your script, display debugging information during authoring, or put up warning message boxes for your end user. Its authoring dialog is shown in Figure 6.15.

When you are using the AUI, the Authoring Messages window is always available to display error messages that come from the Server. If you run an object or a script from the AUI and the Server finds an error, it will be reported in this window. The Authoring Messages window saves all the error messages in a list which you can scroll through to see what happened and when.

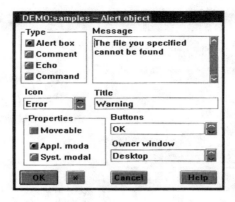

Figure 6.15 The Alert object authoring dialog. The dialog is shown in the "Alert box" mode.

You can force a message to be displayed in Authoring Messages by creating them as an Alert Echo object at any point in your script. You can also display values of variables for debugging by setting up a Variable object with the Query option turned on.

The other mode of the Alert object is to display message boxes during your application. A message box presents a window with a text message to the user and demands a response before your application continues. You can author the message contents, the message box style, and the type of button choices that will be shown. Following a message box, you can set up to perform different actions based on which button the user clicked in the message box.

The Input Object

The Input object is the principal object for implementing a controlling activity in MEDIAscript. Its authoring dialog is shown in Figure 6.16.

A properly designed MEDIAscript application will spend most of its time sitting in Input objects, as this is the only way the application can be responsive to the user. An Input object waits for *events*, which are either actions by the user or system events such as the occurrence of a particular frame number.

When authoring an Input object, you specify a list of events to which you want to respond. The event types are:

- any keyboard or mouse action,
- specific keyboard actions,
- click specific buttons in specific windows,
- time out of this Input object,

Using an Authoring Program 99

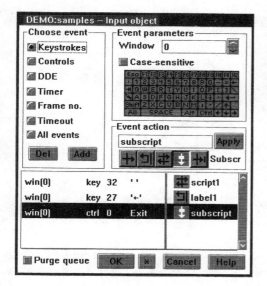

Figure 6.16 The Input object authoring dialog.

- system timers that can repeat over and over,
- DDE events, and
- frame numbers in video or audio while playing.

Then you specify for each event the action which should take place if the event occurs. There are five actions that you can specify for any event:

- **LINK** – quit this script and run another.
- **GOTO** – jump to another place in this script and continue.
- **CALL** – run another script and return to this object.
- **SUBSCRIPT** – execute a list of objects and continue this object. This is the most general action type; in a subscript you can do *anything*, even another Input object. At the end of the subscript, the system returns to this Input object to await further events.
- **QUIT** – exit from this script.

One Input object can respond to any number of events. There is also an event called "all events," which is just a way to specify an action that you want to occur regardless of which event happens. This can be used at the same time you specify a particular action for each event.

Most of a script's action usually occurs inside of an Input object. And no matter how many items there are in an Input object, it will still appear as a single icon in its parent script. To see the contents of that item or to make changes, you must open the Input object.

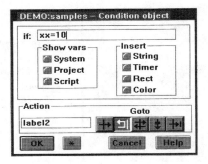

Figure 6.17 The Condition object authoring dialog.

The Condition Object

The Condition object lets you create a controlling activity by testing MEDIAscript variables and specifying an action to occur when a test is true. The Condition dialog is shown in Figure 6.17.

In the Condition object you specify a logical test on a MEDIAscript variable or an expression, using any of the comparison operators: =, >, <, =, !=, &&, ||, !, &, |, and ^. When the condition is true, an action is performed. The same five actions described for the Input object are available.

The Variable Object

MEDIAscript has many types of variables; all their values are assigned using the Variable object. Its dialog is shown in Figure 6.18. In this dialog, you specify the name of a variable, which may be a system variable (predefined), a script or project variable (defined by the author), or a string, timer, color, or rectangle variable (predefined arrays). Then you put in '=', followed by the desired assignment, which may be either a constant value, or an expression.

A single Variable object can have up to eight separate assignment statements, so you can perform complex operations in one object. Usually, you will have a Variable object combined with a Condition object; the Variable object performs the processing of variables, and the Condition object tests the results and acts accordingly.

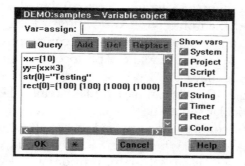

Figure 6.18 The Variable object authoring dialog.

The Message Object

The Message object lets you send commands to concurrently running processes; for example, you can tell a running video to pause. The Message authoring dialog is shown in Figure 6.19.

Messages can be sent to audio or video files that are open, windows that exist, window controls, existing animations, or DDE. We won't cover all the possibilities here, but you can adjust most of the parameters of audio and video dynamically this way, as well as showing, hiding, or destroying windows or their controls individually, adjusting an animation, or sending DDE messages to another application.

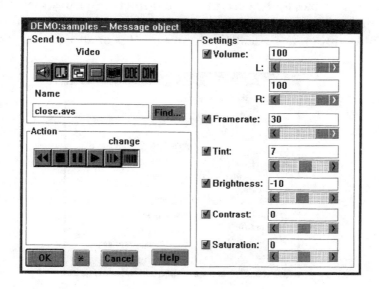

Figure 6.19 The Message object authoring dialog. The object is set up for a video control message.

The DDE features in the Message object, combined with DDE features in the Input and Data objects, let you author a DDE link to another application that can send or receive data and commands. These features are general enough to build any kind of protocol as required by the other application. If you have the Excel spreadsheet on your system, for example, through DDE you can have MEDIAscript tell Excel to start up and open a particular spreadsheet, and then tell Excel to change some cell values. Or, you could tell Excel to read back to MEDIAscript the values in a specific range of cells. When you are finished with Excel, you can tell MEDIAscript to close it. MEDIAscript provides a collection of sample scripts and macro scripts to facilitate the setup of DDE communication with many different applications. These are currently available for Excel, Microsoft Word, Toolbook, Visual Basic, Object Vision, and Easel, with more being added for both OS/2 and Windows programs.

The Data Object

The Data object provides a collection of features for data file I/O to hard disk and printer. It also has commands for doing text searches on MEDIAscript string variables or disk files. Its dialog is shown in Figure 6.20.

MEDIAscript supports printing of text information created or specified during an application. The Data object can send the contents of a group of string variables to the current system printer, or it can specify a file to be printed. By using the **write** action of the Data object, you can also have MEDIAscript create a text file from a group of string variables. For

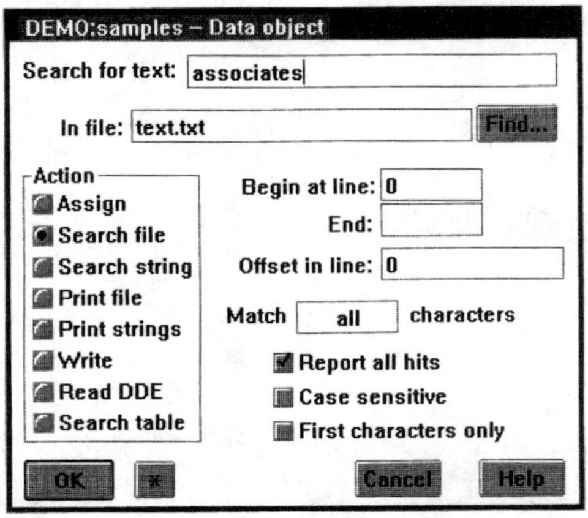

Figure 6.20 The Data object authoring dialog.

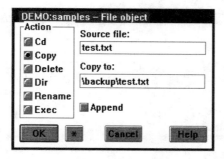

Figure 6.21 The File object authoring dialog.

graphical printout of screens or windows (PM plane only), the OS/2 system tools can be used.

The File Object

The File object provides a collection of features for file management. Its dialog is shown in Figure 6.21.

MEDIAscript Capture Tools

The acquisition of assets (audio, video, images) usually becomes a major part of the task of authoring an application. Often, some of the assets are available in a non-computer format, such as analog audio or video tape or still photographs. The task of capturing these into digital form on the computer is non-trivial. Therefore, audio, motion video, and still image capture tools are built into MEDIAscript OS/2. They are accessible from the menu bar of the Projects or Project windows, and from the respective object dialogs. These tools will not be described here, but each of the asset types are covered in detail in Chapters 10, 11, and 12.

The MEDIAscript Organizer

An application (a project) usually consists of many scripts, which run one after another according to the overall architecture of the application. In MEDIAscript, you can set up that architecture using the Organizer tool. Figure 6.22 shows the Organizer window.

All the scripts in the project are listed in the Organizer, along with a listing of their *links*. Links are named exit points in the scripts, which can be created by Input or Condition objects using the LINK action. For example, each choice of a menu might be given a link name. In the

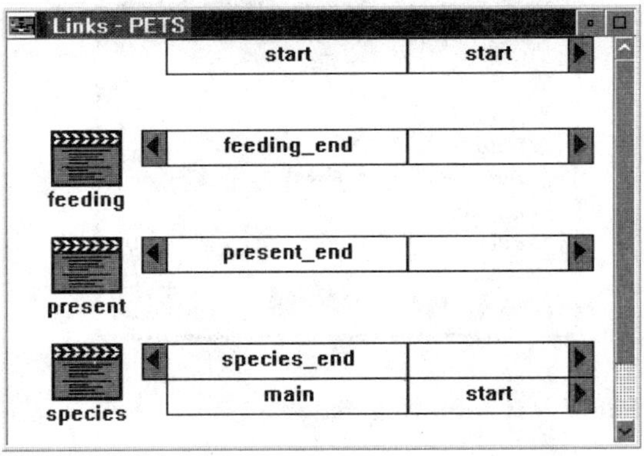

104   *Designing Interactive Multimedia*

Figure 6.22 The Organizer window.

Organizer window, these named exit points can be connected to another script simply by clicking on the script's icon. The name of the connected script then appears in the block to the right of the link name. The project files will store the link connections for use when the project runs.

Every script is automatically given a link name for its end, indicated by the suffix "_end" in the Organizer window. These points are thus accessible even when a script contains no Input or Condition objects. If a project's execution reaches a link which is not connected to another script, the project will automatically end.

In order to follow the flow of execution through a project, an author can use the arrows to the right or left of the link statements to move either forward or backward through the project. The Organizer window will automatically scroll to the next item when you click the arrows. Notice that the Organizer metaphor places no limitations on how the scripts of a project are connected. The project architecture may be any kind of multidimensioned structure or network.

SAMPLE OF AN AUTHORED SCRIPT

Figure 6.23 shows a script that simply displays an image and gives the user a button to click when she is finished looking at it. Since the loading of the image may take several seconds, a "Getting Ready" message is put up first. When the user clicks the button, all the windows are destroyed.

The sequence of objects for this sample script is as follows:

- A window is created for the "Getting Ready" message.
- The "Getting Ready" text is drawn.

Using an Authoring Program 105

Figure 6.23 Sample of a script that displays an image. The script also "waits" for user input.

- The image display window is created invisible.
- The image is loaded to the Display window.
- A Message object tells the Display window to show itself.
- A Message object destroys the "Getting Ready" window.
- An Input object then waits for the user to click the button. When the button is clicked, a GOTO action moves to **label1**.
- **label1** is shown in the script.
- A Message object destroys the display window.

Authoring of a script like this takes only a few minutes to complete. Although you could display an image with fewer objects (actually just two: a Window object and an Image object), this script does it more smoothly; it gives the user immediate feedback, and it cleans up all windows when it is finished.

CHAPTER SUMMARY

You can see from this quick overview of the MEDIAscript authoring environment that it is very powerful. Despite its apparent degree of complexity, MEDIAscript's structure can be used by nonprogrammers and programmers alike. The preauthored sample scripts can be used as examples that will help beginners not only to get immediate results, but to progress; and the features available in the objects allow experienced authors to tackle more difficult problems, still without having to learn a new language.

7

User Interfaces

user: one who uses the services of a computer system.
interface: a shared boundary.
　　　　　IEEE Standard Directory of Electrical and Electronics Terms, 1988

If you have ever struggled through the programming of a VCR to record a television show, you know the importance of a good user interface. The usefulness of a product depends entirely on the customer's ability to successfully operate it. If a user can't figure out how to run the product, the interface is automatically a failure.

Interaction with a product is through its *user interface*: What you do with the product, what you see and hear, and what the product does, are all part of the product's user interface; in short, it is a face-to-face conversation.

User interfaces—some good, some bad—are all around us. The kitchen stove, the coffee maker, even the bathroom sink have user interfaces. We take them for granted because we know them and how they work. At a more complex level, significant time is spent learning another important user interface—the automobile. It also becomes an integral part of our life.

But as we move up to even more complex devices, especially electronic ones, we are often dismayed at the difficulty of the user interfaces, and often we do not want to make the effort to master them. We expect things to be intuitive, and when they are not, we may abandon the device. And at the top of this arduous heap is the personal computer. Because of its programmability, the personal computer is unique: Its physical controls—keyboard, mouse, etc.—are reasonably well standardized, but what they *do* may be *anything* depending on the software running at the moment. Because of the many varieties of software, the user interface can change drastically from one instant to the next. This is not only confusing, it taxes our intelligence (and patience) to remember all the interfaces.

Some computer manufacturers have tried to deal with this problem by setting standards for user interfaces. The most successful of these is the Apple Macintosh. Apple addressed the user interface when they were developing the machine; they wrote standards *before* any software was written for it. Then they asked all software developers to follow the standards. To encourage compliance, they added significant functionality to the operating system to support the standard user interface, which made it easier for a software developer to use the standard interface than it was to write his own from scratch. The result is that the Macintosh is recognized for the most consistent user interface of any personal computer.

In the case of the IBM-compatible PCs, no user interface standard was available at the start; standards were written later as the PC world began to transition to the graphical interfaces of Windows and OS/2. Both of these products have user interface functionality built into their systems, and they provide documentation on how to use it. The best reference on this is the *Common User Access Advanced Interface Design Guide* published by IBM. This excellent document (often referred to as the *CUA Guide*) was written for OS/2 designers, but it is equally applicable to Windows designers. It contains fundamental advice that applies to any computer system with a graphical interface. Additional references for user interface design are in Appendix D.

This chapter discusses the design of user interfaces for multimedia applications.

TYPES OF MULTIMEDIA USER INTERFACES

The user interface of a multimedia application is that part of the application that presents choices and requests to the user, receives input from the user, and provides the user with feedback about status. For user interface purposes, we can divide all multimedia applications into two categories: those that want to look like a computer, and those that don't. This division depends primarily on the type of end user: If the intended user is the general public, the system should not look like a computer; other users, who are primarily professional and business people (we'll call them the *professional* audience), don't care what the system looks like—a computer metaphor is fine.

As mentioned before, a large segment of the general public is not comfortable with computers. They relate much better to television. For this audience, it is best to use a full-screen metaphor, showing one thing at a time like television, and do not use any of the computer-style control gimmicks. On an ActionMedia II system, a television look is accomplished by using the DVI plane as much as possible for the interface, because DVI images look just like television, with many colors and smooth gradations of color.

For the general audience, do not assume that the user will have any previous knowledge of user interfaces. All information about what to do next should always be available, either on the screen or in the audio. This restriction is both good and bad. On the one hand, it provides more flexibility to design different interfaces because we explain the interface to the user right there. On the other hand, we have the obligation to build the explanation into our interface.

With the professional audience, we can assume that they are familiar with CUA conventions, and that they know how to work with a windowed environment. But because multimedia has so much flexibility, we must be careful with design because it is easy to depart from CUA rules and make non-standard interface elements. And when an application needs to do that anyway, we have to be sure to provide the information so the professional user can figure it out.

USER TASK ANALYSIS

The key to designing a successful user interface is to have a complete understanding of the target user. This includes not only the demographics of the user, but a full appreciation of what the user will do with the interface and the application. How will the user use the application? What steps will he follow to get the results he expects from the application?

A good way to answer these questions is to study the user in action: develop serveral scenarios describing different ways of interfacing with the application and then think through how the user will do the necessary work. Take the user's point of view. This process is sometimes called *user task analysis*, and the more complex the proposed application, the more important task analysis becomes. Once you have developed a road map for how the user's work will progress through the application, you are ready to start design of the user interface.

CONSISTENCY

The overriding consideration of a user interface is *consistency*. When the same thing is done in two parts of an application, it must look and operate exactly the same in both places. Once we have taught the user how to do something, it should work the same way every time.

With general audience applications, the consistency rule applies rigorously inside of one application; for that audience, however, consistency is less important *between* applications, because we require that each application is self-sufficient and teaches its own interface anyway. This is based on the assumption that the general audience never sees more than one application at a time. If, on the other hand, the environment is such that the same user will be running more than one application in the same session, then obviously we should have consistency between those applications. It would be better still if there were standards for this use, and there could be. We will be discussing some of the issues later in this chapter, and make recommendations that are a step toward consistency between applications. With industry standards activity in this area, we may someday be able to assume that the general public knows a standard interface.

SIMPLICITY

A general principle of all types of design is that simple is better. It certainly applies to multimedia applications and their user interfaces. If we have a simple application concept, then the interface can also be simple, and therefore easier for the user. If you spend time thinking through the architecture of your application and what features you will and will not put into it, it will pay off in the design of the application itself and also in the ease with which you can build the user interface. Especially for a general audience, carefully weigh whether there is real need for all those bells and whistles, which greatly complicate the user interface and may not be used anyway.

If you must have a lot of complex features in your application, then at least try to make it *look* simple. The best way to do this is to make a list of all the features that have to be accessed by the user, and prioritize them by frequency of use. Features that are used often should be directly accessible, with as few selection steps as possible. Lesser-used features can be hidden in submenus, such as "Options," "Configure," "Tools," etc. (These are names from the MEDIAscript AUI submenus, which are an example of a user interface for an extremely complex application.)

With a simple application and a simple interface, the user does not have to think about what the application is doing in order to figure out what to do next. The behavior should be natural, and the correct next action of the user should be obvious based on what he sees and hears. He should not have to think about what is "under the hood."

Simplicity does not happen by itself. If you don't pay attention to it, you probably won't get it. No matter how complex your application has to be, you can still benefit from thinking about how to simplify it, or at least how to simplify the user interface. Remember: Simpler for the user means harder for the designer. But it's worth it.

METAPHORS

An important principle in interface design is to use approaches that are similar to something the user already knows. Thus, if you are creating an interactive video player in your application and you want the user to be able to start, pause, stop, and rewind the video, it would be natural to use the type of control buttons that are used on VCRs. This is a well-known metaphor which most users will instantly recognize and know how to use.

Some applications use a computer-style scroll bar for positioning a random access start point in a video or audio, or to show the relative point in the audio or video that is currently being played. This is a different metaphor, one that is not as familiar to general audiences as the VCR example. (The equivalent in the VCR metaphor would be the tape time readout.) However, if you do choose to use the scroll bar metaphor and teach your user how it works, then use the same metaphor everywhere else it applies in the application. The principle of consistency is even more important than using a familiar metaphor.

USER CONTROL

The user will be most comfortable with an application when he feels that he is in control. The application should do his bidding—start when he wants, stop when he wants, retrace steps when he wants to back up, and most important: never do something he doesn't expect. Many of the principles already discussed contribute to this feeling, but you have to do some special authoring to achieve some of these features.

For example, if you are going to provide an escape path for the user in every part of your application, you are going to have to author that everywhere, and provide additional controls for escapes on-screen. This is non-trivial work, but the result is that your user always has control. You should plan for this feature in the initial design of your user interface.

THE TELEVISION-STYLE INTERFACE—TOUCH SCREENS

We have already said that a general audience user is more comfortable with something resembling a television; which means, try *not* to use a keyboard or a mouse in the user interface. The usual alternative is a *touch screen*, an interface that is either built into a display monitor or is an overlay placed over the display screen. Either way, it does not interfere with viewing the screen, but makes the screen sensitive to touch. When you touch the screen, the position of your touch is reported to the computer, much like what happens when you click a mouse button.

A touch screen is different from a mouse, however, in that you do not normally have a cursor (pointer). Therefore, you don't know where the user is pointing until he actually touches the screen to make a selection. There have been some attempts made to incorporate a dynamically touch-sensitive screen on which you drag your finger; a cursor follows your finger. To make a selection, you just press harder. This is a nice idea, but it has not gained much acceptance yet, probably because this is making the touch interface more complicated for the user. We assume then that you do not drag objects around on a touch screen.

The first step for a general audience user who is approaching a touch screen is that he has to realize he must touch it. People don't normally go around touching television screens, so this is not natural to the user. Recall from Chapter 3 that the "attract" stage of a general user application must tell the user to touch the screen. Once the user has done that, we can proceed with the user interface.

Usually, this is some kind of main menu screen, on which the user has to touch some part to make the first selection. The screen or the audio has to tell him that. After this, he will probably understand the metaphor and it won't be necessary to tell him again that he needs to touch.

An important consideration to remember when designing touch applications is that the user has to be standing within arm's length of the screen so that he can reach it. This means that the viewing distance between his eye and the monitor is 18" to 24". Since touch monitor screens are in the range of 14" to 19", the viewing distance is much shorter than that at which we normally view television screens of that size. You can express this as a *viewing ratio*, where you take the ratio of the viewing distance to the screen height. The numbers above represent viewing ratios between 1.5 and 3.

Television images are designed to look best when viewed at ratios of 4 or more. If we show television video full-screen at too-small viewing ratios, the tendency is for the user to step back so that it looks better. The result is that he can no longer reach the screen to touch it. You can effectively use full-screen video during the attract mode, when you are trying to attract a user who is presumably farther away anyhow. However, once you have brought the user close to the screen, it is not a good idea to show full-screen motion video. A quarter-screen (half-width by half-height) video window will be more satisfactory, and the user will not step back from it.

In a touch application, there should always be a timeout that activates if the user does not touch for a certain length of time. The timeout will cause a preplanned action, which might be to proceed with some part of the application, or to return to the attract mode on the assumption that the user has walked away.

SELECTION METAPHORS

Once the user is hooked up to an interface, the principal task is usually to get him to make one or more selections. There are various strategies for this; they depend mostly on how many selections there are, and how difficult it is to explain to the user what each selection means. Normally you don't want to present the user with too many selections at once—that can become overwhelming. If there are a large number of choices, use some type of hierarchical approach to present them.

A hierarchical menu structure requires several actions in order to make one selection, depending on the number of levels in the hierarchy. This may prove awkward if selections have to be made often. Figure 7.1 shows the relationship between the number of choices available at each level of a hierarchy vs. the total number of selections that can be made using all the levels.

It is best to not have too many selections in a single menu. This is primarily associated with the need to adequately identify each item in the menu. Generally, a menu should be self-sufficient; that is, it should contain all the information needed by the user to understand what the items are. This is most important at the first-level menu, where the items are most likely to be quite different from one another. As you move down the hierarchy to the lower levels, you are inherently moving into items that have been grouped together somehow, and it becomes easier to identify each item.

114 *Designing Interactive Multimedia*

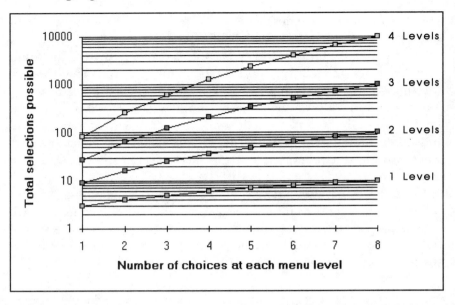

Figure 7.1 Hierarchical menu number of selections versus number of choices at each level.

For first-level menus, a good rule is to have no more than six selections. This assures that you will have enough screen space to identify each item and to provide directions for use of the menu. However, this is not a hard-and-fast rule; if the items are easy to identify, you may have more. For example, in the hypothetical application about pets that was mentioned in Chapter 5, it is possible to select a type of pet from the main menu and not have to use a hierarchy. Since animals, birds, fish, etc., are easy to recognize from pictures, it is reasonable to provide just photographs of each one in the main menu and have the user select directly on the photos. There could be as many as 20 choices in such a menu.

The pets menu just described is an icon menu. Icons are a good approach only when it is clear what the icons mean. This is no problem with pets, since everyone knows what they look like, but computer programs often use arcane icons whose meaning has to be learned. This approach is not recommended for multimedia applications, and if your audience is the general public, *don't do it*. Unless your application has some other extraordinary appeal, indecipherable icons are enough to turn off your potential users.

When you are selecting from a list of items that can be arranged in a logical sequence, such as text items arranged alphabetically, a scrollable list box is an effective selection device for up to 100 items or so. Alphabetical sorting of the items in a scrollable list is critical; without it, a user does not know which way to scroll. Of course, nothing keeps you from scrolling lists with more than 100 items, but somewhere around that number the process begins to get tedious. It is better to figure out a way to categorize your items into groups of not more than 100—select the group with menus, and then scroll within the group.

IMMEDIATE FEEDBACK

Often the result of a selection by the user is something that will take some time to complete. Because of this delay, it is very important that the user get immediate feedback indicating that his selection was accepted, but that the result may take a while. There are various ways to do this. One common technique is to have the menu item highlight when it is selected and accepted, indicating that the computer recognized the selection. This is a task that can be accomplished quickly, and can be immediate if it is the first thing the application does after receiving the selection.

If the result will be available in one or two seconds after the selection, highlighting is enough. If, however, it is going to take longer than that, tell the user, and provide the opportunity for him to abort the operation. The most friendly approach is to calculate the time needed and tell the user, "This is going to take 31 seconds." You could even put up a clock that counts down during the operation. What you definitely don't want to do is leave the user hanging for 31 seconds—he'll probably decide that the application has crashed and give up. In order to convince the user that you have not crashed, display something that changes periodically during the processing time: a button that blinks every three seconds, for example. Often it is not practical to calculate the processing time, and the blinking button approach will solve the problem. Of course, whatever approach you use, you have to author it in your application.

WINDOWING ENVIRONMENTS

Most multimedia today will be running in a PC environment that supports windowing. As already indicated, for a general audience, you may want to hide that for a less "computer-like" appearance. However, that does not mean you don't use windows—in fact, you may have to. (MEDIAscript inherently requires windows, for example.)

Actually, what makes windows look like a computer are not the windows, but the borders around the windows and the window controls. Usually, you can specify windows that do not have borders, and you can

116 *Designing Interactive Multimedia*

Figure 7.2 TV remote control metaphor implemented on a multimedia computer.

choose to not use window controls. Instead, custom draw your controls in the PM plane, or create DVI images for controls. That way you can create controls that look like something more familiar to the user, such as a TV remote control (see Figure 7.2) or the controls on a microwave oven, etc.

But, if your user is perfectly comfortable with computers, then use the windows, because (among other things) it will make your job easier. The following guidelines for using windows will help you get the most from the windowing environment.

1. Don't use too many windows at the same time. Windows are intended to help the user separate multiple processes that are running concurrently. If there isn't a need for concurrency, it's better to hide a previous window rather than leave it lying around on the screen. Unused windows clutter up the screen and the user expects that he can click in them and they will come back alive, which may not be what you intended. A good rule is to have just two windows open at a time: a window for the current presenting activity and a control window.

    If you want your application to have the full attention of the user, have a full-screen window that is there just to blank out everything else on the desktop. This way, when your application is running, other windows and icons will not be distracting. If you have a full-screen window like this, it is also desirable to have minimize or restore controls on it so that the user can get behind your window if he wishes. Of course, he can still do it by using the Task Manager, but your application may lose control if he does that.

2. The second guideline to using windows is: Don't provide window control functionality that you don't need. This refers to size borders, title bar (for moveability), minimize/maximize, and system menu features. It is easy to author a default window, which provides all of these features, but unnecessary features are just going to cause problems for you. For example, if you provide a small window and make it sizable by having a size border, the system will allocate enough memory to support a full-screen window, because the user might go to full-screen with the size border. Unless there is a need to resize that window, remove the size border. Then the system will allocate only enough memory for the small window.

It is also undesirable to have sizable windows when a window contains controls. By resizing the window, a user may cause controls to be covered up. Of course, you could author so the controls moved to stay visible, but that is more work. Another liability of sizable windows is that you may have to redraw the window contents other than the controls—also more work for the author. The moral is: Don't have size borders when you don't need them.

The computer's windowing environment provides extraordinary flexibility which can support many kinds of applications. That doesn't mean that you have to use all of it in your application. Remember the rules of simplicity and consistency, and choose only those windowing features that will service your application without adding excessive frills. Figure 7.3 shows an example of a control panel built using the standard window controls.

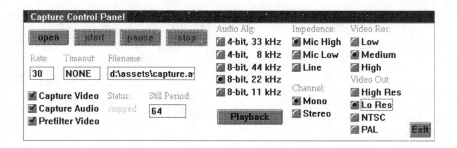

Figure 7.3 Example of a control panel built from window controls.

CHAPTER SUMMARY

The user interface of an interactive multimedia application is as important as the content of the application. Without a good user interface, your user may never be able to get to the content at all.

Multimedia user interfaces can be made to look like a computer, or like television screens for general audiences.

Important principles of user interface design are:

- Make it easy to figure out.
- Make it consistent.
- Make it simple.
- Use metaphors.
- Give the user control.
- Provide immediate feedback.

A good user interface goes half of the way to a good application.

8
Designing an Application's Style

style: n.: distinction, excellence, originality, and character in any form of artistic or literary expression.
Webster New World Dictionary, 1988.

The television screen constantly gives us examples of visual and aural presentation. In fact, our familiarity with television causes us to expect a certain appearance whenever we see a television screen. However, we have very different expectations about appearance when we look at a computer screen. We need to understand these differences, which are in the area defined as *style*, because with multimedia we will be working with computer and television metaphors *on the same screen.*

THE INGREDIENTS OF GOOD STYLE

Style refers to the manner in which something is done and the way it looks; good style implies excellence, elegance, originality, or character in an implementation. Certainly we would like those words to be associated with our application designs. What are the ingredients of good style in multimedia? Here's a list:

- The application should *work*—it should accomplish its purpose, all features should belong there, and they should be successful.
- The application should *look* professional—things should work smoothly and correctly, all the elements should be well designed, and everything should make sense to the user.

- The user interface should be designed to *suit* the intended user group—users should have no trouble understanding the application.
- The application should be *consistent*—whatever choices are made in the style-determining elements of the application should remain the same throughout.
- The application should give the user a good feeling. This last item in the list expresses the intangible aspect of style—when something has good style, you somehow just *know* that it is right. Everything about it is successful, all the parts clearly belong together; it just "sings."

In this chapter you will find out about dozens of components that contribute to expressing the style of a multimedia application. As you read these, think about how the items might fit into the things you want to do. With experience in multimedia, you will start deciding on certain features that you like, things that you use all the time. These will become your personal multimedia style.

Examples of style, both good and bad, are around us all the time. As you become aware of style considerations, you will start seeing things in television, movies, or your colleagues' presentations that you never noticed before. Try and rate them for style: Think about why something is done a particular way, or if it could have been done better. This will help you learn what is good and what is not so good.

THE TELEVISION LOOK OR STYLE

As mentioned in Chapter 7, an application designer should decide at the beginning between a television or a computer look for her application. When you know who your audience is, that decision becomes easy—it simply depends on what is going to be the most comfortable to the audience. This decision in turn simplifies another choice: If the application is to have a television look, then it should be a full-screen application; if the application has a computer look, you have the choice of going full-screen or not, and you can use windowing if you like. Television is always full-screen—it actually is *more than* full-screen, because television images always go beyond the edges of the screen mask. This is called *over-scanning*. Also, television doesn't really use windowing; although some of the split-screen effects on television may look like windows, they do not represent windowing, which implies user interaction.

If you choose the television look, there are certain aspects of style that you should maintain in order not to upset the metaphor. First, use primarily full-screen photographic quality images or motion video. Computer graphics or text may be used, but they should be designed to be overlays on top of a photographic image. Text should be done with proportionally spaced fonts like you see on TV, not with a monospaced computer font. This is equivalent to the use of titles on television. Any use of a full computer screen is going to break the metaphor.

Television *always* has audio, and your television-style application will be enhanced if you have real audio at all times. In fact, audio always enhances an image, so it should not be neglected in computer-style applications either.

There is a problem in displaying motion video on a television-style application for a touch screen kiosk. As explained, full-screen video may make the user step back from the kiosk to the point that she can't reach the touch screen. You can avoid this by playing the video in a quarter-screen window. This is an exception to the guideline "don't use windows." Do it the same way they do on television: Put some kind of picture frame border around your video window, or just provide it with a shadow so that it appears as a video picture on the wall. TV news shows do that all the time.

THE COMPUTER LOOK OR STYLE

The computer look is achieved by using mostly graphics or text, and you can also use windows with standard PM controls. Real images should always be presented in windows, as the user may become confused about what she is watching if you go to full-screen real images without borders. In this kind of application, it is good to always have one or more computer-style objects visible on the screen. This can take the form of a small control panel that overlays otherwise full-screen images, maybe in one corner. At least you are telling the user that the computer is still there.

As multimedia becomes more widespread, users will learn that computers can combine television images and video with computer screens. Once there are a lot of applications that do this well, perhaps the general public will no longer be afraid of computers. After all, computers now have the "beloved" television right inside of them!

SCREEN DESIGN

The visual aspects of style are determined by considerations that can be grouped under the heading of *screen design*. A screen is the visual face of your application. At any time, your user is looking at only one screen, even though there may be hundreds or even thousands of screens in the complete application. Screen design is the task of planning all those screens so that they accomplish the visual part of telling your application's story.

It is important to think about screen design considerations and make global decisions for your application. Setting good screen design rules in the beginning will solve one of the main problems of achieving consistency throughout the application. It will also give you a basis on which to plan the scripting of the application to make both the scripting process and the application itself more efficient.

How Much in One Screen?

Before going into detailed screen design issues, you need to decide about how much material should be shown in one screen. The upper boundary of this is determined by the viewing ratio at which your user will see the screens. For example, touch screen users have to view at ratios between 1.5 and 3 in order to be able to conveniently touch the screen. Desktop computer users are at ratios between 1.5 and 2; and if you are doing a presentation for a large audience, the viewing ratio at the back of the room may be 10 or higher. As shown in Figure 8.1, which is based on text displays, the amount of material that can effectively be shown in one screen drops rapidly as the viewing ratio goes up.

The values in Figure 8.1 represent a screen that is filled completely with text, with the character height taking about 75 percent of the line pitch. In fact, you may want to plan on considerably less than this amount of text in order to allow space for headings, logos, or control panels to also be on the screen. Also, you can make the screen more pleasing and easier to read by reducing the number of lines still further so that you can put more blank space between the lines. For example, a good choice is to make the character height be only 50 percent of the line pitch. However, do not reduce the character *size* in order to get more space between lines—the text will become too small to read at the desired viewing distance.

If your application screens will be shown in a window that is smaller than full-screen, reduce the values in Figure 8.1 in proportion to the height of your window.

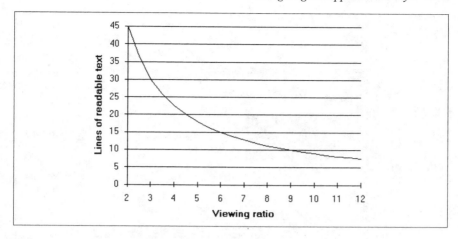

Figure 8.1 Lines of readable text on the screen vs. viewing ratio.

Screen Elements

Figure 8.2 shows a drawing of a typical screen and calls out the nomenclature for the elements that make up a screen. The drawing shows all of the elements that you might use, although you would seldom use all of them in the same screen. In fact, the simplicity rule also applies to screens: Don't put more in a screen than you need. If there is not a good reason for having them, don't clutter up your screens with borders, headers, logos, or other cosmetic features. Simple is best here, too.

Screen Backgrounds

Every screen has a background; it is the only style element that is mandatory. The possibilities are endless; here are a few background choices:

- solid colors
- dithered colors
- graded colors
- patterns
- drawings
- still images
- moving backgrounds

The solid color background is the simplest case and it is also the easiest to do. Simply specify a color from the color palette and go. However, if you use the PM plane (which is the easiest), usually you will have only 16 colors to choose from; and except for the grays and white, each color

124 *Designing Interactive Multimedia*

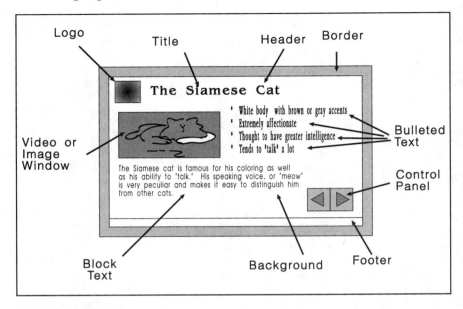

Figure 8.2 The elements of a screen.

makes a very strong statement. A background is something that fills the space between the objects that you want the user to see, and a bright color will draw attention away from those objects. Therefore, backgrounds usually should be low-key or dull.

In the PM plane, you can achieve some dull tones by using *dithered colors*, which are non-palette colors that PM makes by using several different colors in adjacent pixels of the screen. Because the pixels are close together, the human eye tends to see an average of the colors. This can produce a wide range of colors, but sometimes it also produces patterns that may be too distracting because the eye is not really averaging. You have to experiment with dithered colors to decide about that. In MEDIAscript, a color mixing dialog for creating dithered colors can be called up anywhere a color is to be entered. For example, in the Window object, you can author a background color that is different from the default by clicking on the Mix... button, which brings up the dialog shown in Figure 8.3.

The three horizontal sliders let you adjust the proportions of the primary colors (red, green, and blue) that go into your dithered color. The resulting color appears in the small window to the right. As you move the sliders, MEDIAscript keeps redrawing the color box so you can see what you are getting. You will see that some colors have strong patterns and some don't. For a background you will usually want to choose a color that doesn't have too much pattern. And because colors sometimes look

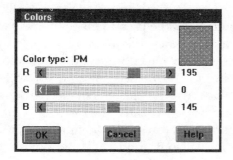

Figure 8.3 The MEDIAscript color mixing dialog.

different when they are shown in large areas, transfer the color to your sample window and view the full window before you finalize on the color. Notice that when you hit a color mixture that actually exists in the palette, PM will choose the palette color directly and present it without any dithering.

Solid colors can also be produced in the DVI plane, which has a vast palette of colors that enables you to choose anything you want without dithering. However, color filling of the DVI plane is not supported by the ActionMedia II system software for OS/2. Therefore, MEDIAscript OS/2 can't create a colored DVI background directly; what it can do is display a DVI *image* of a colored background. Such images can be created by using a DVI painting tool program, which currently is available only under MS-DOS. However, the DVI file format is the same for DOS or OS/2, so you can use the DOS tools to create images to display under OS/2. This procedure is described in Chapter 11.

In choosing any kind of background, you also have to consider the matter of contrast between the background and the other material you will be showing, particularly text. If you choose a bright background (white, for example), then you are going to have to use dark colors or black for text or drawn objects on that background. Similarly, if your background is dark (dark blue works well), then your text has to be white or yellow to get the contrast you need. Therefore, it is a good idea to test the appearance of text when choosing a background. You will probably want to choose background and text color(s) at the same time.

In general, backgrounds that are shades of gray work well, except it is difficult to achieve contrast if you choose a middle gray; therefore, choose dark gray or light gray. All shades of blue work well, and most beige colors. Colors based on red or green are problematical because these colors have mid-brightness and your choice of other colors that will give contrast becomes limited. Always test color selections carefully under all the conditions in which they will be used to make sure you like the result.

Graded (or shaded) backgrounds are sometimes very effective. These cannot be done in the PM plane because of the limited color palette, but they do work well in the DVI plane. However, you will have to use the technique discussed to create an image. A shaded background makes the contrast problem more acute because the range of colors in the shading has a range of brightness. If you shade too much, you will not be able to find a single color that will look good at all locations on the background. Another consideration in graded backgrounds is that you may get a pattern of lines in the background (technically called *contouring*) because the color display being used does not have enough different colors to produce a smooth gradient. You may have to experiment to avoid this problem.

Solid colored backgrounds are best when you are trying to avoid patterns. However, sometimes a pattern may be just what you want. Patterns can be made by replicating drawings or images. You can perform the replication process by starting with a small image or drawing and creating a loop of transitions that does the replication in two dimensions, if necessary. This process can be done at runtime; or to simplify your scripts, you can do it during authoring and save the replicated background as a single image. Loading a single image at runtime will place the background. In MEDIAscript DOS there is a function that automatically fills a rectangle or the entire screen with a pattern made from a DVI image.

Using a DVI image for a background is very effective, especially if you have chosen the television look. However, you will often have a problem with the contrast or color brightness of an image background. In television production, they can't do very much about that except control the depth of focus of the camera or the lighting; but in multimedia, the background is almost always a separate image from the foreground objects, and we can use digital image processing techniques to independently change the contrast of the background (or the brightness, tint, or saturation for that matter). In MEDIAscript, adjustment of these parameters (only on a DVI image) can be done during an instantaneous transition (copy) operation. Thus, you can load an image to an off-screen window and adjust its brightness, contrast, and color parameters in the process of copying it to an on-screen window.

- A technique that is effective on an image background is the color wash. To get a wash, first convert an image to monochrome by setting its color saturation to 0, and then add a new color over the entire image, for example: light blue. The effect is that the whole image is now displayed in shades of blue, which serve to suppress the detail of the image enough that it becomes a non-obtrusive background but still conveys the message of the original image. For example, if you are displaying a specification sheet for a video camera, you could use a washed image of the camera as the background for the specification text. This way, the screen is more interesting than just a screen full of text.

Screen Borders

Television screens never have borders—they wouldn't be seen on most receivers anyway because of the over-scanning. However, a border is a way to add some character to a computer-style screen. A border is also needed on a motion video window in an otherwise full-screen application in order to set off the video from the background.

A border on a full-size screen is a non-essential element because the screen already has edges. An additional border adds a degree of formality to the style, which you may want. However, you should realize that there are other ways to add formality, such as headings, logos, or footers. One or more of these may be essential elements for other reasons. If you think about all of that and decide that you do want a border, here are some of the possibilities.

The simplest border to author is the PM window border, which has a number of options. But be aware, that this immediately ties you to the computer metaphor, which you may or may not want. The PM borders have other meanings, too; for example, if you like the look of the PM size border, you can't have it without it being active—you may not want the user to be able to resize the window. Thus, the PM window borders lack flexibility, and if you are interested in a border, you probably want to design your own.

The next simplest border is one of a solid color different than the background. This can be achieved with graphics: in MEDIAscript use the Draw object to make a border in the PM plane. There are two ways to get a rectangular border with graphics:

1. Fill the whole window with the border color (choose it for the window background), and then fill the window again with a slightly smaller rectangle in the desired background color. This leaves the border color around the edges. If the background is an image, you may be able to achieve the same effect by making the image appropriately smaller than the window. The biggest disadvantage of this approach is, if you are building the window on-screen, the whole window will flash in the border color. This is not a problem if you build the window off-screen.

2. Fill the whole window with the background color or image, and then do four graphics calls (all in one Draw object) that draw four narrow rectangles around the edges of the window in the border color. This happens quickly, and gives an interesting effect when done on-screen. For the best effect, the four operations should move around the screen in one direction.

Borders can be built with all of the same options described for backgrounds. You can use dithered colors, shading, images, repeating patterns, etc. There are also some possibilities that are unique to borders: for example, shadowing or beveling.

Shadowing is achieved by placing narrow dark rectangles just outside of the bordered area on two adjacent sides—most commonly the right and bottom. It is only possible when the shadowed window is less than full-screen; on a full-size screen there is no place to draw the shadow. When you have a right/bottom shadow, it implies a light source for the screen that is at the upper left. If you have multiple shadowed objects on the screen, obviously they all should be shadowed the same way or it will be unnatural. This also applies if you are using shadowed text. If the background for the shadowed object is an image, you can reduce the brightness just in the shadowed area, rather than going all the way to a solid color. This gives a more realistic effect. Also, if a shadowed object is moveable by the user, you will have to program to move the shadow whenever the user moves the object.

A beveled border is achieved by drawing four polygons around the window to give the appearance of mitered corners. To give the proper effect, you have to draw the four polygons in four shades of the same color. This creates a shadowed effect that gives depth to the bevel. Figure 8.4 shows examples of shadowed and beveled windows.

Screen Headers

Often you will want to title your screens. This may simply be some text at the top of the screen, but sometimes you might like something a little more formal than that. There are many possibilities.

Probably the simplest thing you can do is draw a line across the screen just below where you will put the header text. The line creates a separation, indicating a distinction between the heading and the rest of the screen. You can get a similar distinction by using slightly larger text for the heading, and drawing it in a different color. A bit trickier is to use a different font for the header (see the discussion about fonts below).

Another simple header approach is to fill the top part of the screen behind the header text with a different background color. This can either

Designing an Application's Style 129

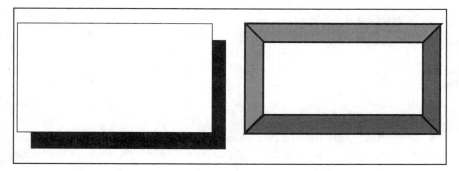

Figure 8.4 Shadowing and beveling for window borders.

bleed off the edges of the screen on the top and sides, or (more formal) have a rectangular heading area that does not go to the edges of the screen. In either case, you might want to set off the separation even further by drawing lines at the demarcation. (But remember the warning about overdoing the style.)

When you use a rectangle instead of a bleed to set off a header, you are opening the door to a more global style possibility where you divide the whole screen into rectangles and use a separate rectangular color background for each working area of your screen. If your screen can be sensibly divided in this way, it produces a very precise and mechanical looking style.

Of course, if you want really dramatic headers, use shadowing, beveling, or images to make the header more exciting. Except in special situations, however, this is probably going overboard.

Screen Footers

Footers are used less than headers. Typically, they are provided as an area to give prompt messages to the user, or to report status items about the application. Sometimes in business presentations, a footer is used to hold the company name or the name of the presentation. Normally, in a footer you would use the smallest readable text for your viewing situation. Although you can use any of the means described for headers to set off the footer area, this is unusual except for status lines.

Text

There are more options for text than any other element you will use in your screens. Whole books are available about the proper use of text. Most of these deal with printed text as used in publishing of books, magazines, and newspapers; a lot of that applies to our purposes as well, but on the video screen there are also some special considerations, covered here.

Text Fonts

The first choice you have to make about text is the font or face. The font is identified by a name, for example, Courier or Helvetica, and it defines the basic shape and style of the characters. In publishing, there are tens of thousands of text faces; however, almost everything is done with a small handful of these—maybe 20. For most computer screen types, hundreds of fonts are available, but again only a small number of these serve most purposes. The greatest danger in choosing fonts is using too many—another reminder of the simplicity rule!

For computer displays there are two classes of fonts:

1. **bitmap fonts**—in these fonts, a pixel image is stored of each character, usually in some kind of array that the computer can easily access. The advantage of a bitmap font is that no special processing is needed to display it; the computer simply copies the pixels of each character to the desired location in the screen memory. This is a fast operation.

    However, bitmap fonts do have some serious disadvantages. First, the size of the font is determined by the number of pixels used to represent the characters. If you want a different size, you need a completely different font, created with fewer or more pixels, depending on the size. Another problem is that bitmap fonts are wasteful of storage, especially when you consider that you have to have separate fonts for each size that you want to use. Regardless of these problems, bitmap fonts are widely usd because they are so simple to apply.

2. **vector fonts**—(sometimes called *outline* or *stroke* fonts)—vector fonts store a mathematical description of the outline of each character. This typically takes less storage than a bitmap font, and it has the major advantage that the font can be displayed in any size by having the computer calculate the pixels to display each character at the time the character is to be displayed. This process of calculating the character from its mathematical description is called *rendering*.

    The disadvantage of vector fonts is that the rendering process is compute-intensive and can be slow. However, computers have gotten fast enough that even slow is often fast enough; consequently, vector fonts are being used more and more. Also, remember Moore's law—computers will continue to get faster in the future, and this technique will become even more practical as that happens.

Designing an Application's Style 131

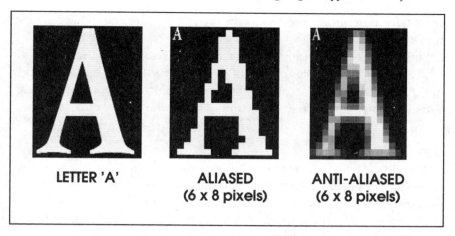

Figure 8.5 The text character "A," showing (a) an ideal character, (b) aliasing, and (c) antialiasing. View this figure from a distance of about six feet to see the effect most clearly.

MEDIAscript OS/2 supports both vector and bitmap fonts, but only on the Presentation Manager plane. Text in the DVI plane is supported only by DOS programs, and there we can also use both kinds of fonts. The DVI plane, with its larger number of colors, can support *antialiasing*, a technique for rendering characters that minimizes the tendency to have jagged edges, particularly on diagonal lines. This is most noticeable when you look at an italic font, where almost all the lines are diagonal. Antialiasing varies the color intensity of the pixels around the edges to cause an apparent smoothing effect. Figure 8.5 shows a character blown up in size to demonstrate the effects of aliasing and antialiasing. The use of DOS DVI tools to draw DVI text is covered in Chapter 11.

Another property of text fonts is the character spacing technique. Fonts can be either proportionally spaced or monospaced. Proportional spacing means that the characters are spaced according to their width—it is the most common technique in book text, and it is used in what you are reading here. Monospacing is what we are used to seeing on computer screens—characters are spaced evenly along the line, regardless of their actual width. This gives a rather uneven look to a line of text, as shown by the example below, which is in the Courier monospaced font:

```
This is an example of Courier monospaced text.
```

As you can see, monospaced text is somewhat harder to read than proportionally spaced text. You will probably want to use proportional spacing on most multimedia screens, unless you have some special requirements for exact character alignment, such as the display of a table of data. Even there, because most tables involve numbers, proportionally spaced fonts generally use monospacing for their number characters so that tables of numbers will align.

Still another consideration of font selection is whether to use a *serif* font or a *sans serif* font. Serifs are the little extensions that appear at the ends of the lines that make up each character, as in this text you are reading. Sans serif fonts do not have these lines, as shown in the example below:

SERIF   SANS SERIF

The choice between these is mostly a matter of preference. Most people think a serif font is more traditional, probably because they associate it with the text carved on Roman ruins. San serif fonts are considered more contemporary. There are also ongoing arguments about readability, but they seem to be inconclusive.

If you are using small sizes of text (where the character height is less than 16 pixels), then the ability of the computer screen to reproduce the fine lines of serifs becomes important. You cannot display a line on a computer screen thinner than one pixel wide or high, so once the character gets small enough that its serifs ought to be thinner than one pixel, you are forced to choose between no serifs, or serifs that are really too fat. Of course, a sans serif font avoids that problem.

Text Size

The minimum text size is determined by the viewing distance consideration discussed earlier. You should not use text smaller than the size that would fill the screen according to Figure 8.1; however, it is fine to use larger text. Decide on text sizes and then use them consistently for the same kinds of screens throughout the application. You can begin consideration of size by working with the same font for all the text. Once you have established the size relationships you like, then consider whether to use a different font for headings, for example.

In paper publishing, text size is expressed in *points*: one point represents 1/72" on the printed page. Points make sense on a computer screen only when there is a stated relationship between the size of the computer screen and the size of a printed document made from the screen. For example, if we print the screen 1:1 onto paper, then 1 point will also equal 1/72" on the screen. If the screen has 72 pixels to the inch (corresponding to a VGA screen that is 6 2/3" high—about a 13" diagonal display), then 1 point will be exactly 1 pixel. If a VGA screen is made larger than 6 2/3" high, there will be fewer pixels per inch, and theoretically 1 point when printed at 1:1 would correspond to less than 1 pixel. This is confusing.

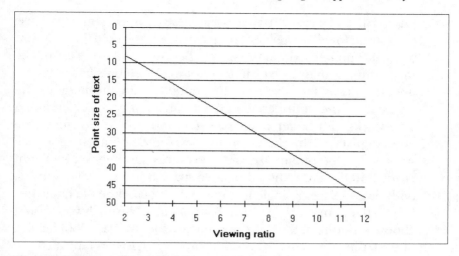

Figure 8.6 is Figure 8.1 revised in terms of point size.

Most multimedia systems cut through the confusion by saying that 1 point is always equal to 1 pixel, regardless of screen size or printing ratio. So 12-point text is always exactly 12 pixels high. That is what is done in MEDIAscript OS/2.

Figure 8.6 is similar to Figure 8.1, but with another scale that gives the point size of the text which will produce the specified number of lines of text in the screen height. (This conversion applies to VGA screens only.) So, if we are designing for a maximum viewing ratio of 6, we can have 15 lines per screen height. On a VGA screen, this is 32 pixels per line, and with the 75 percent text to line pitch ratio, we would use 24-point text.

Text Styles

Having chosen a font type and point size, we still have the option of choosing a text style such as bold, italic, shadow, outline, underline, etc. Most of these options may also be combined, leading to a vast array of text styles. A brief description of each style and its uses follows:

- **bold**—draws the text with thicker lines, giving an enhanced appearance. It primarily provides emphasis, which can be used to highlight a word or phrase in a block of text, or to make a heading stand out.
- **italic**—draws the text with a little slant to the right on each character. It is used for highlighting that is more subtle than bold. It can be used for headings, too, but you probably would want to increase the point size as well to provide more distinction to the heading.
- **shadow**—draws a shadow beneath the text. Usually the shadow is darker than the text; the shadow makes the text appear as if it is

raised off the screen. It is an elegant style; often you would use shadowing for all the text in a screen, while using bold, italic, or size to create emphasis within the screen. Because shadowing cannot be made thinner than 1 pixel, it does not work well on small text.

- **outline**—draws the text as a thin outline, with the body of the characters either transparent or filled with another color. Outlining only works with larger point sizes (24 and up), where there are enough pixels in the characters to allow for the double-lining of all strokes that the outline treatment requires. Outline is a highlight effect, and therefore should be used sparsely, for special emphasis.
- **underline**—places a single line beneath the baseline of characters. It is used for emphasis, much as bold or italic. Normally you should choose only one of the three approaches for emphasis (bold, italic, or underline), and use that exclusively. Trying to combine all three in the same screen can easily lead to confusion about what the different styles mean.

All of the above options are available for text drawn by MEDIAscript OS/2. In addition, one further option is to angle the baseline of the text, over a range of ±90 degrees from the horizontal. This is primarily useful for putting labels on drawings or graphs, where you want the text to follow an angle in the drawing, or to be vertical.

Text Blocks

A text block is a number of lines of text that are intended to be read contiguously; for example, each paragraph on this page is a text block. In addition to the text character styles already discussed, a block of text has its own block format. Ordinarily you can define a rectangle that encloses the text block; the text is formatted to stay inside of that rectangle by *word-wrapping* it. When the computer displays the block of text, it determines, before displaying the text, the maximum number of full words that will fit on each line. Then it displays the text with line breaks at those full-word points.

When displaying the word-wrapped lines of text in a block, there are four choices of formatting:

- **left-aligned**—all lines of text begin at the same horizontal position on the screen. This means that the variation of line length caused by the word-wrapping appears all on the right; the right edge of the text block is said to be *ragged*. Left-aligned text blocks are the most common format.

- **right-aligned**—in this case, the lines are aligned at the right and the left edge is ragged. This is often used if the text block is up against something on the right, such as when putting the caption for an image to the left of the image instead of below it.
- **centered**—in this format the raggedness is equally divided between the left and right edges of the text block. Centered text can also be justified.
- **left-right aligned** (or *justified*)—this format aligns both edges of the text by adjusting the space between words and often the space between characters, too. The paragraphs on this page are justified.

The MEDIAscript OS/2 Server supports text blocks, but you need the Professional Edition of the AUI to author them.

Bulleted Text

The technique of *bulleting* is often used to set apart the individual items of a text list. A bullet is a symbol set to the left at the beginning of each item in the list. Bullets can be text characters, such as the asterisk or the dash, or graphics objects, such as rectangles or circles. Even more elegant bullets can be made with small images.

All the bullets in a list should align at the same horizontal position, and all the text (whether single lines or blocks) should left-align at a position a little to the right of the bullets.

Logos

A logo is a small symbol or image that represents an entity. A logo should be easily recognizable, because its purpose is to visually represent its owner in an elegant way. Familiar logos are associated with automobiles, companies, software products, computers, and almost every other well-known item in the marketplace.

Logos are used for the same purpose on multimedia screens—to help us associate the application with its owner. For example, the product logo might occupy a prominent location on every screen of a selling application. This helps build recognition of the logo for the user, who will go away with the logo firmly in mind. Later, if she sees that logo in another context, we want her to immediately recognize it. The logo and the header text should be sized appropriately to go together.

When a logo is used on a multimedia screen, it is usually placed in one of the corners. The upper left-hand corner inside the header area is a good location. Another good location is the lower right-hand corner, preferably with nothing else close to it on the left.

Many companies have elaborate rules for how their logos are to be used, including a list of things you *cannot* do with their logo. If you are working with such logos, learn the rules and follow them. This is especially important if the owner of the logo is your client or your boss!

Control Panels

Another visual style element is the *control panel*, which is an area of the screen devoted to giving the user interactive control of the application. Depending on the type of hardware, the control panel is operated by clicking the mouse button(s) when the pointer is on the controls, or by the user touching the screen over the controls. The panel's design and size should be compatible with the way it is going to be used.

An application ought to have a general control panel style for *navigation*, which carries through all the screens of the application. Navigation is the process of interactively moving from screen to screen of the application. At times, there may be screens that offer additional choices beyond what the user can do with the control panel. For example, a menu screen could have numerous choices, whereas the control panel might only offer a default selection from that menu.

The control panel style is introduced to the user at the beginning of the application, and from then on she is expected to know how to use the navigating controls. Ideally, the general control panel is fairly simple so that it is easy for the user to learn and remember. The choices of the control panel should work the same way on all screens. For example, an entire application can be designed to be navigated with just two buttons: forward and reverse; or three buttons: forward, reverse, and exit. Of course there will be places where you will need many more choices than this, such as on menu screens. On a menu screen, the control panel is still present, but the forward button will automatically choose something from the menu based on a default, or based on choices the user has made previously.

At the start of the application, the user would be told to click on the right arrow to proceed. From that prompt, she will know what to do, and will probably know what to do the next time she sees the panel, including realizing that the left arrow will back up. The two-button approach is desirable because of its simplicity and ease of learning; however, it may be too simple for many applications. For example, in a multimodule training program, you might want to have these controls available in each module (see Figure 8.7 for examples):

- forward (in this module)
- reverse (in this module)

- exit this module to menu
- restart this module
- help

This example would require a five-button control panel, which is not excessive except that it will be difficult to find five symbols that are as easy to understand as two arrows. It just means you will have to devote a little more effort at the start of the application to make sure the user understands what the controls do, and present them in such a way that helps the user to remember the symbols.

Another control panel approach is to have one button on the standard control panel that is simply called "Options." On screens that need additional controls, clicking on "Options" will open another control panel that has additional special controls (fully labeled) for that screen. If you have some screens on which there are no options, you can gray out the "Options" button to clue the user that there are none for this screen. This last point is important—whenever a button is not going to work, indicate it in some way so the user knows that.

Control panels can be built with PM pushbuttons or other PM controls, or they can be built from drawings of images. Figure 8.7 shows some examples of control panel styles.

When you use the PM control types in your panel, the click or touch area of the control is defined by Presentation Manager. However, when you use a drawing or an image, PM does not know where you want to put the click areas. In those cases, you must separately define a *hotspot* for each control. In MEDIAscript OS/2 this is done by using the hotspot control style in the Window object, which you author exactly the same way that you author PM control types. Hotspots get hooked up to Input objects in the same way that the PM controls do.

Dynamic Effects

The way in which you transition from screen to screen, or the way that you change objects within a screen is also a part of the visual style. Most multimedia systems give you many possibilities for dynamic effects, and there are important considerations about how you use such capabilities.

Computer people are used to seeing screens build step by step as the computer figures out what to draw. Television people are not used to that—they want to have a fully drawn screen wipe smoothly onto the tube. From the standpoint of elegance and professionalism, the televisiom people are right. The way a computer draws a screen is distracting.

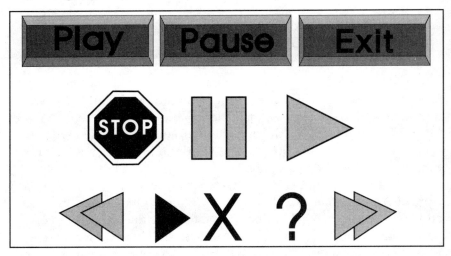

Figure 8.7 Control panel styles.

It is possible to produce the television effect with a computer; it is just a little more complicated. First, draw the screen to an area of memory that is not being displayed (called *off-screen*), and then separately display it. In MEDIAscript OS/2, do that by defining a window that is invisible, drawing your screen to it, and then using a Transition object to copy the invisible window's contents to another window that is visible.

The Transition object has a number of choices for the dynamic effect. This works well except for the very first time you show the visible window. The problem is that all windows are created by Presentation Manager, and PM only knows the computer-style way of displaying things. You can minimize this by creating the window as invisible, and then using a Message object to show the window. You will still see a little flash while PM shows the window, but once that window has been shown, you have full control of its contents, and you can prevent any further flashing in the window. Therefore, it is a good idea to establish the application's main window right at the start, and then reuse the same window from then on. As explained later, this is also a good technique from the point of view of maintaining uniformity of style.

Layout of Screens

There are some rules for how you arrange the various elements on a screen, which will help the appearance of your screens. First, it is usually desirable to avoid symmetry in a screen layout. Symmetrical screens are uninteresting; however, you don't want the screen layout to appear random, either.

The layout should make sense for the items involved, and it should be designed to look simple. Try to group similar items together; for example, if your screen has a lot of pushbuttons, it looks better if they are all together in some kind of array rather than scattered all over the screen. This also will prompt you to make all the buttons the same size and design, which also supports simplicity of style. When you are using a touch screen, the buttons or button array should be at the bottom of the screen, so the user does not have to reach too high or cover the rest of the screen with her hand to touch a button. With a mouse, the location of the button array is less important, although the bottom is still a conventional and logical location.

Many screens are made up of rectangular items, and the rectangles should be sized so that they fill the entire screen, with a uniform amount of space between each of the rectangles. The space between rectangles does not have to be the same as the space left around the edge, which can be larger or smaller. If some of the rectangles involve a group of items, such as an array of buttons, the space between the items in the group does not have to be the same as the space between groups—in fact, it is usually better that the spaces inside a group are smaller than the spaces between groups. This helps to visually group the items. As much as possible, horizontal or vertical edges of groups that come close to being aligned should be adjusted so they do align. This will also help affect the simplicity of appearance. Examples of these layout rules are shown in the sample application style designs at the end of this chapter.

ELEMENTS OF AURAL STYLE

The way you use audio is just as important as the way you use the video display in establishing the application's overall style. Audio adds immeasurably to the realism and effectiveness of still images or motion video. Do not neglect it. Of course, motion video with audio is the most realistic, but it is also expensive and difficult in several ways. First, motion video uses at least 10 megabytes of storage per minute, while good audio can be presented with less than 1 megabyte per minute. Second, good video is more difficult to produce than good audio. Third, you can produce better image quality with still images than you can with motion video, and the data rate is far lower, even when you change images fairly rapidly; for example, showing a new image every two seconds would use only about 1.5 megabytes per minute. And fourth, showing motion video means that you have to allocate space for it on the screen, which may not always be available. Audio can add to the presentation and it doesn't use any of the screen area. For many purposes, a presentation made with still images and audio will be more effective than anything you could do with motion video.

You do need to make some choices about audio style. First, you have to choose between mono or stereo. If your audio is going to be only voice, there probably isn't any reason to use stereo. But if you will have music, you may want to consider stereo. Stereo will double the data rate, and it will also make the audio production more difficult. There is more discussion of these choices in Chapter 10.

Another question to answer about audio style is: When do you use it? For a true television style, you should use audio all the time, but this may prove expensive, especially if you try to fill waiting times caused by the user. You can deal with this by looping (repeating) some audio on menu screens, for example, but if you do too much of that—especially if you loop a clip of audio that is too short—the user is either going to become bored or annoyed. It is probably best to present your audio message once for a menu, and if you want to loop something there, loop some music.

Music in your application can add a lot, but the music has to come from somewhere. If you plan to copy existing music, you have to worry about the rights to it, which can be a nasty problem. The other possibility is to make your own music—if you are up to that, it is a great approach. The best choice for most low-budget operations is to stick to voice, a voice that you or your colleagues can record yourselves. Chapter 10 tells you more about that.

We have covered the major elements of both visual and aural style. Now let's look at a few examples of different kinds of applications and their style decisions.

STYLE FOR A BUSINESS PRESENTATION

Let's suppose your boss is making an important speech at an industry convention and you have offered to do visual support for her in multimedia. You offered because it gives you a chance to show what you can do with multimedia—and she will have to send you to the convention, too.

Your boss has already written the speech; it is 20 minutes long, and you and she have mapped out about 40 separate visual screens (about one every 30 seconds). There won't be anything dynamic in the visuals themselves, but you would like to present them with dynamic transitions and, of course, timing is important—each visual must appear exactly on cue as your boss speaks.

The conference is providing a VGA video projector and an 8-foot-high screen for the meeting room, which is 80 × 80 feet. Thus, the maximum viewing ratio in the room will be 10:1.

In looking through the list of visuals, you see that they can be divided into three groups:

- text bullet charts,
- full-screen images, and
- graphs in a window with text captions.

However, your boss also wants the company name and logo discreetly displayed on each chart, and she wants an elegant, formal style to all the charts. She also wants a title slide that embodies the same style.

We'll discuss only the style issues here: Figure 8.8 shows the four screen types that were designed, and we'll discuss the considerations below.

The style is introduced in the opening screen, which has a narrow double-line border and a solid blue background. The title is written in large italic Times Roman text, which is white with a black shadow. Below, the speaker's name and title are written in smaller Times Roman normal (not italic) text with the same color and shadow. The company logo appears in the lower left-hand corner with the company name just to the right in Helvetica type, as required by the corporate logo rules.

On the transition to the first screen of the speech, which will be a left-to-right horizontal wipe, a heading block also wipes in, and this remains for the rest of the talk. The heading block is a horizontal panel of dark gray at the top of the screen and extends all the way across the screen inside the border. The heading text is Times Roman in the same colors used on the title screen. The company logo and name remain in the lower left.

For text bullet charts, the bullets and text are also white with black shadows. The 10:1 viewing ratio in the meeting room means that there should not be more than about 6 bullet lines per chart to maintain visibility. For image screens, which will all be DVI images, the image is displayed inside the border, using all the area below the heading block. The company logo and name will overlay the image at the lower left.

Graphs are displayed on the background color in the same area occupied by bullet lists. For graph captions, a band of the heading background color is placed across the screen below the graph, extending from the left border to the right border. The caption text is written in white in this area. Again, the company logo and name remain in the lower left.

All transitions between screens except the first one are vertical wipes, from top to bottom.

142 *Designing Interactive Multimedia*

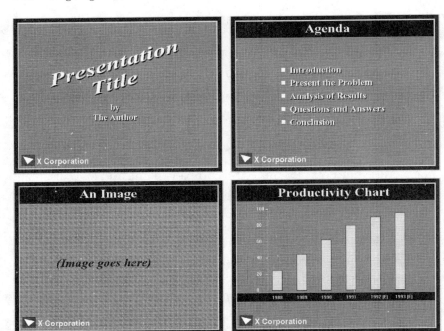

Figure 8.8 Screen styles for a business presentation: (a) title screen, (b) bullet-list style, (c) image style, (d) graph style.

You can see how the several elements of the style lend a continuity to this presentation: the double-line border, the company logo and name, the text font and color, and the heading block are constants. Subtle changes are made to accommodate the three different types of screens.

STYLE FOR A SELLING APPLICATION

Figure 8.9 shows the style elements of the camcorder selling application described in Chapter 3. This application has an attract screen, an introduction screen, a main screen that also displays the camera output, and a detail specification screen. It is a touch screen kiosk.

The attract screen is full-screen motion video, which plays a looping video of TV commercials for the cameras. It has a rectangular overlay at the bottom, which is blue with a white border, and it contains the words "TOUCH THE SCREEN," in Helvetica.

When the user touches the screen, the video stops and a wipe transition changes to the introduction screen. This screen is set up for a canned audio and still image presentation showing the features of the four

Designing an Application's Style 143

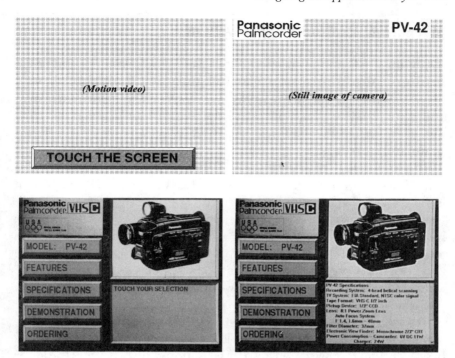

Figure 8.9 Camcorder selling application styles. (a) attract screen, (b) introduction screen, (c) main menu, (d) features screen.

cameras in the product line. This screen shows full-screen DVI still images of the cameras; but as features are described they are highlighted by text-block overlays which come and go as the audio indicates. The camera type number shows in an overlay box at the top right of the screen. The manufacturer's name overlays in the upper left of the screen. Each of the overlay windows is light gray with a beveled border, and all text is Helvetica dark blue. The camera photographs are all taken with the same neutral background.

At the end of the introduction, the screen wipes to the main interactive screen. This screen has a marbled gray background. However, the working areas of the screen use light gray rectangles with beveled borders and dark blue Helvetica text just as in the introduction. A special quarter-screen window shows the output from the live camera in the kiosk. The manufacturer's name is at the upper left.

One of the choices on the main screen is to switch to a full-screen view of the sample camera's output. When this button is touched, the screen transitions to a full-screen view of the camera video, but with a touch button at the bottom containing the word "Menu." This button returns to the quarter-screen camera view and the rest of the menu screen shows.

STYLE IN A TRAINING APPLICATION

A training application is proposed for teaching soldering techniques to new workers in an electronics manufacturing plant. The application will be presented at an interactive workstation that has a touch screen display and actual soldering equipment so the worker can practice the techniques presented in real time. The style design for this application is shown in Figure 8.10.

The application opens with a title screen, which is a drawing of a soldering iron with the title text overlaid. The background of this screen is the same as that used on later screens.

When the student touches the screen, it changes to the main menu screen, which has a shadowed heading rectangle at the top. Below that is a menu of four items, which is simply bulleted text. The text items are also hotspots. A prompt at the bottom of the screen says "Touch an item." There is an "End" button at the lower right-hand corner of the screen that will end the application.

If the student selects "Introduction" from the main menu, an introductory full-screen video with audio is played, showing soldering theory and basic techniques. This screen has a three-button control panel at the lower right, giving the student the opportunity to pause, resume, or end the video. Ending the video returns the student to the main menu screen.

For any of the other main menu selections, a formatted screen appears, a heading block, a menu, an image or video window, and a text block. Depending on the menu selections that are made, images are shown, video is played, and the contents of the text block are changed. An "End" button at the lower right returns the student to the main menu.

The background color, block color, the shadowing approach, and the font styles remain the same throughout this application.

STYLE MAINTENANCE

In a large application with many scripts and many asset files, the maintenance of uniform style can be a real problem. This is especially so if changes are made to the style specification after the application has been partially or completely built. If you do not carefully plan the handling of style, you may find that style changes have to be made in hundreds or even thousands of places. Fortunately, there are several techniques to help you avoid these difficulties.

Some of the style attributes are contained in the windows used by your application. The best way to handle windows is to create all the visible

Designing an Application's Style 145

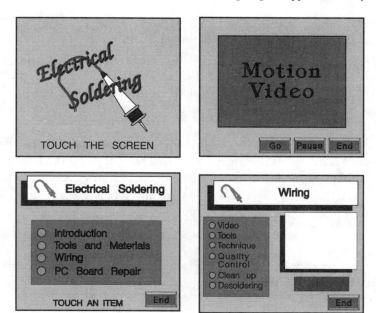

Figure 8.10 Training application styles.

windows at the start of the application, and then leave them alone, reusing the same windows over and over. Then, if you need to change a widely used window at a late stage, you need to modify it in only one place. If some of the windows are not visible all the time, be sure that you hide them to make them invisible—do not destroy them (which would require recreating them when you need them again). Similarly, the initial window definition should also include definition of all the fonts you plan for the application. In MEDIAscript OS/2, font definitions are part of windows anyway.

Of course, if this approach for your application requires too many windows, you may have a problem with memory usage if you try to keep all the windows defined all the time. In that case, use one of the other suggestions below for managing the windows.

An approach that applies more broadly than just to windows is to place style-determining elements into one or more scripts by themselves. These scripts are called whenever you need to build a screen containing the standard style. You call the script first to get all the standard elements of the style, and then add functions to incorporate other elements or to make local changes to the style. Again, put all style-determining functions in one place where it is easy to make changes that will globally affect the application.

When you are dealing with the style of a screen, you can often encapsulate the standard style elements into an image. Then, every time you create a screen, you begin by loading this standard image, after which you add the local elements on top of the standard image. This approach is especially effective if the basic style is complex, where it may be faster to load one image than it would be to draw the standard style from scratch every time you need it.

The last suggestion for localizing style elements applies when you are using data-driven engine scripts for parts of your application. In this case, you should put (or call) style-determining elements in the engine scripts. Again, you have localized the style parameters to one place in the application.

CHAPTER SUMMARY

Style is an important contributor to the success of your application. It will make the application more pleasing, easier to learn and use, and it will make you look better, too.

Choose either television style or computer style at the beginning of the design process. Much of the style of an application is contained in the way it uses audio and video, and in the design of its screens. With the objectives of the application in mind, plan the application's screens using the rules of good style, simplicity, and uniformity presented in this chapter.

Part of the style-design process is to think about where the style-determining items will be located in the structure of your application. It is important that style determination be localized to as few places as possible in the application's scripts so it is easy to achieve uniformity.

9

Multimedia Assets

asset: n. a valuable or desirable thing to have.
Webster's New World Dictionary, 1988

Audio and video are two *assets* of multimedia. However, you cannot have audio and video without the files in which to store them. Therefore, these files are called the assets of a multimedia application. In fact, all of the non-program files used to present a multimedia application (audio, video, image, animation, and data) are included in the assets of the application. This chapter discusses each of the asset types and some of their special considerations. The acquisition (capture) of audio, images, and video is covered further in subsequent chapters.

ASSET FILES

All assets are stored in files on your hard disk or CD-ROM. All asset files (except for text files) contain *file headers*, which are data structures placed at the start of the file to tell the file's user some things about the file. The software that is going to use a file must know the format of its header in order to read the actual asset data from the file. If you attempt to read from a file type that your software does not know about, errors result, your system may tell you the file is incorrect, and sometimes you may even cause a program crash. Therefore, it is important that your asset file types match the capabilities of your software.

Unfortunately, the multimedia industry has not matured to the point that there are universally accepted standards for asset file formats. Each asset type comes in a variety of formats, some of which are listed in the discussions below. In many cases, multimedia software will know about and can use several different formats, and some software even is able to convert between formats—it reads an asset file's data into memory, and then it writes the data back to disk using a different format.

To help you keep track of asset files without having to open them to read header data, many file standards use a *filename extension* code to identify the file type. A filename extension is a period and one to three alphanumeric characters placed at the end of the file's name. This is a very useful feature for management of asset files. Of course, you will still have problems if the filename extension code does not actually match the file's type. You should never change a filename extension when renaming asset files.

AUDIO ASSETS

The audio for a multimedia application is primarily produced from real audio sources: voice, music, sound effects, or any other sound, natural or synthetic. Usually, sounds are recorded by conventional analog means such as cassette tape, and then separately transferred to a computer format. It is also possible to record from a live source directly into the computer; this is a preferred technique for desktop multimedia because it is so quick and inexpensive. However, it is difficult to achieve the most professional sound in this way.

Synthetic computer-generated sounds, such as computer-generated music or speech could also be included here; however, these are not used as much as natural sounds, probably because multimedia applications so far are striving for the realism that is the multimedia PC's unique advantage over other computers. As this early thrust wears off, there will be greater use of computer-generated multimedia sound because it requires substantially less data than recorded natural sounds and therefore, with a given amount of storage, we could have more sound. In addition, the sound hardware of a multimedia system today can do a better job of computer-generated sound than the artificial sounding computer voices we have heard in the past.

MIDI

A special case of computer-generated sound is MIDI audio. MIDI is an acronym for *Musical Instrument Digital Interface*, which is a standard originally developed in the electronic musical instrument industry for interfacing between music keyboards, synthesizers, and computers. By attaching one or more music synthesizers to a MIDI port on a computer, high-quality music can be generated from MIDI control files on the computer's hard disk. A complete orchestra can be synthesized this way.

MIDI control files are created by using special *sequencer* software which allows MIDI codes to be captured while a musician plays on a MIDI keyboard that is interfaced to the computer. Once in the computer, the MIDI musical score can be displayed and edited by the musician. This is great if you are a musician, but it won't be much help if you are not. As with other asset types, there are companies who offer libraries of MIDI music for distribution under license.

The advantage of the MIDI music approach is that a MIDI file is many times smaller than a digitized audio file for the same music. A disadvantage is that it requires the synthesizer peripherals, which could cost as much as the whole computer itself. The Multimedia PC specification calls for a MIDI port and a rather minimal synthesizer to be built into every Multimedia PC. This is a nice feature, but it may not really be cost-effective considering the limitations of the minimal synthesizer. However, some Multimedia PCs being offered include much more than the minimum synthesizer.

Audio Capture

Capture of real audio (called *digitizing*) requires an audio card with audio inputs to one or two analog to digital converters, depending on whether you want stereo or mono capture. The DVI ActionMedia II card has this capability, and several other audio-only cards are available that will also do it (see Appendix A).

Digitized audio files for multimedia are often *compressed*, meaning that the audio data has been processed to reduce its data rate. There are many different approaches to audio compression, which are called *algorithms*. Different algorithms offer a range of sound quality vs. data rate or degree of compression. In the case of DVI ActionMedia II, compression is performed at the same time audio is digitized. The algorithms used for DVI audio compression are discussed further in Chapter 10.

There are two principal digital audio file formats:

Format	System	Type
.WAV	Windows	WAVE audio
.AVS	DVI	DVI audio (see below)

Depending on your audio capture hardware and software, you will capture in one or the other of these formats. There are tools for editing in either format, and there are some tools for limited conversion between them. All of these are discussed in Chapter 10.

THE DVI .AVS FILE FORMAT

Audio asset files for DVI technology are stored in only one format—the **.avs** format, which is a DVI special format. An **.avs** file is very flexible; it is able to store one or more assets of one or more types. Thus, for a motion video clip, a single **.avs** file stores both the audio and the video. The two data types are referred to as *streams* in the **.avs** file, and because they are interleaved in the same file, it is easy to play them in exact synchrony. An **.avs** file is able to contain additional synchronous streams; for example, a motion video file might have multiple audio streams for different languages—at play time the user could select the one he wants to hear. Similarly, the video file could have one or more data streams, which might be presented during playback; one application for a data stream is to hold the data needed to present text subtitles as the video plays.

An **.avs** file can also store one or more still images. These can either be by themselves in the file, or they can be combined with other streams. For example, one interesting use is to have an audio file that also contains a series of images to be displayed along with the audio. The **.avs** file will support this, and a player designed for this feature would be able to simply "play" the file to deliver an audio and still image presentation.

While not all existing DVI software supports all of the features of the **.avs** file format, the examples here show how the file format has been designed to be expandable in the future.

MOTION VIDEO ASSETS

A DVI motion video asset is an **.avs** file that has at least one motion video stream, and it may optionally have one or more audio streams or data streams as described above. Since motion video is produced by rapidly (30 times a second) displaying a sequence of video images called *frames*, a video **.avs** file has a frame structure to it. Each frame includes the data needed to produce the next video image to be displayed. There are two general approaches to producing the next image: create the next image from scratch, called a *reference frame*, or produce the next image by modifying the previous image, called a *delta frame*.

A video file must begin with at least one reference frame to create the first image. After that, the frames can be either reference frames or delta frames. Note that delta frames take substantially less data than reference frames, since they only contain the parts of the image that have changed from the previous frame. Unless there was a camera switch, there is typically very little change between adjacent motion video frames. Therefore, for maximum compression of the video data, use delta frames as much as possible.

Sometimes you would like to jump into the middle of a video file and begin playing it. This is called *random access*, and you can do it by specifying a *frame number* on which to start. But remember, you cannot begin playing video except from a reference frame, because there is no way to create the first frame from delta frame information only. Consequently, video files that are intended for random access playback must have reference frames inserted periodically to create potential start points. On the average, reference frames take about three times more data than delta frames, so a video file made entirely of reference frames would be three times larger than one that had all delta frames. Unless there is a definite need for random access to any frame number, a compromise is in order. Most times, it will be satisfactory to place reference frames about once per second, or every 30 frames. This does not significantly increase the file size, and still gives one-second accuracy to random access. Note that the insertion of reference frames into the video stream has no effect on the normal playback of the video.

An **.avs** motion video file contains an index of all its reference frames in the file header. If you want to random access to a particular frame number, the internal software looks first at the frame index to see if the desired frame number is a reference frame. If it is, it seeks to that frame in the file (using the offset value from the frame table) and begins playing. If the desired frame number is not a reference frame, the software will usually seek to the next reference frame and play from there. This strategy depends on the exact software you are using to play the file; what is described above is the MEDIAscript OS/2 method. Obviously, you need to take this into account if you are going to use random access of video files.

The frame structure described for video is also used for audio, although audio itself does not inherently have frames. Although the **.avs** format allows other possibilities, usually the audio is divided into 30 frames per second (the same as the video), so a "frame" contains the data to make one video image plus the data to play 1/30 second of audio.

IMAGE ASSETS

Still images can be in a variety of formats, which support display on either the DVI or the PM planes. We'll discuss them separately.

Images for the PM plane can be in two basic types—bitmap or vector—the same as described for PM font files. A third type of file, known as a *metafile*, can contain a combination of bitmap and vector information; for example, a metafile might contain a bitmap image in combination with some vector drawing commands which draw on top of that image. Bitmap image files contain the data from all of the pixels in the source image. A bitmap is *device-specific*, meaning that it should be displayed on a system that has the same screen and pixel format as the system that created it. A bitmap file can be made device-independent if its header contains a complete definition of the bitmap format. This way, a program that loads the bitmap into a different system will know what the format is and can make its own decisions about how to display it. When a screen is simply saved as a bitmap, the file is usually in the **.bmp** format. There are **.bmp** formats for both Windows and PM, but beware: They are different. They both contain complete header information that supports device-independent loaders.

PM bitmap files can be created either by paint or draw programs. *Paint* programs work directly with a bitmap and directly manipulate pixel values. A *draw* program works with *objects* such as rectangles, lines, or polygons that you can place and size on the screen. The draw program saves its data as a vector file, although most draw programs can also save the drawing as a bitmap. Paint programs can save their work only as bitmaps. Some programs contain both paint and draw functionality in the same program.

Bitmap files can be produced from your screens by screen capture programs, or they can be captured from real images. In the latter case, the results are severely affected by the limited number of colors (usually either 16 or 256) available in the PM plane. For capture of real images, the 16-color mode is not particularly usable unless you want a psychedelic or silhouette effect. With 256 colors, minimally acceptable results are possible if you let the capture software create a custom palette of colors for each image. This is workable if you will be displaying only one image at a time. There also is software available that will examine two or more images and create a compromise palette to display them all together, but the best method for display of real images is to use the DVI plane.

As a result of competition among draw and paint programs for both PC and Macintosh computers, there are a large number of formats for

VGA or PM image files. Some of the more important ones are listed here, with an outline of their principal characteristics:

- **PCX**—This is one of the most widely used bitmap formats; it is supported by almost all draw and paint programs. Although it usually supports up to 256 colors, it does provide for custom palettes. Extensions to PCX have recently been made for full-color operation, but few tools support them yet.
- **TIFF**—This is the *Tagged Image File Format* for bitmap files. It is one of the most flexible, and also one of the most complicated, formats. There are many versions and no application supports all versions.
- **PICT**—This is the Macintosh metafile format, used for interchange of graphics data among nearly all Macintosh applications. It is not widely used on PCs, but some file conversion programs do support importing of it.
- **TGA**—This is the TARGA image format, first used with the Truevision TARGA real-video boards. It supports up to 32 bits per pixel and is widely used for distribution of photo-realistic images. It stores RGB information directly and therefore does not require color palettes.
- **MET**—This is the PM metafile format. It is specific to OS/2 Presentation Manager, and supports both bitmaps and vector data.
- **BMP**—This format is used for both PM and Windows bitmaps. However, the format is slightly different between Windows and OS/2. It stores a device-independent bitmap. For either 4 bpp or 8 bpp it has a built-in compression method. It supports up to 24 bpp, but uncompressed.
- **EPS**—This is the Encapsulated PostScript format, developed for use with PostScript printers. It is a metafile format and is very flexible; it is supported by many drawing programs.
- **HPGL**—This is the Hewlett-Packard Graphics Language vector format. It was originally developed to send commands to a line-drawing plotter.
- **CGM**—This is a metafile format which is a national standard supported by the American National Standards Institute (ANSI). It is widely used in the publishing, CAD, and graphics markets.

This list is only a small subset of existing image formats—there are at least 50 different formats in use. Because of this, most image creation or processing programs have the capability to import or export images in a number of formats. Programs that do not directly support a particular format can also rely on *file conversion* utility programs, such as *Hijaak* by

Inset Systems. This PC-based utility can convert between more than 50 different image file formats.

MEDIAscript OS/2 and other DVI authoring systems face yet another problem—the file formats for DVI images are also unique. MEDIAscript provides for conversion between **.bmp** and DVI images, but it currently relies on external utilities for conversion of other formats to either DVI or **.bmp**. (Network Technology is working on built-in conversion from other file formats for inclusion in a future release of MEDIAscript.) Using conversion tools, you can generally import any type of image into a MEDIAscript application. You will find DVI image formats described in Chapter 11.

ANIMATION ASSETS

There are a number of animation tool programs that create their own special asset formats. Generally, a special driver or *Dynamic Link Library* (DLL) is required to present the animations. These drivers or DLLs must be supported by your main multimedia program. Since there will continue to be new animation techniques developed in the future, a flexible approach is needed so that various types of animations can be included in your multimedia programs. The MCI interface discussed in Chapter 2 addresses this problem. Some of the different animation tools are:

- Macromind Director
- Autodesk Animator
- MEDIAscript OS/2.

These tools use a variety of animation approaches, and some of them support several of the techniques. It is useful to examine each approach more closely.

Macromind Director

Director uses an extremely flexible approach called *cast animation*. You specify *cast members*, which can be individual images, graphics, or text objects. Then you work with a *score*, which lays out a series of *frames* that will be displayed in sequence. In each frame of the score, you can specify which cast members are to be displayed and where and how on the screen (called the *stage*) they will be shown. When the animation is played, all the resources of the animation are first loaded into system RAM, then the CPU creates the frames one at a time as specified in the score and displays them. This is very effective and allows a much longer and complex animation to be produced from a given amount of memory.

The Director system includes a language called *Lingo* which allows fully interactive animations or presentations to be built with the product. There is also audio capability built in. Although Director runs only on a Macintosh, Macromind has created a player that operates under Windows 3.1 on a PC and can play Director files which have been created on the Macintosh and converted to PC format with a special tool. The Windows 3.1 Multimedia Extension supports the Macromind player directly and through MCI. Macromind has also introduced *Action!*, a PC-based animation product.

The principal limitations of Macromind animation are the amount of system RAM to hold the animation data, and the CPU speed for processing the images. At present, color formats go up to only 8 bpp (256 colors), but Macromind is working on support for DVI Technology, which should extend the color and motion video capabilities.

Autodesk Animator

Animator creates graphics or animations based on a frame-by-frame authoring metaphor. Individual frames are produced by drawing and by assembling bitmaps.

MEDIAscript OS/2

MEDIAscript OS/2 is a full authoring environment with a graphical interface and an underlying language. Its animation capability is based on the frame animation approach. Ten or more animations in either the PM or DVI planes can run simultaneously; the limit is dictated by CPU speed and memory capacity to hold the source images. Animation techniques are covered more fully in Chapter 13.

GRAPHICS AND TEXT ASSETS

You have a choice with graphics and text—either create (draw) them at the time your application runs, or draw them during authoring and save them as bitmaps for display at runtime. In the latter case, they become image assets, and are handled just like any other images.

Text and graphics to be drawn at runtime are stored as commands in a script, in a vector image file, or in a metafile. All of these have the advantage that the commands for a drawing usually take less storage than the resulting bitmap image. However, depending on the contents of the drawing, it may take longer to render (draw) the drawing than it takes to load an image. This is a tradeoff that you must weigh according to the needs of your application.

One case that requires you to draw at runtime is when the object to be drawn is based on data collected or created during the running of the application. For this, you set up variables in your application to hold the values from the application, and the actual drawing of the object is done with parameters calculated from those variables. With MEDIAscript OS/2, you create the necessary variables in the project or the script, use a variable object to assign the variables with values collected during runtime, and then use a Draw object in which you authored the variable names or expressions for the drawing coordinates and other parameters. This way the exact drawing is dynamically determined at runtime.

Some special considerations apply to using text and graphics in the DVI plane. DVI text and graphics can only be created or drawn using the MS-DOS version of DVI software. (Hopefully, this will change some day.) If you are working with DVI in an MS-DOS system, graphics and text work the same as described above; but if you want DVI text or graphics in the OS/2 environment, you must create them with MS-DOS tools and save the results as DVI images. Since DVI image files are compatible between MS-DOS and OS/2, there is no problem with this. However, if you need the dynamic determination of DVI graphics or text at runtime, that is possible today only in an MS-DOS system.

DATA ASSETS

Data assets are files such as engine control files, assign files, or database index or data files. Their exact formats depend on how your authoring system handles data I/O and the specific needs of your application. In some cases, you will want to bring data into memory for processing or display, and in other cases, you may be able to perform operations on the files themselves.

In MEDIAscript OS/2, data I/O is handled through the string variables array. If you require information in memory, you can load text files into the memory string array by using the **assign** option of the Data object. Once data is in the strings, you can search it, or process it with a full range of string-manipulation functions. The result of such processing can be displayed either by the **text** option of the Draw object, or it can be read back to disk using the **write** option of the Data object. MEDIAscript OS/2 can perform data search actions on either disk files or strings. Depending on the needs of your application, choose from these capabilities, and develop your data strategy and the data file formats you will use. There are some examples of this in Chapter 14.

Sometimes the data search or processing requirements of an application will be too much for these simple functions. This would occur, for example, if you were dealing with a large CD-ROM database such as an encyclopedia. In that case, you would probably choose to communicate with a separate data retrieval program. In the OS/2 or Windows environment, that could be accomplished by using DDE capabilities to control a separate data retrieval program that was installed on the desktop. In MEDIAscript OS/2 you could do that by using the **execute** option of the File object to start the other program, and the DDE options in the Input, Message, and Data objects to establish and work the DDE connection.

USING THE ASSETS

Many situations will arise in your applications that require you to decide among several assets that you could use to accomplish a given point. For example, you could teach your user a particular procedure using any of the following approaches:

- Create an animated drawing with audio voice-over.
- Present a series of slides with audio.
- Do it all with motion video and sound.

How do you decide which one to use? There are many considerations that you must weigh to come to a decision. Some of the more important ones are:

- data usage
- time schedule
- existing assets
- asset facilities
- asset skills
- special needs
- available funds

We'll take up each of these subjects in detail below. Although the decision-making process requires common sense, there are some issues that may not be completely obvious. Some of these are brought out by the comparisons in Table 9.1.

158 *Designing Interactive Multimedia*

Asset	Data Usage Per Minute	Cost to Create	Presentation Effectiveness	Time Cycle
Video	9 MB	High	High	Long
Audio	250 K	Low	Medium	Short
Images	500 K	Medium	Medium	Medium
Animation	10 K-100 K	Medium	High	Medium
Text & Graphics	10 K	Low	Low	Short

Table 9.1 Comparison of assets

Data Usage

You can see that motion video is the largest user of data; it is high in cost, but it gives high effectiveness (when well produced, of course). Because of the high cost in data and dollars, you ought to use video only where it will do the most good or where the other approaches are not adequate for the material to be presented. Still images (based on about 10 DVI images per minute) are medium range in all categories. Audio is medium for effectiveness and data usage, but it is low in cost (if you do it yourself). A good combination is images plus audio—this duet gives good effectiveness at medium cost. The lowest cost approach is to use text and graphics; it is easy and inexpensive to produce, but it also provides the least effectiveness. A better choice is to use text and graphics with audio.

Time Schedule

A short time schedule often forces you to choose a simple approach, one that you can do easily, and where as many of the pieces as possible are already available. This may also mean that it is not the best approach in terms of the needs of the task, but it is necessary for you to meet the schedule. An important point to keep in mind when thinking about schedules for multimedia projects is that they have a habit of taking longer than you expected. This is especially true when the details of the job are not completely planned out in advance. In such cases, extra features and extra work have a habit of creeping in. Actually, you can say this about any kind of project (not just a multimedia project)—if you don't plan well up front, you will have no control over the scope of the work.

Existing Assets

Obviously, it costs nothing and takes no time to use something you already have. However, what you already have may not be the optimum for the current task. This is something you must weigh: Will the sequence be good enough if I use existing assets for it? Of course, you still have the opportunity to edit or touch up existing assets to make them more suitable to the current project. You have to decide.

Working with Existing Assets

Existing materials include assets that you already own and assets that you can purchase from others. There are many companies that offer libraries of audio, images, or video. Sometimes a library is offered for sale and you are given unlimited rights to reproduce and use the material. These are usually called "clip" libraries.

In other cases, you will have to license the use of someone else's material on an individual item and/or a per use basis. Such licenses must be individually negotiated and can sometimes become very expensive. And do not overlook the fact that such acquisitions take time.

The important point to remember about using other people's assets is that you **must** obtain proper permission to use it. This is obvious when the material is offered for sale or license; however, it may not be so obvious when you find the material in a book or magazine, on TV, or on a CD. In all these cases, the material is copyrighted, and may not be copied or displayed for any purpose other than what is expressed in the copyright notice on the item, unless you have received permission to do so. *In all cases, obtain proper permissions for materials before you use them in your applications!* If you have questions, consult a lawyer specializing in intellectual property rights.

Also take into consideration that when you use existing material, many times it will not be in the proper format for use directly by your application. It may be in analog form: on tape or film, or as analog hard copy. If it is already in digital form, it still may not be the exact format that you can use. Thus, your planning process must take into account the time and cost of doing media preparation: the digital capture, format conversion, or other processing needed to prepare the material for use. This can become a major task, especially when there is a large volume of material. It may require the acquisition of special tools or special programming to facilitate a large media preparation task.

Asset-Making Facilities and Skills

Another consideration about the type of material to use for your project is whether the necessary facilities are available to create your own assets. For example, if you decide that you want a video clip for the project, you must have access to the equipment and skills to produce that video. If you can't do it yourself, there is still the possibility that you can hire a video production crew and studio to do it, which requires funding.

Special Needs of the Application

Some applications just naturally call for a certain type of presentation. For example, it would be difficult to teach someone how to speak a foreign language without using some audio. Similarly, simulation of a chemical process really benefits from animation, so that the user interactively controls the parameters of the process and the animation runs accordingly. If your application has such a special need, then your decision is probably already made for you: You have to do what is required.

Available Funds

Obviously, your available budget of funds and time also affects your approach to the application. As shown in Table 9.1, different types of presentation have different costs. You may not be able to afford the most effective approach, especially if you will have to pay others to do the work. The bottom line is: The final choice of approach must fit your budget for the project.

CHAPTER SUMMARY

The audio, video, image, or data files for an application are called its assets. Asset files are not well standardized—there are many formats, and you often face the problem of format conversion in order to incorporate materials into your application.

There are many different ways to present a given subject, using different combinations of assets. You must decide what approaches to use in your application before you can go after the needed assets.

When you use assets owned by others, be sure to obtain the necessary permissions and rights from the owner of the assets.

10

Producing Your Own Audio

natural: adj. produced or existing in nature; not artificial or manufactured.
Webster's New World Dictionary, 1988

The ability to capture *natural* sounds and bring them into your multimedia applications is the real purpose of digitized audio. But there is more to this than setting up a microphone and telling the computer to capture. A well-produced sound track will do more to support the realism and effectiveness of your application than almost anything else.

Sound recording has been practiced for more than 50 years in audio records, motion pictures, and broadcasting. The techniques are highly developed, and many specialties have been defined. An unbelievable array of equipment and processes is available and used daily in the industries mentioned above—far more than you could ever deal with as an individual. This discussion focuses specifically on the kind of audio work you might consider doing by yourself, but gives enough of a broader view so that you will know what else is available if you decide to bring in sound experts.

This chapter will tell you what facilities you need to capture your own audio and how to best use those facilities to obtain high-quality audio for your applications.

EQUIPMENT FOR AUDIO CAPTURE AND PROCESSING

Since natural audio is basically analog, and most audio sources (microphones, tape decks, records, radio, or TV) are also analog, you must have a capability for analog to digital conversion to capture audio into the computer. This is normally available on an add-in board for your PC, although as multimedia becomes more widespread it will probably become a built-in feature. The DVI ActionMedia II card with the capture adaptor is the best choice, because it offers a digital signal processor (DSP) that gives a wide choice of audio capture methods, including real-time audio compression. ActionMedia II also provides video as well as audio on the same card. However, there are numerous other cards for audio-only that provide basic capture functionality. (See Appendix A.)

An audio capture card in your PC is only the beginning—you will need other equipment to deliver audio signals to the card, and to provide control of those signals. A starting equipment list includes one or more of these items:

- microphone,
- audio mixer,
- audio tape deck,
- audio amplifier, and
- speakers.

Depending on your needs for audio quality and ease of use, available equipment ranges from home-quality (you can purchase a setup for as little as a few hundred dollars), to setups designed for amateur musicians at around $1,000, to professional audio or broadcast equipment costing many thousands of dollars. The more expensive equipment offers higher audio quality (up to CD audio quality), and many features that make it easier to get precise results in audio capture and editing. Figure 10.1 shows a medium-priced audio setup utilizing an integrated stereo mixer and tape deck by Yamaha.

If you are going to capture live audio with a microphone, such as taping a live speaker (possibly yourself), you must have a quiet place to do it. You do not want the background noise of an office or workroom to disrupt your application's audio. In a large office complex, you can usually schedule a quiet conference room for this; but better still is a real audio studio. As more multimedia is done in business, it will make sense to have studio rooms available for this purpose.

BASICS OF AUDIO PRODUCTION

Unless your audio requirements are extremely simple, such as a voice-only track, you will want to produce your audio first on analog audio tape. Once you have the complete sound track assembled on tape, you will then

Figure 10.1 Typical inexpensive audio mixing and tape recording setup, the MT-120 by Yamaha.

digitize it with the computer. The reason for using analog production is that the tools for assembling, modifying, and editing of audio are more complete, easier to use, and lower in cost than current tools for processing of audio after it is digitized. That will change in the future, but today you will want to do most of your audio preparation in the analog world.

A typical sound track is made up of one or more of these four elements:

- **ambience**—the background sounds of the environment or location. This is what you hear when no other sound element is active.
- **voice**—(also called dialog)—the voice of the performers or the announcer. This element, when it exists, usually carries the principal message of the scene.
- **music**—usually added for effect. If there is no voice track, the music track may be carrying the message of the scene.
- **effects**—sounds other than music or voice. Because of this definition, ambience is often considered to be part of effects. Effects can be real sounds created by the action in the scene, or they can be other sounds added for "effect."

If you listen carefully to the sound for a TV show, you will easily recognize each of the elements. For the most flexibility, each element is recorded (produced) separately and then the elements are combined into the final sound track in an editing or *postproduction* session. In order to do that, you first must plan your sound track by making a time line diagram that shows how and when you want each element of the sound track to come in. This diagram can then serve as the basis for producing

Figure 10.2 Plan for sound track for introduction sequence.

each element, and it tells the editor how to put the elements together. Figure 10.2 is an example of such a plan for a simple sound track.

ACHIEVING AUDIO-VIDEO SYNCHRONIZATION

The need to synchronize picture and sound will often affect the way that you produce the audio. For example, if someone is speaking on camera, you will need to achieve lip synchronization between picture and sound. The easiest way to do that is to capture both at the same time and keep them together. This works well for synchronization, but it may not let you achieve everything you want in the sound track. You may still need to separate the sound track from the video and modify it to add ambience, effects, or music.

In movie or television production, sometimes even the dialog track itself is replaced by using a technique called *automatic dialog replacement* (ADR). In ADR, the performers in the scene go into a special studio where they see and hear their original performance over and over by looping it (ADR is sometimes called *looping*). By practicing repeatedly, they eventually can speak their lines in sync with the original; their voices are then recorded, but this time in the controlled environment of the studio. This way, a perfectly clean dialog track can be produced in sync with the original.

In professional sound production, effects are often added by a technique similar to ADR. A special sound stage called a *Foley studio* is equipped with devices for creating all kinds of sound effects. A sound-effects professional watches the video of the scene and uses the Foley equipment to make the necessary sounds in sync with the images.

In cases where the important sound for the sequence is not coming from on-camera action, such as with an off-screen announcer, it is often easier to produce the sound track first, and then shoot or edit the video to fit the sound. The sound track becomes the time line for the video production. If the video consists of a series of stills, the audio-video timing process is done as part of authoring. The author simply plays the audio track and finds the frame number cues for each still image according to the plan for the sequence. Then she authors the images to be displayed on the frame number cues.

EQUIPMENT SETUP

If your sound tracks have only one element, you do not need any mixing capability, and it is reasonable to work with a home-type cassette deck for recording from microphones or other sources. The principal requirement is that you have a way to control and monitor the audio level (volume). Most tape decks have some type of volume indicator display or meter, which will be adequate. However, if you expect to do some mixing of multiple elements in your sound track, then you need a more elaborate facility like the one described below.

Figure 10.3 is a block diagram of a modest setup for monaural audio recording and mixing, using a 4-channel mixer and a 4-track tape deck. Each of the units can be separate or combined in one piece, such as the combined mixer-recorder that was shown in Figure 10.1. This diagram is for a small operation; a larger activity would have more mixing channels for more microphones or tape sources, additional tape tracks, and many more boxes for effects and processing. Most equipment today provides the means to deliver stereo output by allowing controlled mixing of each channel of the mixer to either stereo channel. The controls that do this are called *pan* controls.

The basic purpose of the mixer is to allow you to connect any input to any output, with control and monitoring of the amount of signal through each path. Thus, you can activate just one path through the mixer, such as connecting Microphone 1 to the Track 1 input of the tape deck; or you can set up more elaborate structures, such as taking the playback of Track 1, adding additional sounds coming in on Line 1 and Line 2, and recording the combined result on Track 2 of the tape deck.

Your setup must include the means to monitor (listen to) your results as you work. Most mixers have some monitoring capability built in so that you can select whether to monitor the input to the mixer, intermediate points in the mixer, or the output of the mixer. The monitoring lines can be connected to headphones or to a separate amplifier and speakers. The choice is up to you.

168 *Designing Interactive Multimedia*

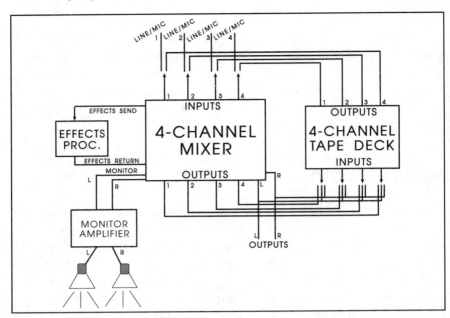

Figure 10.3 Setup for monaural audio recording and mixing.

An optional, but very desirable feature, is to have some audio effects processing capabilities. Effects processing is different from sound effects mentioned earlier; it is special processing of an existing sound to add an effect such as reverberation, whereas sound effects are completely new sounds that are added to the track. Most mixers have the means to extract signals from the input and pass them through an external effects processor and then add the processed signals back into the output of the mix. This is used to introduce reverberation, delays, chorus, flanging, or other effects to the output. Effects are widely used in music production and they can be easily added to your productions with simple equipment.

Another facility that is often valuable is equalization. This is normally placed in-line in the output of the mixer and may be part of the mixer unit or separate equipment. It allows frequency-range distortions to be corrected, or for special frequency-range effects to be produced, such as cutting the highs and lows to make a voice sound like it's coming over the telephone.

As you can see in Figure 10.3, even a simple audio system contains many interconnections. The cables and connectors are an important part of the system and should not be overlooked. In a professional audio system, all of the interconnections use *balanced lines*, which is a system that uses two signal wires in each cable. The two wires have opposite polarity signals on them; when a balanced line signal is received, the signals on the two wires are subtracted, which causes them to add up because of their opposite polarity. However, any interference picked up on the wires is typically the same on each wire, and therefore interferences will cancel in the receiver processing. The result is that hum, crosstalk, and noise pickup in a large system can be minimized. Balanced interconnections are expensive because of the special processing that must be at each end of a cable, and because the connectors (XLR type) are more expensive.

Inexpensive audio systems use mostly *unbalanced* interconnections, in which there is one signal wire and one ground wire. This is satisfactory if your system is small, you do not have long cable lengths (more than 10 or 20 feet), and cables are kept away from sources of interference such as motors, high-power audio sources, or video displays. Most low-cost audio systems use RCA-type phono connectors, or the 1/4" or 1/8" phone plugs often used for headphones. You should use only high-quality audio cables, and make sure that all of your equipment is properly grounded.

AUDIO PRODUCTION TIPS

The following tips are based on the example of producing the sound track shown in Figure 10.2.

Setting Audio Levels

The most important paramater of an audio signal is its *level*, or amplitude. It corresponds to the volume of the reproduced sound. In order to get the best quality from an audio recording, the maximum level of the sound signal should be set close to the maximum level that the recording channel can handle. Getting the level too high will cause distortion, and having the level too low will cause the noise level from the tape to be higher relative to the audio.

Audio level is measured in *decibels* (dB), which is a logarithmic unit that expresses a level relative to a *reference level*. A logarithmic scale is used because the amplitudes in an audio signal can cover an extremely wide range—more than 1,000,000 to 1—which would not be well described by a linear scale. Also, the human ear has a logarithmic response to sound, and therefore a logarithmic scale actually represents a scale of audibility. Since a dB scale is relative, meaning that it represents the ratio of one signal level to a reference level, the definition of dB is: **dB = 20 log(E/Eref)** for voltage ratios. Thus, if the signal voltage is 10 times the reference voltage, it is a 20 dB level. Table 10.1 gives some other values. You can see

Voltage Ratio	Decibels
1000:1	60 dB
100:1	40 dB
10:1	20 dB
2:1	6 dB
1:1	0 dB
1:2	-6 dB
1:10	-20 dB
1:100	-40 dB
1:1000	-60 dB

Table 10.1 Voltage ratios and dB values

the the dB scale from –60 dB to +60 dB conveniently covers a range of 1,000,000:1.

Most recording equipment has some kind of meter or display that shows dynamically what the audio level is doing. As music plays or someone speaks, the level will vary over a wide range; what is most important is the level of the highest peaks of the signal. The peaks must be set so that they do not exceed the capability of the recording channel. Usually, a level metering system is designed to help you set the level so that typical peaks in the signal come up to the 0 dB mark on the meter, and occasional peaks will not go beyond +3 dB on the meter. However, the techniques vary, so you should follow the advice in the instructions for the equipment containing the meter.

Ordinarily, it is preferable not to continuously adjust the level while audio is being recorded (this is called *riding* the level). Doing so is very difficult to get right, and it will remove some of the dynamics of the audio. Therefore, levels are usually set by running level tests before starting a sequence; then they are left alone for the duration of the recording. Only in the case of some predictable extreme fluctuation would you do any riding of the level during the recording. A better strategy is to set up for the peaks you expect and record the live source without level control; then plan to do any riding as a postproduction step. That way, you will be able to retry the level changes until you get them right.

Microphone Technique

As with many other things in audio production, proper use of microphones is as much art as science. Certain audio engineers are much in demand because of their skills in *miking*—the technique of microphone selection and placement. Fortunately, most of the things you attempt by yourself do not require some of the more arcane techniques; however, a little theoretical discussion will help you understand what factors affect microphone performance.

When you are sitting in a theater watching a live performance, the sound you hear is distinctly affected by the acoustics of the surrounding environment. Your ears are receiving sound waves *directly* from the source (the actors or the orchestra); plus, you are hearing *delayed* sound that has been reflected from distinct parts of the theater structure. Finally, you are also hearing *reverberation*, which is the decay that is caused by repeated reflections with partial absorption around the theater after a sound ends. The sound waves have a complex spatial structure combined with several temporal structures.

A certain amount of reverberation is desirable—it contributes to the liveliness of the sound. Reverberation is measured by the time it takes for a sound to decay by 60 dB (to 1/1000 of its original intensity). Typical studios for speech have reverberation times in the range of 0.5 to 1 second, and theaters designed for musical use have reverberation times in the range of 1 to 2 seconds. A space with no reverberation at all is considered *dead*—typically a large level space with no objects such as walls and ceilings (or trees and mountains, if you are outside) to reflect the sound. Playing music in such a large outdoor space requires a lot of electronic processing to add the reverberation that makes the music more life-like.

The opposite situation is also a problem: If there is too much reverberation, speech becomes unintelligible. You probably have experienced this problem in a large sports arena; if the sound system does not have the proper characteristics to overcome the arena's reverberation, you cannot understand the announcements. Simply placing microphones at your seat in this kind of theater usually will not capture what you think you are hearing when you are actually there. The reason is that microphones respond differently than your ears to the various sound waves coming from different directions.

In the example of the theater here, it usually is better to move the microphones up very close to the stage and try to capture the sound of the performance without any of the room ambience in it. The ambience factors can then be added in controlled amounts during postproduction. In extreme cases, such as rock concerts, the performers carry their own microphones, and the entire effect for the audience is achieved by electronically combining all the sound parts and adding special effects.

Returning to the simpler situations that you might face, a typical case is recording a single voice for narration of your application. The first concern is selecting the speaker. Depending on your application, you may do the speaking yourself, but if you want a real professional sound, hire someone who has been trained for narration. Such people are widely available; there even may be someone in your organization who can do it. Otherwise, consult with local sound production companies to find such people.

For the recording, choose a small, quiet room that contains a reasonable amount of sound-absorbent furnishings. Set the narrator up with her back about three feet from one wall, with a desk or podium in front. Place a microphone, preferably a directional one, immediately in front of the narrator, not more than six inches from her lips. Although this may sound very precise, it's not; what you want is to devise a setup that gives you recordings that sound natural when played back in your application. Once you find a setup that does that, remember it and use it again when you have more recording to do.

Continuing with the recording session: The narrator should practice reading the script while you set the levels for recording. When that is done, proceed with the first take. The recorder should be started first, and then cue the narrator to begin. Record until the script is finished.

Your first take undoubtedly will have some problems and you will want to do it again. You can just rewind the tape and record over the first take, but doing so requires that you decide on the spot whether you have a satisfactory take. A better approach is to simply continue running the recorder and add the second and subsequent takes after the first one. If you do that, however, you need a way to identify and locate each take. This can be achieved by taking notes of the tape timer readings at the start of each take, and by adding a brief announcement—such as, "Take three"—just before you cue the narrator. Then you can continue with takes until you think you have a good one. Later, you can replay the tape and make a final selection before you do the digitizing. It may turn out that the last take wasn't the best one, and you will be glad that you have all the takes to choose from.

Editing Technique

Audio editing is another one of those disciplines that has its artists in the professional world. Elaborate editing requires professional equipment and can be time consuming. A skilled editor can even do things like replace one word in a take with a word from another take or remove an unwanted sound. If you need fancy editing, hire professional help. For our purposes, we discuss the simple editing you will have to do to identify the exact start and stop points for the take that you are going to digitize.

In professional editing, the equipment is normally controlled by a *time code* track, which identifies locations on the tape down to 1/30 second—one video frame. The equipment is computer controlled and can reliably seek to an exact frame number and play out an exact number of frames. However, the low-cost equipment that you probably have does not do time code, and you will have to locate and repeat tape positioning by simpler means.

Locate the start of your take by playing the tape up to a point just before the take and stopping it—this is called *cueing*. With simple equipment you have to do this by trial and error, using the tape deck forward, reverse, play, and stop controls. Most tape decks have a *zero-stop* feature, which lets you command the tape to return to zero on the tape counter. When you think you have found the proper start point, zero the tape counter at that point. Then roll the tape forward a few seconds to get away from the zero point, and reset the tape deck automatically to zero. Once the tape is back at zero, you can preview the result by listening carefully as you begin playing the tape from the zero-stop position. Proper cueing is achieved when the speaker begins between 0.5 and 1 second from the time you start the tape. If you don't get it the first time, repeat the cueing process, reset the tape counter, and try again. You don't really have to locate the end point of the sequence now; this can be done during the digitizing process.

Mixing Technique

Mixing is the process of combining several different elements into a complete sound track. In the professional world, this can become quite complex, and may even have several intermediate steps or *premixes*. For the situation here, things are much simpler; the most you may need to do is combine a music track with your narration, or maybe insert some sound effects. Let's examine the task of adding a music track to your narration, as shown in the sample sound track plan of Figure 10.2.

Because the music track begins before the narration track, you have to use a separate tape deck to do this mix. The separate tape deck must contain the narration track (you ought to record it originally on this deck), and it will start after the recording of the music track has begun. An alternative is to record the narration track with the right amount of quiet time before the narrator begins speaking, which must be done in each take. This is awkward, but if you have just one tape deck it is the only way you can do it.

The process is easiest when done in two steps: First record both the music and narration onto separate tracks of the multitrack recorder, but with the proper relative timing (the narration begins 10 seconds after the music begins). Then do the final mix—combine music and narration into a recording on a third track. Notice that this approach causes the music to be recorded and replayed twice in getting to the final mix: once onto a track by itself, again in the mix process. The narration is recorded three times: once for the original recording, the second time to put it on the multitrack in proper timing, and the third time in the final mix. Each step of rerecording is called a *generation*; the narration goes through three generations.

Because analog noise and distortion accumulate for each generation, you should avoid too many rerecordings. (Digital recording does not have that problem.) You could reduce the narration generations by one if you played the external tape deck into the final mix instead of first recording it onto the multitrack. However, that makes the mix more difficult to handle because you will have to manage not only the control of the mix, but the timing of the other tape deck in real time. If you can find someone to help, you might try this, but it is too much to try by yourself. Nevertheless, three generations with our equipment is probably OK, so let's proceed.

First record the music track onto Track 1 of the multitrack recorder; do this at normal level and starting at the beginning of the tape. Then, set up to record from the external tape deck onto Track 2, also at normal level. With the external tape deck cued at the take you are going to use, start Track 2 recording from the beginning of the tape. After 10 seconds, start the external deck playing, and continue playing and recording until the end of the take. Stop the external deck at this point, but let the multitrack run a little while longer, so that it goes beyond the end of the music on Track 1.

Now set up for the final mix, which will be done by playing Tracks 1 and 2 while recording on Track 3. The signals will be controlled by the fader controls 1 and 2 on the mixer. To begin the mix, simply start the multitrack from the beginning of the tape; immediately push up the fader on Track 1 to bring in the music to normal recording level. After the desired 10 seconds, simultaneously push up the fader on Track 2 to bring in the narrator and push back the fader on Track 1 to reduce the music volume so it does not override the narrator. At the end of the narration, move the faders back to the first position and continue recording the music to the end. At the end of the music, stop the tape.

The mix is on Track 3; rewind and play it to see how it sounds. You will probably need to practice this several times until you get a pleasing result;

but that's no problem, because you still have the original materials on Tracks 1 and 2 so you can repeat the mix as many times as needed. When you are satisfied, you are ready to convert the contents of Track 3 to digital.

DIGITAL AUDIO CAPTURE

Digital capture of audio can be done with a number of different boards and software. Here, we will use the DVI ActionMedia II board and the MEDIAscript OS/2 software. This combination provides a choice of audio capture algorithms as shown in Table 10.2.

The 4-bit algorithms use ADPCM (Adaptive Differential Pulse Code Modulation) compression, while the 8-bit algorithms are uncompressed PCM (Pulse Code Modulation). The result of this is that at the same sampling rate, the 4-bit algorithms may produce better sound quality because the decompression expands to nearly 16-bit quality. The 4-bit 8268 algorithm should be used only for speech; its bandwidth is too low for most music. All the other algorithms are usable for speech or music, but with different degrees of high-frequency response, as indicated by the bandwidth figures.

The 8-bit algorithms are data-compatible with the Microsoft WAVE format specified for Windows multimedia. However, at present, DVI audio and WAVE have different file headers. MEDIAscript OS/2 can play either file format, but can create only in the DVI file format. Notice that using the stereo format doubles the data rate. The stereo channels are

Bits/Sample	Sampling Rate	Bytes/Minute	Audio Bandwidth	Stereo
4	8268 Hz	248 Kb	4 kHz	no
4	33072 Hz	992 Kb	15 kHz	no
4	8268 Hz	496 Kb	4 kHz	yes
4	33072 Hz	1.98 Mb	15 kHz	yes
8	11025 Hz	662 Kb	5 kHz	no
8	22050 Hz	1.32 Mb	10 kHz	no
8	44100 Hz	2.65 Mb	18 kHz	no
8	11025 Hz	1.32 Mb	5 kHz	yes
8	22050 Hz	2.65 Mb	10 kHz	yes
8	44100 Hz	5.3 Mb	18 kHz	yes

Table 10.2 DVI audio algorithms

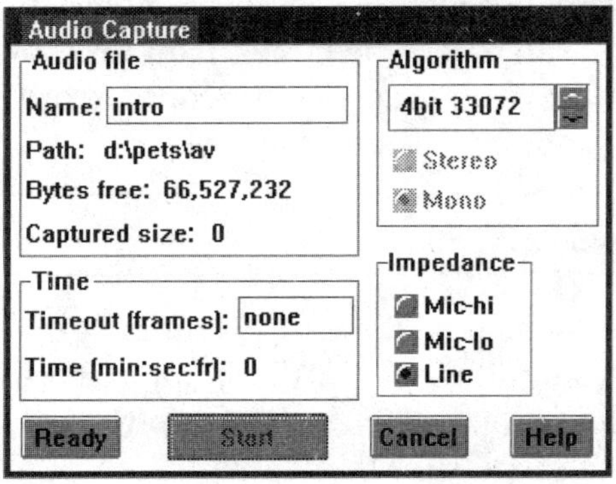

176   *Designing Interactive Multimedia*

Figure 10.4 MEDIAscript OS/2 audio capture dialog

completely independent channels and could be used for other purposes, such as two language tracks.

To do audio capture, connect the audio output of the multitrack recorder to the input of the ActionMedia II board. Then start the MEDIAscript OS/2 Server and AUI modules. To get the capture tool, select **Audio capture** from the **Tools** pull-down menu of either the **Projects** or a **Project** window. The dialog shown in Figure 10.4 appears.

Notice that the **Ready** and **Start** buttons of the dialog are grayed out. This is to alert you that you have to do something before they will become active. In particular, you must enter a filename for the audio file to activate the **Ready** button. The reason is that audio capture is directly to disk (even when compressing), and therefore nothing can happen until a filename is specified. If you are satisfied with the default path shown, you have to enter only a filename—no path or extension is required. The path shown is the default audio path for the AUI unless you are using capture from a Project window; in that case, it is the audio path for the project. The **Bytes free** field shows the amount of free disk space on the drive indicated by the current path.

At this point, you also may choose a different algorithm from the default one shown; and if you want it, choose **Stereo**. Radio buttons also let you choose the nominal input condition with the **Impedance** selector: microphone or line. For a tape recorder signal, choose **Line** impedance. The remaining option is to specify a timeout for the digitizing. If you want an exact number of frames to be digitized, enter the value in the **Timeout** field; capture will automatically stop at this number of frames. If there is no timeout value given, or the word **none** appears, digitizing will continue until you stop it or until you run out of disk space.

Once the filename is entered and you have chosen the appropriate options, select **Ready**. This begins the capture software in the monitor mode, which passes the audio input through to the output of the ActionMedia II board, while processing the audio exactly the way it will be done when capturing and playing back the digital audio. The **Start** button also now becomes active. This is the state at which you can set levels before digitizing.

Setting levels for digitizing is very critical for two reasons. First, the overload behavior of a digital channel is not at all forgiving; if you exceed the capability of a digital system by even 1 dB, a loud crashing noise typically occurs. This is not tolerable, even briefly. Therefore, you have to set the level so that overload *never* occurs. However, you can't be too conservative about this either, because when the level is too low for digitizing (especially with the 8-bit algorithms), you get a distortion called *quantizing noise*, which causes an annoying "crunchy" character to the sound.

The best way to deal with this is to preview your entire sequence and keep pushing the level up to the point of overload. When that happens, back off just a little. Then preview again and make sure that overload no longer occurs anywhere in the piece. You can do this with the MEDIAscript OS/2 capture tool while in the **Ready** mode. This is another good reason to record your complete audio first on analog tape—so you can play it repeatedly to set the best digital level.

Once the level is set, reposition the tape at the start of the segment and run the digitizing. For that, simply start the tape playing and click the **Start** button on the capture tool at the same time. (The capture can also be started by hitting the **Enter** key on the keyboard.) Note that as soon as you start, the **Start** button changes to **Stop**; this is so you can start and stop with two strokes of the **Enter** key. While digitizing is running, the Capture dialog shows you approximately how large an audio file is being generated, and it displays the duration of the capture in minutes, seconds, and frames.

When digitizing is completed (stop it at the end of the audio), you can replay the digital file by using the **Audio player** from the **Tools** menu. If there is anything wrong with the result, you can immediately correct it and rerun the digitizing, writing over the same file, if you wish. Note that if your audio file is too long at either the start or the end, you can fix it during playback in your application; but if it is cut off at either end, you must fix it now.

This discussion has given you an overview of the steps of audio production and postproduction for a fairly simple application. It also has indicated where more elaborate things are done in professional audio production in order to help you understand what the possibilities are when you use professional help. Either way, audio production can be very rewarding, and it is a lot of fun.

CHAPTER SUMMARY

A wide range of audio equipment is available for both amateur and professional use. The most suitable equipment for desktop authoring use is equipment designed for use by musicians. If you need very elaborate facilities, it is probably best to use professional audio production houses.

The best approach is to produce your audio on analog equipment and prepare a complete analog sound track before digitizing.

Audio production and postproduction have many detailed steps; however, by proper attention to those details, you can produce your own sound tracks.

The last step is to digitize the sound track into the computer. This can be done with the ActionMedia II card and MEDIAscript OS/2 software.

11

Producing Your Own Still Images

reproduce: vt. specif., to make a copy, close imitation, duplication, etc., of (a picture, sound, writing, etc.).

Webster's New World Dictionary, 1988

The objective of an image reproduction process is to make images that look just like the original. Until recently, PC-based image reproduction had to make a severe compromise because most PCs could display at most 256 colors in one image. Now, with facilities such as true color boards or DVI Technology, images are easily displayed with 65,000 or more colors. This means the computer's palette of colors no longer limits the display of photo-realistic images, and difficult processing to make color compromises is not necessary.

Digital images are obtained by digitizing photographs or video camera scenes; or they are created by painting them with special software for drawing and manipulating images. This chapter covers techniques for obtaining digital images, particularly for DVI Technology; we also discuss the equipment and software required for these techniques and how to use it.

DVI IMAGES

DVI images come in two pixel formats: 16 bits/pixel (bpp) and 9 bpp. There also is hardware support for 24 bpp, but it has not been widely used. The 16 bpp format delivers high-quality images with almost enough colors for any purpose. The reason for saying "almost" is that 16 bpp

180 *Designing Interactive Multimedia*

delivers only 65,536 colors, which is not always enough to reproduce smoothly shaded natural images without visibility of contouring.

The 9 bpp format is really a name for a more complex arrangement that yields 24-bit color, but with the compromise that the color information has fewer actual pixels than the monochrome fine detail information. This is accomplished by actually having three bitmaps to display a picture: one full-resolution bitmap that holds a full-resolution monochrome image, called the *luminance* image; the Y bitmap; and two lower-resolution bitmaps to hold color difference information, called U and V. When these bitmaps are displayed in real time by the DVI chip set, the U and V bitmaps are interpolated up to full resolution and displayed along with the monochrome image. This is shown in Figure 11.1. The result is a full-color image that looks perfectly normal for photographic images. It works because the human eye does not perceive fine detail in color as well as it does in monochrome. This technique is also used in NTSC and PAL color television; in fact, it was first developed for color TV.

The name 9 bpp comes from the fact that there are 8 bpp for the Y image, but the number of U and V pixels is reduced 4:1 in each direction (called *subsampling*). There are still 8 bpp for each of the U and V bitmaps,

Figure 11.1 DVI 9 bpp image format. The full color image is made from separate bitmaps for Y, U, and V components. The U and V bitmaps are 1/4 resolution in each direction; they are interpolated up to full resolution by the DVI chips when the bitmaps are displayed.

but since their pixel count is reduced by 4:1 in each direction, there are 16 times fewer pixels, and each one only adds 8/16 or 1/2 bpp for each Y pixel. When you add all this up: 8 for Y + 1/2 for U + 1/2 for V, you get 9 bpp! This is a form of image compression.

Although the 9 bpp system is good for natural images, it does not work well for artificial images; which have highly colored thin lines or sharp colored edges such as can be created with computer graphics. The subsampling and interpolation processes cause thin colored lines to lose color and sharp colored edges to become fuzzy. For that reason, you should not use 9 bpp for graphics; instead, the 16 bpp format is preferable because it does not have subsampling. You may choose either 9 bpp or 16 bpp for displaying still images, but when you are playing motion video, you must use 9 bpp, because DVI motion video compression depends on the 9 bpp mode. However, a 9 bpp screen can still display a 16 bpp source image because the DVI software performs automatic conversions.

DVI Image Files

All digital images are stored on disk or CD-ROM as files, usually one file per image. Image files for PM or VGA images were covered in Chapter 9. In this chapter we primarily are concerned with DVI image files, although some of the techniques discussed also can apply to image files for other display media.

Historically, there have been several DVI image file types because the technology originally specified different filename extensions for different bpp and compression methods. Also, the 9 bpp images formerly had three files per image, corresponding to the Y, U, and V bitmaps. This is being superseded to simplify file management. In particular, all new DVI image files are created in the AVSS file format—the same one used for motion video and audio. This file format needs only one file per image, regardless of what kind it is; in fact, the format can support multiple images per file (that's what motion video is), but we do not recommend using AVSS files for multiple still images because it limits flexibility. In case you should run into them, Table 11.1 lists the older DVI image file formats. Current DVI software such as MEDIAscript OS/2 still supports these old formats as read-only.

As mentioned in Chapter 9, motion video and audio files use the filename extension **.avs**, denoting the AVSS format. Image files could use the same extension, but it would be confusing to keep track of the various file types if they all had the same extensions. Therefore, MEDIAscript OS/2 has adopted the convention that assigns **.a9** extensions to 9 bpp images, and **.a16** extensions to 16 bpp images. These extensions are

bpp	Compression	Name Extension
16	none	.i16
16	lossless	.c16
9	none	.imy, .imu, .imv (3 files)
9	DVI	.cmy, .cmu, .cmv

Table 11.1 DVI Image formats (old)

unchanged whether the image files are uncompressed or compressed with any of the algorithms. The file header contains all the information needed to load images of any type.

FILE FORMAT CONVERSION

With all of the file formats shown in Table 11.1 plus the new ones, there was an imperative need for a DVI image file conversion utility. Intel provided for this in their toolkit for DVI developers using MS-DOS. The utility is called **vimcvt**, and it can convert between all of the formats in Table 11.1, the AVSS format, external formats like **.tga** (Truevision Targa), and **.pix** (Lumena, a painting tool by Time Arts, Inc.). Thus, a developer using **vimcvt** can import any of these file formats, convert them to AVSS format, and rename them to **.a9** or **.a16** to bring them up to date.

The only problem with **vimcvt** is that you have to buy the Intel toolkit to get it, and it runs only under MS-DOS. To alleviate these problems, MEDIAscript OS/2 is developing built-in file conversions. For example, you can load any of the Table 11.1 file formats into memory with MEDIAscript OS/2, and then save them back to disk as **.a9** or **.a16** files. Similarly, you can load a **.bmp** file into a DVI plane with automatic conversion occurring, and then save that as a true DVI image. Of course, if the **.bmp** image only has 16 or 256 colors, the conversion will also have the limited color palette. With MEDIAscript OS/2 you can also load a 16 bpp image file into a 9 bpp window, and the conversion will happen automatically. The reverse, 9 bpp to 16 bpp is not supported, however. Network Technology Corporation is developing further image conversion features for future releases of MEDIAscript OS/2, including DVI to BMP conversion and support for the Targa TGA formats.

IMAGE COMPRESSION

Image files get very large; for example, a 9 bpp 512 × 480 image is 276 Kb, and a 16 bpp 512 × 480 image is 492 Kb. Since many applications need hundreds or thousands of images, these numbers eat up storage very fast. Fortunately, there are many ways to compress images, and file sizes can be reduced by 10:1 or more without serious image degradation.

Compression methods can be divided between *lossless* and *lossy* compression techniques. Lossless methods compress and decompress the image without any actual loss of digital data—the final image is *exactly* the same as the original, bit for bit. There is a lossless DVI compression algorithm for 16 bpp images, which typically achieves 2:1 or more compression. The actual performance depends on the amount of fine detail information in the image. (The more detailed an image is, the harder it is to compress.)

Lossy compression techniques do lose some information from the image, but they do it in ways that are difficult for a user to see when viewing the image. For example, the 9 bpp method described earlier is a lossy compression method; it loses some fine detail in the colors, but that is hard for the human eye to see. There is a DVI lossy compression algorithm for 9 bpp images that achieves up to about 10:1 compression on most images. It has parameters you can adjust to tailor the compression method to suit each image if you wish. The parameters are stored in the file header along with the compressed data, so the decompressing software knows how to interpret the data.

Another lossy compression technique is the JPEG standard (for *Joint Photographic Expert Group*, the industry body that standardized it). JPEG compression can achieve 10:1 or more compression on 9 bpp images with very good results. Thus, compressed file sizes can be reduced to 20 Kb or so per image. An advantage of JPEG is that it is a worldwide standard which is being implemented on a wide range of platforms and display hardware (not just DVI Technology). The standard is also parameterized and can be applied to fields other than video display, such as teleconferencing and data communications.

EQUIPMENT FOR DIGITIZING IMAGES

Image digitizing is done with a video camera and an imaging board such as DVI ActionMedia II, or it can be done directly with an image scanner. Both methods are covered below.

Capture with a Video Camera

The photograph or scene to be captured is placed in front of a video camera, and the output of the camera is connected to the video input of the digitizing board. Any video camera can be used, but some are better than others.

Selecting a Video Camera

The first consideration when choosing a camera for image capture is its resolution. Camera resolution is usually expressed in *TV lines per picture height,* or just *lines.* The number refers to the number of black and white lines that can be distinguished by the camera in a horizontal distance on the screen equal to the picture height. For example, low-priced consumer cameras made for use with home VCRs may have a resolution figure around 200–250 TV lines. This kind of camera will make a fuzzy picture at 512×480 pixels because it cannot distinguish as many lines as the pixel structure can. For good results with still images, the camera resolution should be at least 500 TV lines. You will not find a consumer camera with that kind of resolution.

Almost all video cameras today use solid state pickup devices, and many of those are the CCD (Charge-Coupled Device) type. With these devices, resolution is sometimes specified in terms of *number of elements,* which is the total count of all sensing areas in the device. This is something like pixels in our digital displays, although all sensing elements in a CCD are not necessarily independent of each other as are the pixels in a digital display. Typical numbers of elements range from 250,000 to over 400,000. Since a 512×480 display contains only 245,760 pixels, you might think that a single-CCD camera with 400,000 elements in its pickup device would be good enough. That's not necessarily the case because some of the elements in the CCD are used for sensing color and do not contribute to the full resolution performance. Depending on the design of the camera, up to two-thirds of the elements may be for sensing color, so the resolution turns out to be substantially lower than the number of elements suggests.

Another consideration for camera selection is the type of output signals that are provided. Most consumer cameras deliver their output in NTSC format, which is the standard for color TV in the United States. NTSC is a *composite* format, which means that all the monochrome and color information has been combined into a single signal. NTSC works well for color television, but it is a serious compromise for digitizing in that it further contributes to loss of resolution of a still image. Although most digitizing boards do support NTSC signal input because so many signal sources provide it, it is not the best approach.

In spite of all of the above, if your budget is limited, you may still decide to look at consumer cameras for possible use in still image capture, especially because (as we will see in Chapter 12) they probably will be satisfactory for motion video capture. If you want to consider them, be sure to look for cameras with the highest resolution numbers or the highest number of elements. Then *by all means* try the camera in an actual digitizing setup before you purchase it to make sure you will be satisfied with the results. The best way to evaluate a series of cameras is to use a photograph as the source image and digitize the same photo with each camera, comparing the digital images that result. To establish a standard, try to have someone digitize your test photograph with professional equipment or with an image scanner. That way you can see what the ultimate performance is.

The foregoing discussion implies that there are better kinds of cameras available—and there are. The highest quality cameras are ones designed for broadcast station service; however, they cost tens of thousands of dollars, which is prohibitive for small multimedia users. A lower-cost range of cameras priced in the thousands is made for commercial, educational, or industrial users. You can find cameras in this range that do have resolution numbers over 500, and they have some other features that are just as important.

The most important feature to look for in a camera is an *RGB output*. This means that there are three signals coming from the camera, representing the three primary colors: red, green, and blue. (See *RGB* in the Glossary, Appendix C.) RGB output avoids the compromises inherent in the NTSC signal and insures that the full camera resolution is delivered for each of the colors. This contributes noticeably to improving the sharpness of the image, especially when you digitize in 16 bpp or 24 bpp.

Another desirable feature is a *three-sensor* design, which means that there is one CCD sensor for each of the three color channels. You do not *have* to have three sensors to get an RGB output; RGB can be obtained from a single-sensor camera by appropriate signal processing, but be aware that this approach may not deliver the highest resolution. Unfortunately, a three-sensor camera is substantially more expensive, not only because of the cost of the additional sensors and optics needed, but because the sensors have to be kept in alignment, called *registration*. You can expect three-sensor cameras to be nearly double the price of an equivalent single-sensor camera. This is the price you have to pay to get the best performance.

Figure 11.2 Digitizing setup with camera and tripod.

There are many other characteristics to consider when purchasing a camera. An important feature is the lens: You should get a zoom lens, with a macro feature for the close-up work you will do when digitizing photographs. The zoom feature also will be valuable when you use the camera for shooting motion video.

For digitizing from hard copy, you might consider some kind of copy stand. These are devices that enable you to mount the camera overhead and have a table below to hold the copy you are working with. Lights are provided to uniformly illuminate the copy. However, a copy stand is not cheap either and, more importantly, it takes a lot of room and will not fit on your desktop! We have found that it is satisfactory for most work to simply use a tripod that you can set on your desk with the camera facing down, as shown in Figure 11.2. You will have to jury rig something for lights, but usually you can develop a satisfactory setup this way. Also, the tripod will have other uses when you need to take the camera out on location to shoot stills or video.

One camera parameter that gets a lot of attention in the consumer market is camera sensitivity. This is actually not an important feature for most of the work you will do for multimedia, however, because you will usually have plenty of light. Also, when you are going for the highest quality, you should arrange for plenty of light anyway—even the most sensitive cameras deliver a degraded picture when operating at low light levels. In general, almost any camera's sensitivity will be adequate unless you have some special situation that requires you to shoot with insufficient light.

Doing the Capture

We'll begin with capturing from hard copy or photographs, using the ActionMedia II board with MEDIAscript OS/2 software. The camera output is connected to the video input of the ActionMedia II board. If you have an NTSC camera, there is one connection to make; if you have an RGB camera, three cables must be connected. In your initialization of the ActionMedia driver software, you have to specify whether capture is enabled and which type of source you will be using. Then, when you boot up your computer, the correct setup of the driver software and the board will automatically occur. Consult your ActionMedia II documentation for the details of doing this.

Next you must start up the MEDIAscript OS/2 Server and AUI modules. From the menu bar of the **Projects** window of the AUI, select the **Image capture** item from the **Tools** pull-down menu to activate the capture software. The dialog box shown in Figure 11.3 will appear.

To view the output of the camera, click on the **Ready** button. This causes a small monitoring window to appear; it displays the camera signal as shown in Figure 11.3. The monitoring window can be repositioned or sized to suit your convenience, although you will find that the image

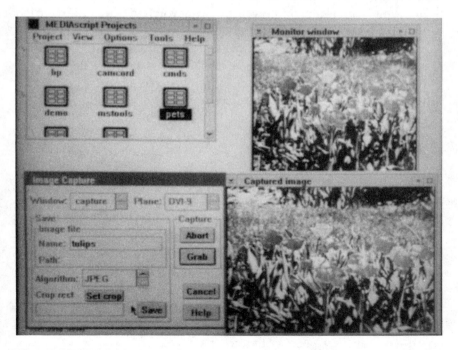

Figure 11.3 MEDIAscript OS/2 Image capture dialog. The Monitor window is open to the right.

cannot be made larger than quarter-screen. Using the monitor window, you can set up the camera positioning and focusing to suit your needs.

Normally, you should make the image fill the monitoring window, with no blank spaces around the edges. If you intend to crop a section out of the image for final use, do as much of that cropping as possible with the camera. This will give you the best final quality. Don't worry if you intend to display the image less than full-screen in the final application; that will be taken care of later. Right now, the objective is to get the best full-window picture that you can.

The thing that is difficult to do at this point is to set the video level. Video levels are standardized and most cameras do not have adjustments for levels. The level will be determined by the circuits in the camera which automatically set the iris of the lens. To check whether the automatic system is doing the best it can, turn off auto iris and then manually adjust the iris up and down to see if you can get a better picture. Normally, if anything can be improved, it will probably occur by opening the iris a little to get some more output. If you go too far, something will overload—either the camera circuits or the digitizing board. In either case, it will show first in the highlights of the picture by washing out or changing to totally wrong colors. Close down the iris until you eliminate such effects. If the result is not much different from what you had with automatic iris, turn auto iris back on and forget about it.

In the professional video world, video levels are monitored with *waveform monitors*, which are *oscilloscopic* displays that show the actual video waveforms. These are expensive and complicated equipment, and unless you are already a TV engineer, they are not recommended for use on the desktop. However, if you have trouble in your initial setup and don't think you are getting the best picture you should, you might call on a TV engineer to help you optimize the setup. The person who sold you the camera would be the place to start.

Once everything is set, capture the image into memory by clicking on the **Grab** button. This grabs the image and opens a second display window that shows the grabbed image—now a still. The monitoring window will continue to show the live camera input. The captured image window can be maximized so you can see how the result looks full-screen. If you are not satisfied with this and want to change something, restore the window to normal size and make your changes. Hitting the **Grab** button again will make a new copy of the image containing whatever you changed. At this point, your image exists only in memory on the ActionMedia II board—nothing has been written to disk.

To save the image to disk, you must enter a filename into the dialog, which will cause the **Save** button to become active. If you then click **Save**, a full-screen image will be saved to disk in the directory shown by the path field of the dialog. It does not matter what size the display window is when you save the image. However, you may want to choose a different algorithm, or crop the image before saving it. Also, you might want to choose 16 bpp rather than the default 9 bpp imaging. This latter choice has to be made before you click **Ready**.

If you examine the **Algorithm** spin button, you will find (for 9 bpp) a choice of no compression, DVI compression, or JPEG compression. The no compression choice will deliver the file sizes mentioned earlier in this chapter, and the DVI and JPEG choices will give much reduced file sizes. You should experiment with each of these to decide what is best for your application.

If you wish to crop the image, click the **Set crop** button after you have grabbed an image, but before you save it. This will enlarge the grabbed image window to full-screen and place a small rectangle on it. Using the mouse, drag and size that rectangle to enclose the exact area of the image you want to save. Once you are satisfied, click the right mouse button to accept it. A set of four numbers will appear in the **Crop rect** field, corresponding to the crop you selected. Now, when you select **Save**, only the cropped rectangle will be saved to disk. If you want to cancel the cropping, you must erase the numbers in the **Crop rect** field. Note that a cropped image will always be displayed less than full-screen; you can display it smaller than actual size, but you cannot enlarge it.

Capturing Live Scenes

Sometimes you may need to take your camera out and capture images on location. The easy way to do that is to simply go with a camera and VCR or a camcorder and tape the scenes you need. Then you could come back to your desk and at your leisure play the tape into the computer and grab stills from the video for the images you need. Although all that will work, it is not a good idea. Individual frames from motion video never have the quality of a still digitized directly from the camera. The most significant loss comes from the VCR, which has reduced resolution and poor noise performance. Also, if there is even a little motion in the frame you grab, there will be loss of resolution due to the motion. If you must capture images on location, the best approach is to use photography, and then digitize from prints of the pictures. The only other choice is to drag your whole computer setup out to the location—if it is important enough, maybe you should do that.

When you are shooting photographs for later digitizing, there are some things you can do to improve the end result. First, shoot with print film, not slides. It is very common for photographs to have more contrast than the digitizing video system can handle; this happens especially with slide film. Print film is naturally lower in contrast, which helps. Also to reduce contrast, make sure you have good lighting; bright scenes without dark shadows are going to look better when digitized. If the scene contains shadow areas that have important detail, try to get some light into the shadows by using reflectors or auxiliary lighting.

When setting up the camera, make sure that you photograph the scene as close as possible to the framing you want to finally use. Get good closeups that won't have to be cropped in digitizing. In general, practicing good photography pays off in the end.

IMAGE PROCESSING

One of the advantages of digital imaging is that you can use the computer to process images to make them better, but you can never achieve the same result that you get from a good image to begin with. The best approach always is to try to fix the image at the source; don't get into a situation where you have a lot of images that need work, because it is never easy. However, when you do have to fix up an image, the computer may be able to do it for you. With DVI Technology, there are several approaches to image processing.

In the MS-DOS world, you can use a DVI paint program such as Lumena from Time Arts to touch up an image or adjust the parameters of an entire image. You can also do this with MEDIAscript's DOS version. With either of these packages, you can adjust the contrast, brightness, tint, or color saturation of images. You can also perform processes such as posterization, mosaicing, washes, tints, warps, keying, or titling to create unusual effects.

Similar processing can be achieved by using an image conversion program to convert a DVI image to a format such as **.tga**, for which there are a number of image processing packages available for PC or Macintosh computers. When you have achieved the result you want, use the conversion tool to bring the image back to a DVI format. Although all the file conversion is tedious and time consuming, it may be the only way you can get the effect you want. But remember, the best approach is to plan so you need to do as little of this as possible.

IMAGE SCANNERS

We have concentrated on using video cameras to capture images, but there is another device that can do an even better job if you have hard copy or photographs. That device is the image scanner, which scans across an image with sensors and directly creates a digital representation of the image. No digitizing board is needed. The resulting digital file can be converted, processed, or displayed using any of the techniques we have already discussed. Figure 2.2 showed a photograph of a typical image scanner.

Scanners are special-purpose devices; they only do still images from hard copy (or sometimes slides). Because they serve only this one purpose, they seem to be expensive; they are priced in the several thousand dollar range. However, when you consider the quality that you can get, a scanner is a good investment if you have enough work to keep it busy. Most scanners come with a hardware interface to the computer, software for capture, and sometimes image processing. Few of them support DVI Technology at this time, but that will soon change. In the meantime, you may have to adopt a file conversion regimen to get DVI images from a scanner.

IMAGES FROM PAINT PROGRAMS

You don't have to settle for only real images; you can also paint or draw them, for which you need suitable painting or drawing software, the same as mentioned in the section above on image processing. With file conversion, you can use any software package working on any hardware and in any image format, and still end up with a DVI image. Of course, if your original hardware has limited colors, that's what you will end up with—file conversion can't add colors that were not present in the original.

Text and Graphics

Paint and draw tools also let you use graphics and text in DVI images. Although a DVI image is an expensive way (in terms of data) to present text, there are cases where it may be the only way to display the fonts, styles, or colors that you want. However, you will want to limit this because of the large amounts of data that it will take compared to more direct ways of presenting text.

With MEDIAscript DOS, you can display DVI text and graphics directly by drawing them in real time. This is extremely effective, especially because of the tremendous speed of DVI text—up to 30,000 characters per second and DVI Technology's large color palettes. A full screen of text can be drawn in only one frame time. However, that approach uses bitmap fonts, which means that you must have a separate font for every text size and style that you use. This can become onerous if you want to do some fancy things.

In the MEDIAscript OS/2 environment, there is no DVI text or graphics; the software capabilities in the DOS DVI environment have not been ported to OS/2. However, there is a similar capability available for the PM plane in the OS/2 environment, and it is based on vector fonts, which give much more flexibility. The problem is that it is slow, sometimes drawing only tens of characters per second. This will improve with faster CPUs, but it has a long way to go. The best solution in the long run is to have text and graphics available in both PM and DVI planes; as software evolves, we will eventually get there.

CHAPTER SUMMARY

Most image production is done using a video camera, of which there are many types in a wide range of price, performance, and features.

Once images are in digital format, they can be modified, adjusted, or processed to create different effects. Image scanners are another option for image capture. They provide the highest quality, but at a price.

Image format conversion tools are important because different software uses different image formats.

You can paint or draw images using any of the many tools available.

12

Producing Your Own Motion Video

motion: n. the act or process of moving; passage of a body from one place to another; movement.
                                                     Webster's New World Dictionary, 1988

The most interesting things in nature *move*: people walk, birds fly, fish swim. It is only natural then that when we display these things on a computer screen, we want them to move there also, and a jumpy series of still images does not do it. However, if we have enough stills and present them fast enough, the image will seem to move. Actually, this is what motion video is: a series of still images presented in rapid succession to create the illusion of smooth motion. In spite of that, we usually do not think about motion video that way when we are watching it. We think of it as something continuous, like sound or audio. When we must work with motion video, however, the series structure—the *frames*—dominates our thinking.

This chapter explains some of the characteristics of motion video, and how motion video frames are different from isolated still images. Then we discuss the equipment used to capture video in analog form; and finally, the issues of converting that to a digital format for use in the computer.

CHARACTERISTICS OF MOTION VIDEO

The normal rate for display of motion video is 30 frames per second; this is called the *frame rate*, and it is fast enough to cause the eye to see the display as a continuous image that moves; individual frames are not perceived. But it also means we must display 30 full images per second; if we used uncompressed 9 bpp images at 512 × 480 pixels, that would be a data rate of 8.3 megabytes per second! Obviously that's impractical. Even if we use 10:1 still image compression on each frame, the data rate would be 830 Kb per second or almost 50 megabytes per minute—still impractical.

Thirty frames per second gives smooth motion reproduction of almost any scene. If there is no fast motion in the scene, you can sometimes get away with slightly lower frame rates—20 frames/second or even 15. However, at these rates, the picture will start getting jumpy when anything moves fast, such as a person waving her hands, or almost any kind of sports activity. Motion picture film runs at 24 frames per second, and even at this frame rate, you sometimes see flicker when things move really fast. A truly satisfactory motion video system has to achieve 30 frames per second to fulfill all types of applications.

MOTION VIDEO COMPRESSION

The answer is in video compression technology. But using compression for motion video means that we must decompress each frame in 1/30th of a second in order to keep up with the frame rate. The still image compression algorithms discussed in Chapter 11 that give 10:1 compression take one or two *seconds* to decompress a single image. Here we need much more compression than that to get the data rate down to a practical value. Obviously, we have to do some things differently to achieve the large amount of compression needed and still be able to decompress it fast enough.

What data rate is practical? That is usually considered to be the data rate of a CD-ROM drive, which is 150 Kb per second, or 9 megabytes per minute. At that rate, a CD-ROM can hold up to 72 minutes of motion video. Dividing that rate down, it equates to 5 Kb per frame, 30 times a second. Also, if there is to be audio with our video (which is really important), some of the data rate must be allocated for audio—say 10 percent, or 500 bytes per frame, 15,000 bytes per second. This leaves only 4500 bytes for each motion video frame, or about 160:1 compression compared to a 24 bpp 512 × 480 pixel original. How can we get there?

The solution to this problem is the biggest breakthrough of DVI Technology. It consists of four parts:

1. Recognize that the frames in a motion video sequence are not really completely independent of each other. Unless the camera abruptly

switches from one scene to another, most of the content in one frame is only a small change from the previous frame. If our compression scheme can exploit that fact, we will achieve much more compression than can be done for individual still images, especially when not too much of the scene is moving, or is moving slowly. This is called *frame-to-frame* compression.

2. The second part is more of a compromise: Acknowledge that we just can't do justice to a 512 × 480 pixel image when presenting motion video, and therefore will concentrate on only half as many pixels in each direction—256 × 240 pixels. This is effectively a 4:1 reduction in information content. We will also use the 9 bpp display format, which yields another factor of 2.7.

3. Provide a special processing chip set that is capable of performing the decompression processes fast enough to reconstruct images at 30 per second or faster. (Faster, because we often want to do other things in addition to decompression, such as scaling the video to a different size.) For the greatest possible flexibility, and to allow algorithms to be improved with experience, we'll make the chip set fully software programmable.

4. Perform the compression on a large parallel computer, running several seconds to do each frame. This allows extremely sophisticated algorithms to be used to find the optimum way to encode each frame with the least amount of data, while keeping it in a format that enables the chip set to decompress in real time. Because of the cost of such a facility, we expect that users will send their video to central facilities to have compression done. This approach is called the DVI *Production Level Video* (PLV) compression method; it will be discussed in more detail later.

The result of all this is DVI Technology, a system that has gained an enviable reputation for the motion video image quality it can reproduce. However, there is a surprise: The processing power in the chip set turns out to be enough to do quite respectable compression *in real time* using a desktop PC. This is called *Real Time Video* (RTV) compression, and it makes doing your own motion video compression just as simple as audio or image compression. RTV video quality is not as good as PLV quality, but it is fine for many applications. Since Intel has a continuing commitment to upgrade to faster and faster processing chips, we can expect that the performance of DVI Technology will improve year after year. RTV will get better, and PLV will be able to go to higher resolutions than 256 × 240. DVI Technology is an excellent bandwagon to be on.

There are a number of different DVI motion video compression algorithms, representing different options of RTV and PLV. Because the chip set is programmable, this diversity is handled by simple software changes, and the current chips can play all previous versions of the algorithms. Some of the algorithms, like RTV, provide choices to tailor the algorithm to suit your particular needs. You can specify the frame rate of compression, the resolution to use, and the amount of frame-to-frame compression to use.

VIDEO PRODUCTION

In Chapter 10, we explained that it is usually desirable to produce your sound tracks first on analog tape, and then digitize them into the computer as a separate step. The same recommendation applies to motion video. If you intend to eventually use PLV on some of your video, you must have tape master. If you need any postproduction work done, that works from video tape. In all but the simplest of applications, you'll want to use video tape for your video.

You shoot video using a video camera and a video cassette recorder, or with a camcorder. This equipment is available for home use, for professional use, or for broadcast use—the same as discussed for audio equipment, although video equipment is a lot more expensive than audio equipment. If you will be using only RTV, you can get good results from home camcorders, but if you intend to use PLV, you should seriously consider professional or broadcast-quality equipment.

You might think that shooting movie film would also be a choice; it is, but there are major problems that make us recommend against using film. The problem is that you still have to transfer your film to tape in order to be able to digitize and compress the video. Film-to-tape transfer requires very specialized equipment, it is expensive to do, and there can be performance problems. Since video camera equipment is less expensive and more convenient than good movie cameras, there really is no reason to use film.

VIDEO POSTPRODUCTION

In broadcast or professional video, it is normal to shoot each video element or scene separately and then put the sequence together in postproduction. A postproduction facility includes multiple VCRs, editing controllers, and effects processors. It makes possible a wide portfolio of effects and transitions that can be used to assemble the sequence. However, postproduction equipment is expensive and a small user probably cannot justify having it. The multimedia computer may begin to change that, because the capability to do all the video effects exists in multimedia hardware such as DVI Technology. However, multimedia software is still at an early stage, and there's not much available yet to do video postproduction. That will change over time, and multimedia authoring systems will be able to do video (and audio) postproduction. Meanwhile, you will probably want to plan your video sequences to minimize the need for postproduction, or when you can't avoid it, you will go to an outside postproduction house for it.

PLANNING FOR VIDEO

Just like everything else in multimedia, when you are shooting video, planning ahead really pays off. We will assume that you already know exactly what you want to do—what you are going to shoot, and how long you want the final sequence to be. You should make a storyboard and a script for the sequence. If there is more than one scene in the sequence, plan each scene this way, and also plan how you will put the scenes together.

The first step in planning is deciding *where* you are going to shoot the video: outdoors, indoors, or in a studio? Each of these choices brings different considerations to be faced. Studio shooting is preferred, assuming you have access to a studio for free. If you have to pay for studio time, it can be expensive—often hundreds of dollars per hour, but for that you will probably get better equipment than you may own, and expert help. But paying by the hour for facilities makes planning even more important, because a well-planned shoot will take less time to complete.

If you can't use a studio, indoor shooting is still better than outdoor shooting. That's not to say that outdoor production is bad, it's just that there are more things to worry about, and you will have less control over the environment. In most cases, the needs of your application will determine where you shoot, anyway.

Once you have decided what you are going to shoot and where you are going to shoot it, you can begin planning the kind of shots you want. In doing this, bear in mind the limitations of the medium you are going to be using in the final product. As already described, digital motion video is limited in resolution, and it will work best if there is not too much detail in the picture. This does not mean you can't have detail, but it does mean that if you have a lot of detail to reproduce, the pictures may not look as good or you may not be able to get enough compression to meet your data rate objectives.

In planning your shots, you should use closeup shots as much as possible, concentrating on the things in the scene that are most important. To the extent that you have control, exclude unnecessary detail that does not contribute to your message. For example, if you are shooting a single person speaking, use a head and shoulders closeup if possible. Don't use wider shots unless there is a definite need for them. Also, try for a background that is either very plain, or is partially out of focus so that its detail is suppressed.

Camera movements—panning, tilting, or zooming—can liven up your scenes, but they should always have a purpose. The movement should make sense to the viewer; don't move the camera just for the sake of moving it, and then don't move the camera too rapidly. If you need to use these effects, do them as slowly and smoothly as possible and try them out ahead of time to make sure they will look all right when digitized and compressed.

As we discussed for images, good lighting is always important when shooting video. Well-lighted colors will look better on video than dark ones. But color is just like detail in the picture—don't use it unnecessarily. Bright colors should be used to highlight your main subject, but backgrounds should be more subdued. This is an artistic suggestion as much as it is a technical one.

Once you have an idea of the type of shots you will do, there remain a myriad of details to consider. The following list asks the kinds of questions you should consider in completing your video shooting plan.

- Who will be on camera? If you need other people or professionals, schedule them to coordinate with your shooting plan.
- Will you need any special camera or recording equipment?
- Will you need any props? If so, where will you get them, how will they get to the shooting site, who will set them up, and how much time should you allow for that?
- Will special lighting be required? If so, where does the lighting equipment come from, who will set it up, and how much time to allow for that?
- Who will be operating the equipment? If you need help, you must schedule that with the parties involved.

You can see that a video shoot quickly gets very complicated. It also gets expensive. Once you have been through this a few times, you will be better able to decide at the outset when it is worth using video in your applica-

THE SHOOT

After you have completed the planning and answered all of the questions, you can schedule the actual shoot. When the day arrives, you will begin to find out how good your planning was. Everyone assembles at the site, all the equipment is there, and everything gets set up. Now comes the moment of truth—the first take.

The same approach described for audio applies to multiple takes: Save all your takes and mark each of them at the beginning. In professional video production, a *clapboard* is used to mark the start of each take. A clapboard is a slate on which the take number and other information is written. When the recorder is started, the clapboard is held briefly in front of the camera and a hinged clapper on the top of the slate is snapped down. This makes an audio and a video mark that can be used later for synchronization. You don't have to use an actual clapboard, but the idea of holding up a slate to visually mark each take is a good one. And while you're at it, you may as well make some kind of sound, too. After the clapboard marks the take, the action in the scene commences.

If your sequence can be completed in a single continuous take without having to stop the recorder and restart it, you can accomplish the shoot without any kind of editing or postproduction. However, if the plan calls for repositioning the camera or changing scenes, you must stop the recorder between scenes and shoot the scenes separately. Professionally, the scenes would be shot individually, without worrying about putting them together during production—that would be done in postproduction. However, because we are trying to avoid postproduction with its cost and complexity, let's look at some alternative approaches.

Most video recorders have some kind of on-the-fly editing capability; even the consumer camcorders can do it. The techniques vary, but in general you can stop recording and later restart without any gap in the finished recording. The lowest-priced recorders or camcorders may not do this kind of editing very well—there may be jumps or flashes at the edit points—but the professional recorders do it so there is no interference at all. However, the on-the-fly editing approach requires that you stop the first recording at an exact point so the tape will be positioned there when you resume recording the next part of the sequence. Some recorders allow the tape to be backed up after the first recording to establish a new start point, and with that kind of equipment you can overrun the first part and back up to where you will start the second part.

On-the-fly editing with a recorder also means that you will have to perform the scene change procedure for each take. The fact that there are scene changes creates more chances for errors, so you may need to do more takes to get a good one. And this gets tedious quickly. If your plan requires more than one or two scene changes, figure on using postproduction.

USING RTV COMPRESSION

Once you have produced your video on tape, you can digitize and compress it on your desktop system using the RTV compression algorithm. For simple video, you can also run RTV directly from your camera, but, as we have already explained, producing first on tape is the preferred method for most applications. To use RTV, you must have the ActionMedia II card with the capture adaptor, and you can use the MEDIAscript OS/2 AUI software. The video you connect to the input of the ActionMedia II board will be digitized, compressed, and stored on your hard disk.

Start up the MEDIAscript OS/2 Server and AUI modules. Then select **Video capture** from the **Tools** menu of the **Projects** window. The dialog shown in Figure 12.1 will appear.

The dialog requires that you enter a filename for the video capture before anything becomes active. Enter a filename without extension (**.avs** will be automatically added to the name) and the **Ready** button will activate. However, before you click it, there are some other options you should consider. The first is a choice of video compression parameters. The default is **Normal RTV2**, which performs 30 frames/second RTV compression with a reference frame inserted every 64th frame; for most purposes, this is the best choice. However, if you need complete random access to any frame of the file, select **No frame/frame**, which makes every frame of the file a reference frame. This also makes the file size almost three times larger. A third choice, **Max compression**, increases the degree of compression at some tradeoff in picture quality; use this only if you need to save disk space with your video file.

The second set of options available for RTV compression deal with the resolution. The default is **Medium**, which is 128 × 240 resolution. The other choices are **Highest** (256 × 240) and **Lowest** (128 × 120). The file size and data rate change in proportion to the number of pixels specified here. Note that using the **Highest** position will definitely not work if you are creating files for eventual use on CD-ROM because the data rate will

Producing Your Own Motion Video 201

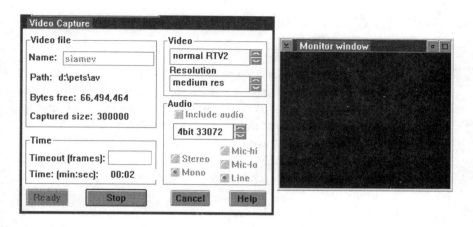

Figure 12.1 MEDIAscript OS/2 Video capture dialog.

be too high, and it requires an extremely fast hard disk in your system to capture without pauses.

You also can choose whether you wish to capture audio along with the video, and, if you do, you can select from the same audio algorithm choices that were available for audio-only capture. Finally, if you want to capture a fixed number of frames, specify a timeout value. If no timeout is given, capture will continue until you stop it, or until you run out of disk space.

Now click the **Ready** button. A monitor window will open, showing the video coming into the board, and the **Start** button will activate. If you are using tape for the input, start the tape, and at the desired start point for the video, click the **Start** button or hit the **Enter** key. At the end of the video, click the **Stop** button or hit **Enter**. That's all there is to it. To preview your compressed video, select the **Video player** tool from the **Tools** menu and play the video. If anything is not right, repeat the process, writing over the old file if you wish (you will get a warning about this, however).

While capture is running, notice that the captured file size grows (it is an estimate), and the captured time is displayed. However, the display of free space on the hard disk is not updated during capture—it remains at the value taken before capture started. Thus, you should compare the free space number and your captured file size to see if you are in danger of running out of disk space.

USING PLV COMPRESSION

You can obtain improved video quality by using the Intel PLV (Production Level Video) Compression Service. However, this has a significant cost, and you have to send your video to a compression facility to have the work done, which takes time. But if you are doing an application for sale or broad distribution, you should definitely consider using PLV. You can wait until the application is almost done before incurring the cost of PLV because you can work with RTV of the same video for all your development and testing; that way, you do not do any PLV until you are sure you have the proper video.

PLV requires that you provide a professional 1" Type C video tape for the compression. Most likely your original tape is not in that format, but you can have a 1" copy made of it at any video postproduction house. In the course of doing that, they should also add an SMPTE time code track and standard headers and trailers as specified by Intel. You will have to use the postproduction house's time code reader to identify the start and end points of your segments in terms of time code values. This will give you all the information needed to fill out an order for PLV. You can get the forms and instructions for making your master tape and filling out the form from Intel Compression Services (see Appendix B).

The PLV compression will take several weeks and the result will come back to you on digital computer tape. Currently, Intel supports only the Archive Viper tape format, although other formats are being explored. You will have to have an appropriate tape drive in your machine to read the PLV tapes that come back. PLV compression currently costs approximately $250 per finished minute of compressed video.

Digital Postproduction

There are some tools for cut-and-paste editing of RTV or PLV files, and more will be appearing soon. Intel has the **vaved** program, which runs under DOS. **Vaved** is a batch type of program, which means that you give it a file of control information, and then it goes off in non-real time and processes the video (or audio) according to the control file. You can use this tool to build one AVSS file from several source files or to change the audio that goes with the video, etc. It's not a very friendly tool, but it does the job.

MEDIAscript OS/2 has a built-in capability to perform DVI audio and video stream editing. This can be used to present combinations of streams from different files in real time during an application, or to do the same thing but save the result to disk as a new AVSS file. To use this, build an *edit decision list* which specifies what streams from what files you want to present when and for how long. Then you can choose to either play that list or capture it to disk. An easy-to-use interface for stream editing is included in the **Custom Tools** menu of the MEDIAscript AUI. By using the language-level interface of the MEDIAscript Professional Edition, similar capabilities can be made part of any application.

CHAPTER SUMMARY

DVI Technology provides capability for 30 frames/second motion video capture and playback on a desktop PC. This is accomplished by means of advanced video compression technology.

Video for multimedia use is normally produced on video tape first, and digitized and compressed as a separate step.

For the lowest cost, try to plan so you will not need to use video postproduction.

You can compress video on your machine with RTV, or for higher quality, you can send it out for PLV compression.

13

Animation

animate: vt. to give motion to; put into action.
Webster's New World Dictionary, 1988

As explained in the previous chapter, a sequence of images presented rapidly gives the illusion of smooth motion. This is the basic principle of motion pictures, television, and digital motion video. In all of those cases, the sequence of images is somehow captured from a natural scene. Animation is the same process—rapid display of images—but the images are not necessarily natural; they may be painted, processed, or completely computer generated. This technique is an important feature of multimedia because of its flexibility to create unusual and dynamic effects, and because it often can produce the illusion of motion video while using far less data than the real thing.

This chapter discusses some of the techniques of animation and how they can be included in your multimedia applications.

FRAME ANIMATION

The simplest animation technique is to prepare a series of images, usually in the form of an array of frames, although you can also animate with individual images. Figure 13.1 is an example of an array image.

The frames represent successive snapshots of the motion; usually they show one complete cycle of motion, such as a complete golf swing, or one complete cycle of a horse's gait. If the frames are successively displayed at the same location, the object appears to be in motion. When the array of frames is displayed repeatedly (returning to the first frame after

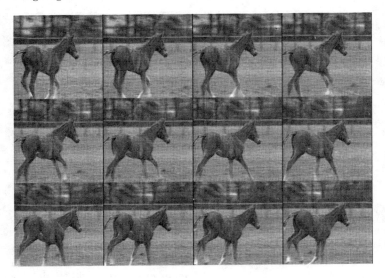

Figure 13.1 An image array of frames.

displaying the last frame) the effect is that the motion becomes continuous—i.e., the horse runs endlessly.

The frames can be real images (for example, taken out of a motion video clip); they can be processed real images; or they can be artificial images created by an artist or drawn by the computer. All combinations of the foregoing are also possible. You can also have the computer perform manipulation of the frames as they are displayed. Many unusual effects can be obtained.

The major requirement for obtaining realistic motion is that the frames must be displayed fast enough—usually at least 10 or 15 frames per second. Slower than that, and the effect is stop action, not smooth motion. This requirement for speed is often difficult to meet; it usually means that all the frames must be in memory before the effect is started. The speed of displaying frames from memory limits the size of the frame that can be animated, and the use of memory limits the number of frames that can be in the animation sequence.

MEDIAscript OS/2 has a built-in frame animation capability, which was described in Chapter 6, Figures 6.12 and 6.13. With it you can run one or more animations at the same time in the PM plane and in the DVI plane. This can be used for simple loop animation as already described, or it can be used to produce pans or rolls by using different combinations of the parameters.

For example, if you create an image that is a panoramic scene (a wide image, larger than you want to display at one time), you can cause the computer to show a moving display as if you were panning a camera across the panoramic image. This is done by telling MEDIAscript that the horizontal pitch between frames is much less than the width of the frame you will display. For example, if we have a panoramic image that is 512×200 pixels, and we want to display it in a window that is 240×200 pixels, we can set up a frame animation where the size of a frame is 240×200, but the horizontal pitch between frames is only, say, 2 pixels. If we animate that at 30 frames per second, it will take $(512 - 240)/2 = 136$ frames to pan across the whole source image, or about 4.5 seconds. Of course, you must stop the animation when it reaches the edge of the source image.

Figure 13.2 shows a MEDIAscript OS/2 script that displays a moving panorama as described above. A Window object creates an invisible window to hold the panoramic image. Then the image is loaded into that window with an Image object. A second Window object creates the visible window that will display the panorama, and finally an Animation object creates the panorama effect, copying from the invisible window to the visible window. The effect runs continuously, until the user does something—an Input object waits for that. When the user hits a key or clicks the mouse, the visible window is destroyed, and the script is ended.

Another use of the horizontal animation effect is to produce a ticker-tape display across the screen.

You can produce a vertical roll effect, similar to the rolling text credits often seen at the end of a TV show, by having a tall source image with all the text credits in it, and then doing an animation that uses a small vertical pitch compared to the height of the display frame. The text credits will roll up in the display window.

The text credit effect brings up the need for transparency in animation operations. Often, you would like the text to roll across an image or video. This can be done by placing the text in the PM plane and the image or

Figure 13.2 A MEDIAscript OS/2 script that shows a moving panorama in a window.

video in the DVI plane. The PM plane is made black, the transparent color; the text must be in another color. Then the DVI image shows through the PM plane everywhere except the text.

Doing the roll in the PM plane highlights another problem—PM operations get slow. With a window that occupies about one-third of a VGA screen, the copying of the entire window to do the animation causes a noticeable slowdown, and the rolling gets jerky. In principle, this can be improved by copying only a small area around each line of text. However, the Animation object by itself cannot do that—some tricky programming is required. It is an example of a task for which a skilled programmer could write a template script, which could then be modified by anyone for a specific application.

These examples show that there is a lot of flexibility in the frame animation technique, but that it is limited by the need to have all the frames prepared ahead of time and available in memory. It would be nice to have a way to create or modify frames while the animation is taking place.

CEL ANIMATION

In frame animation, all the frames exist in memory before the animation is started, but you can also build the frames during the animation. One technique for creating frames as the animation proceeds is called *cel animation*, named for the technique often used to create cartoon animation in the movies. In cel animation in the movies, a background drawing is used, and one or more drawings of the moving character or transparent backing are positioned in front of the background as each frame is photographed. The transparent drawings are called *celluloids* or *cels*—hence, the name.

The same thing can be done in the computer world. An image serves as the backgound and it is copied to each frame as the first step of frame preparation. Then, an image of an animated character is copied on top of the background. The character image should be in a *transparent* rectangle, which is accomplished by telling the copy process to ignore pixels of the color that surround the character in its rectangle; this will make the character appear to stand in front of the background image. You can have multiple characters or *cast members*, as many as needed can be copied to different locations in each image. When all the items are copied to the frame, it is displayed, and preparation of the next frame begins.

To make a character move on the screen, it is copied to a different location in the frame for successive frames. If the character itself has to change, you define additional cast members showing the character in all of its configurations, and use the cast members in sequence.

When you have a sequence where an animated figure does something that has a cycle, such as walking, each frame of the cycle is made a separate cast member. The figure is animated to walk across the screen by cycling through the array of walking cast members while steadily moving the location of the figure across the screen. When the distance moved per frame is consistent with the amount of walking in one step of the cycle, the effect is very realistic. By arranging the precedence of other cast members in the display, the figure can walk in front of or behind other objects on the screen.

Cel animation as described above is implemented in the Macromind *Director* for the Macintosh computer. A very flexible approach, called the *score*, is provided for describing how each frame is built up using the cast members. Director also includes a scripting language which allows complete interactive applications to be built using the animation technique for all display operations, and adding audio and other capabilities. Director animations are called *movies*.

The Windows Multimedia Extensions contain a Player module that can play Macromind Director movies that have been converted from Macintosh to PC format. There are some limitations to this, caused by differences between the Macintosh and the PC, but it definitely adds a unique capability to Windows. No plans have been announced to make this support DVI Technology under Windows. Macromind has also introduced a product called *Action!* that provides some of the authoring capabilities under Windows.

Cel animation is very CPU intensive, especially when several cast members are moving about on the screen, because the CPU has to calculate the repositioning of the cast members for each new frame and also deal with the cases where they overlap. This is a task that would benefit from some dedicated hardware to speed it up. As chip technology advances and we can put more and more on CPU chips, this will be an area to consider.

ANIMATION WITH GRAPHICS

Another technique for animation is to draw an object repeatedly while changing its coordinates or other properties to make it move. A simple case of this is to draw a string of rectangles to make an animated border.

210 *Designing Interactive Multimedia*

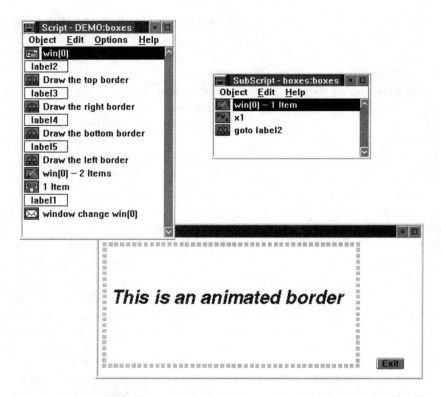

Figure 13.3 A MEDIAscript OS/2 script for an animated border. The second window shows the contents of one of the four loops in the main script. The border is shown in the third window.

Figure 13.3 is a MEDIAscript OS/2 script that draws the dotted border shown in the figure simply by drawing rectangles. The result is that the border "crawls" around the rectangle when it appears. There are four loops used to draw this border, one for each side of the rectangle. The actual drawing script—the contents of one loop—is shown in the subscript window.

The drawing approach to animation can be used many other ways. For example, an object can be made to grow simply by drawing it larger and larger. As long as each new object completely covers the preceding one, this works. However, making an object shrink by drawing it smaller and smaller does not work, because you have to somehow erase the parts of the previous object which will show around the edges of the new smaller one. If you have a solid background color around the object, you can make the object appear to shrink by repeatedly drawing around the edges of the object using the background color.

The use of graphics for animation requires the building of loops in your scripts. In MEDIAscript OS/2 1.0 this is done by making **goto** loops using the Condition object. You have to set up variables to keep track of the values, which change during the loop. Network Technology Corporation is developing other looping approaches for future releases of MEDIAscript.

ANIMATED TRANSITIONS

Most transition effects between images are actually animated copies. For example, a left-to-right horizontal wipe is obtained by repeatedly copying a narrow vertical strip of the new image to the screen. At first the strip is at the left edge of the image, but for each copy, the strip is moved to the right by an amount equal to its width. Both the source and destination strips are moved this way: As the strip moves rapidly across the image, copying all the way, we see a horizontal wipe. This is an animation similar to the animated rectangles of the previous section, except in this case the process is to copy rather than to draw.

A very useful technique is to do an animated effect in the PM plane using the transparent color (black) to reveal the DVI plane. For example, if we use something similar to the horizontal wipe effect in the previous paragraph to draw black strips across the PM plane, the result is that the DVI plane appears to wipe onto the screen. A very nice iris effect is obtained by drawing black circles to reveal the DVI plane. You begin with a small circle in the center of the window, and make it larger and larger until the whole window is showing the DVI plane. These effects can even be done while motion video is playing in the DVI plane.

CHAPTER SUMMARY

Animation is an artificial way to create the effect of motion in an image. There are three basic types: frame animation, cel animation, and graphic animation. All can be done with the computer, and all use less data than required to produce the same effect with motion video.

Frame animation is used when you have an action that can be defined by a small number of frames prepared ahead of time in one or more images and then displayed by the animation routine. Cel animation is used when the frames have to be built dynamically during the display process. Graphic animation is useful when an animated drawn object can be drawn repeatedly to obtain the desired motion.

14

Completing an Application

complete: vt. to make whole, full, or perfect.
Webster's New World Dictionary, 1988

The preceding chapters have taught you how to plan an application and how to collect and design all the pieces (assets) for the application. Now we must put all of those pieces together to complete the project. This chapter overviews that process, and then discusses the completion of several of the sample projects that were mentioned briefly in earlier chapters:

- the Pets information application (Chapter 5)
- the Camcorder selling application (Chapters 3 and 8)
- the Soldering training application (Chapter 8)

Each of these is a major application, sometimes containing more than you will have time to do by yourself. However, in each case, we will design a simple structure that handles all the basic functions of the application—menus, presentations, interactions; this part you can do by yourself. The full application is then built by filling out the data structures for the content material and collecting all the material, which you may need help with.

Before we go into the specifics of the three applications, let's review the steps of the planning process for a major application. If you are doing something simple, such as a short presentation or a demonstration, you probably won't need to use all these steps, but if you are planning an application which grows into a large project, you should consider every step in the list below.

THE PLANNING PROCESS

You must complete the planning process before you can really go ahead with any actual work on the application. This will not only give you the architecture of the whole project, it will let you see how much work it is going to take so that you can determine what help you will need and how long it will take. We've touched on many of the steps in the planning process in earlier chapters, but let's review them all here:

- Define who the users will be. This could be part of the treatment, but it is so important that it warrants being a separate document. It should also include your expectations about what the user's relevant background is (or is not).
- Prepare a treatment for the application. This is a narrative description of the application in a few pages. It should give the purpose of the application and describe the application content and key features.
- List the data to be presented. This is the first pass at the content material of the application, which you must have before you can do flowcharting and further planning. However, this will be an iterative process; the data list will be updated, reorganized, and expanded as the subsequent planning is done.
- Make a top-level flowchart for the whole application. Once you have an idea of the information to be included in the application, start thinking about how it will be presented. How will the user go about accessing the information? How will you structure elements so the user knows what to do? This step should look at the application from the viewpoint of a user, rather than a programmer or author. The way the architecture looks to the user may turn out to be quite different from the architecture used to author the application.
- Design the style of the application. Decide on the major factors that affect how the application will look to the user. Is it a full-screen or a windowed application? Does it have a computer look or a TV look? What kinds of transitions are used between elements?
- Design the user interface. Decide how the user will navigate through the application and how she will make selections along the way. Does the application use the mouse, keyboard, touch, or combinations? Is it menu-driven? What type of controls must be provided?

- Develop the authoring approach. Using the flowchart and the data list, you should now be able to think about how to divide the project into authorable parts. The important thing here is to look for commonality of function that will allow engine scripts to be used to simplify the amount of programming. This should lead you to a more specific design of the content data structure and the layout of individual scripts. List the scripts required with a narrative description of what each one has to do.

- Finalize the data list. This can be done once the authoring approach is decided. Then plan the exact structure of control and data files you will need to let the scripts access all the data. This will also be a specification for whoever is going to acquire all the content material and set it up for use.

- Design the major screens. With the style, the user interface, and the content planned, now start planning in detail for the major screens: the menus and the access screens. Sketch the screens, with notes for the scripting that will create them. A storyboard approach is good for this, although you may want to show more detail about the screen than you would use in a higher-level storyboard.

- Design the presentation sequences. Each presentation in the application should have a storyboard. When engine scripts will be used for the presentations, this design should indicate just what kind of flexibility is provided by the engine, such as choice of transitions or control of timing. The user interface of each presentation should also be defined, and should be consistent with the overall user interface design already developed.

- Estimate personnel and time requirements. With the complete plan laid out—number of scripts to create, amount of content material to collect and prepare—you should be able to estimate time and personnel requirements. Estimating is based on experience. You won't do it very well until you have done a number of projects and have developed a feel for how long processes take. The best estimating technique is to break the project down into as many pieces as possible and then estimate each one and add them all up. At this point, decide whether you can do the project by yourself, or whether the volume of work requires other help. This is a milestone in the project—either go ahead yourself or get the help you need before proceeding.

With this framework in mind, let's look at the Pets application.

CREATING THE PETS APPLICATION

This project, introduced in Chapter 5, is an information delivery application that contains a broad database of information for pet owners. It is probably not something that an individual author would tackle by herself, unless her hobby happened to be photographing birds, fish, and other animals regarded as pets. However, we use it here as an example because the content is easy to understand, and most people will automatically know what such an application ought to do. We'll begin by following the planning steps that we just described.

Who Will Use the Application?

The users of the Pets application are members of the general public. We assume no knowledge of computers and no initial knowledge of the subject of the application. This application could be used on kiosks located in pet stores and animal hospital waiting rooms.

A Treatment for the Pets Application

The Pets application provides information to current or potential pet owners about the different kinds of pets, their characteristics, how to care for them, and how to train them. The information is provided in a combination of media: still images, audio, video, and text.

The opening screen is a menu of major pet classes, including:

- Birds
- Cats
- Dogs
- Fish
- Horses
- Rodents

When the user makes a selection from the main menu, a second screen is built dynamically (see below), with the name of one species of the major class at the top, for example: Parakeet from the Bird class. This is the Species screen. Below that are five menu selections offering information about that species:

- **Life Cycle**—an audio with still images presentation that talks about the life cycle of the species from birth to old age.

- **In Action**—a motion video showing the major characteristics of the species.
- **Grooming**—an audio plus still images presentation about handling and grooming of the species.
- **Feeding**—a text plus images presentation about the eating habits of the species, and how to feed them.
- **Training**—an audio plus still images presentation about how you can train the species.

Each presentation has a default mode that runs by itself, and it has a control panel from which the user can pause, advance, or quit the presentation. The Species screen reappears at the end of a presentation.

The Species screen contains a window that shows photos or video, and an area where a block of text can be presented. It also contains a "Full-screen" button so that the user can choose to see the presentation in full-screen mode. Next to the species name in the Species screen is a button that opens a list from which the user can select different species. When a species is selected, the entire screen is revised for that species. If the user clicks on the image window while in the Species screen, a different image of the species will appear. The number of images available this way ranges from 1 to 10.

When the user makes a selection from the main menu, only then (other times it appears all at once) is the Species screen built. The name of the species appears first, and then an image of the species appears in the video window. The audio explains the choices available on the Species screen as the other parts of the screen appear.

Data List for Pets

For each of the six classes of pets mentioned in the treatment, there are various numbers of species. A first pass of that hierarchy is shown in Table 14.1.

For each of the 34 species shown in Table 14.1 there is a package of data files to support the various presentations. Table 14.2 shows one package. To support the dynamic introduction of the Species screen, there also is an audio file for each of the classes of pets.

You can see that this expands to a lot of data, since there are 34 species, 3 audios, 1 video, 1 text file, and up to 100 images for each species. The collection and preparation of this data will be a large job.

Bird	Cat	Dog
Cockatiel	Burmese	Basset Hound
Finch	Domestic Shorthair	Chow
Mynah	Domestic Longhair	Cocker Spaniel
Parakeet	Manx	Dachshund
Parrot	Persian	Doberman Pinscher
	Rex	German Shepherd
	Siamese	Labrador
	Himalayan	Rottweiler
		Schnauzer
		Sheltie
Horse	**Fish**	**Rodent**
Appaloosa	Goldfish	Mouse
Arabian	Piranha	Rat
Morgan	Siamese Fighting Fish	Gerbil
Thoroughbred		Hamster

Table 14.1 Species list for Pets.

Flowchart for Pets

The structure of this application is quite simple; there are two main screens with five different presentations indicated in the flowchart of Figure 14.1.

Any selection from the main menu except Exit will go to the Species screen. Selections from the Species screen go to one of five presentations of two types, a species select routine, or back to the main menu.

Asset	Number	Use
images	1 - 10	Main Species screen
audio files	3	Life Cycle, Grooming, Training
images	< 26 per presentation	Life Cycle, Grooming, Training, Feeding
text	1	Feeding
video files	1	In Action

Table 14.2 Asset package for one species.

Completing an Application 219

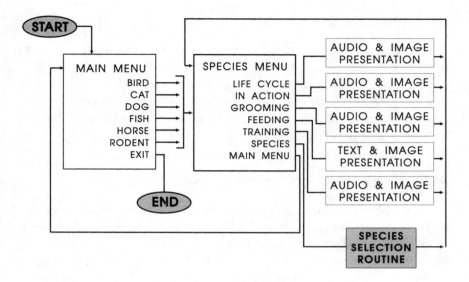

Figure 14.1 Top-level flowchart for the Learn About Your Pet application.

Style Design of the Pets Application

We will make the style of the Pets application fairly simple, in keeping with the overall simplicity of the application itself; this will avoid drawing any attention away from the content. Since the user is the general public, we will go for a television look, and use a full-screen metaphor. Buttons for user selections will be simple rectangles of color with text in them. Presentations will initially appear in windows, but we'll offer the user the choice of going full-screen with them, too.

The menu screens could have been produced entirely in the DVI plane by creating DVI images that held all the buttons and text. However, on the Species screen, we have to change the text for the species name whenever the user chooses another species. In the DVI OS/2 environment, there is no way to do that other than having DVI images of text for all the species (34 for this example, even more if the application is expanded). It is much better to be able to draw the text on the fly, which can be done only in the PM plane; then we do not have to worry about how many species there are.

The problem is that PM text looks different than DVI text, and if we use PM text for only one item on the Species screen, it is going to look out of place. To get around that, we will design the application to use the PM plane for *all* the text on the screens. The DVI plane will hold only the images of pets and the video.

User Interface Design for Pets

The treatment tells us that this should be a menu-driven application, with two levels of menus: Main and Species. Since the user is the general public, a touch interface is preferred; however, we will write the application so that a mouse could also be used. Navigation controls will be via a VCR type of control panel, which the public is generally familiar with; this will be used in all the presentation screens.

Authoring Approach for the Pets Application

From studying the flowchart in Figure 14.1 you can see that the Species menu is the heart of the application. It lends itself to the engine-driven script approach because the same screen is used over and over with different data behind it. The main menu, however, can be a dedicated script since there is only one version of it. We will make that the initial script of the application.

The Species script must know the list of species for the class that has been selected; we'll take care of that by having a data file for each class containing its species list—that's six small files. The user's selection in the main menu will place the name of the appropriate species list file into the first MEDIAscript string variable, **str(0)**.

In order for all scripts to easily find the asset files for the currently selected species, we will use an approach in which all asset filenames begin with a five-letter code that indicates the species. Since the five-letter code may have to be different from the actual name of the species, we will put two columns of data in the six species list files mentioned above. The first column is the actual name of the species that will appear on the screen, and the second column will be the species' five-letter code. Listing 14.1 shows how this will look for the list file for cats: **cats.lst**.

Notice that **cats.lst** uses a fixed format approach, where the second column begins at character position 24 in the file. This makes it easier for the script to parse the file to extract either of the two columns. Since these files are small anyway, this is not any great waste of data.

The presentations called from the Species screen also lend themselves to the use of engine scripts. There are two types of presentations: those that use audio with images, and those that use text with images. We can have one script for each, controlled by a control file that is named with the species' five-letter code. When the user chooses a species, the selection index of the species (which is just the line number in the species list file) will be placed in a project variable called *select*. All the engine scripts will

```
Burmese cat                     burme
Domestic shorthair cat          short
Himalayan cat                   himal
Manx cat                        manxc
Persian cat                     persi
Rex cat                         rexca
Siamese cat                     siame
```

Listing 14.1 Control file cats.1st.

use *select* to index the species list to get the first five letters for all data or asset filenames.

The video presentation for the In Action selection can be run directly from the Species engine script—it is too simple to bother with its own script.

The list of data files shown in Table 14.2 can now be expanded to show the five-letter code approach, and we will also add the control files needed to control the presentations. This is shown in Table 14.3.

The remaining part of the authoring approach is the format for the control files; there are two types, one for audio-plus-image presentations and another for text-plus-image presentations. For the presentations that use audio, the control file simply lists the names of the images in the order that they will be shown, followed on the same line by the frame number in the audio where they will be shown.

Notice that while the five-letter code approach is very elegant, it requires you to have a complete set of assets for every species. If you want to use the same presentation for a number of species or maybe an entire class, you are forced to make copies of all the assets with different names for each species. For example, if you wanted to use the same grooming presentation for every species of cat, you must have copies of the control and audio files for every species. (The images do not have to be copied because they are named in the control file.) Making copies of the control file is not a big deal because they are small, but copying the audio file is a serious waste of storage. We can eliminate that problem by having the first line of the control file be the name of the audio file to use. Listing 14.2 shows such a control file for grooming a cat.

The engine script for these presentations loads the first image, starts the audio, shows the first image, loads the next image but does not show it, and then waits for the frame number to show the next image. As soon

Presentation	Filename
Images used in Species screen	?????N.a9
Video file for In Action	?????V.avs
Control file for Life Cycle	?????1.ctl
Audio file for Life Cycle	?????A1.avs
Images for Life Cycle	?????1C.a9
Control file for Grooming	?????2.ctl
Audio file for Grooming	?????A2.avs
Images for Grooming	?????2C.a9
Control file for Feeding	?????3.ctl
Images for Feeding	?????3C.a9
Control file for Training	?????4.ctl
Audio file for Training	?????A4.avs
Images for Training	?????4C.a9

Table 14.3 Asset files for Pets (for each species). ????? is a five-letter species name, i.e. siame, N is a number from 0 to 9, and C is a character from A to Z.

as that image is shown, it gets the next one, etc. It stops when the audio ends. During the waiting state, the user control panel is also hooked up.

The second type of control file is used for the text-plus-images presentation. This file has to hold the image names, how long to show each image, and the text to display along with each image. The text should also provide the option to have more than one text block for the same image. There are many ways to set this up; here we will use a unique mark to indicate a line in the control file that contains a filename—lines starting with any other character are part of a text block. For example, the character '%' indicates the start of a filename line; the filename follows this mark. Then at position 16 in the line there will be a number indicating the frame count for that image. The next line, if there is one, is the start of a text block. The end of a text block is marked by a line that contains

```
groomcat.avs
siame2a            97
siame2b           392
siame2c           769
```

Listing 14.2 siame2.ctl.

```
%siame3a 150
Cats in the wild are hunters; stalking and killing birds,
rodents, and other small animals. At home, your pet cat
will eat a variety of pre-packaged cat foods and also
certain human foods such as fish, poultry, and meat.
!
%siame3b 150
Your cat should be fed three or four times a day. Although
some cats are happy with a bowl of food available all
the time, other cats will eat too much in this situation.
It is better to present fresh food to them on a regular
schedule.
!
%siame3c 150
It is not a good idea to feed your cat from your own
table. For one reason, it is poor discipline, and the
cat becomes too used to eating human food instead of
its own food. Cats do enjoy an occasional treat of fresh
fish, or liver. Serve it raw, cut up into small pieces.
This will sometimes satisfy some of their hunting urges.
!
```

Listing 14.3 Control file for a text/image presentation.

nothing but an exclamation point. Multiple text blocks per image are simply placed together before we come to the next line beginning with '%'. The engine script will read this format and perform accordingly. Listing 14.3 shows part of a control script for the Feeding presentation of a Siamese cat.

Now we have described how everything works but we haven't explained how the Species name is set. When you come from the main menu, the species script shows just the first species in the list. If the user clicks the More Species button, the entire species list is displayed. A selection from that list causes the displayed species to change, and the value in the variable *select* will be updated. Thus, when the user later makes a selection of any of the presentations, the *select* variable will let the engine scripts find the five-letter code to make names for the proper assets and data.

Design of the Screens for Pets

Figure 14.2 shows a design for the main menu screen. It is a full-screen menu, with a color background and no border—this style will be used for

224   *Designing Interactive Multimedia*

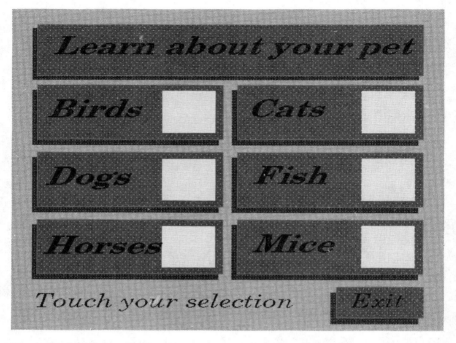

Figure 14.2 Screen design for the main menu for the Learn About Your Pet application.

all the screens of the application. The title of the application, *Learn About Your Pet*, is at the top of the screen. It is highlighted by a different background color. The screen has six buttons for the six classes of pets; the buttons have both pictures and names of each pet. All the buttons use color boxes in the same color as the title. The screen also has an Exit button and a prompt telling the user to make a selection. It is designed for either touch or mouse operation.

Figure 14.3 shows the design of the species menu screen of the Pets application. It uses the same color style as the main menu for background and buttons. On this screen, the name of the currently selected species is at the top, with a selection button for More species to the right of it. Down the left side, five buttons provide for the choices of the different presentations. On the right, there is a quarter-screen window for images or video, and a text block area below that. The image/video window has a "Full-screen" button. At the bottom right of the screen is a button to press to go back to the main menu. Because this screen will often remain up while a selected presentation plays in the images window, selection of a button must have highlighting so the user will know what is selected.

The design of the two menu screens gives a simple, but consistent user interface. It provides self-prompting so the user is able to find out what

Completing an Application 225

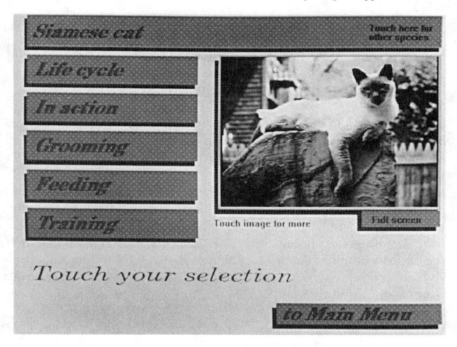

Figure 14.3 Screen design for the Species menu for the Pets application.

to do, and it provides navigation backward (to the main menu or Exit) as well as forward.

Design of Presentations for Pets

The next step in planning this application is to design the audio-plus-images presentations. These presentations show in the quarter-screen image window; or, if the user clicks the Full-screen button, they show full-screen. The full-screen window will show a "Restore" button in the lower right corner; when the user touches that button, the window returns to quarter-screen.

The presentations should enable the user to pause, resume, or quit them. This can be provided by putting a small control panel in the upper left-hand corner of the presentation window. The design of this panel is shown in Figure 14.4. The same control panel will also be used for controlling the video presentation.

A special consideration arises for the motion video presentation. When showing video in a quarter-screen window, we should use the DVI 512 × 480 resolution mode to make the video look the best. However, if the user clicks the maximize button to go to full-screen, we must switch the DVI

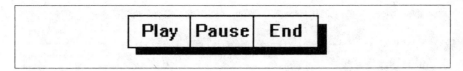

Figure 14.4 Control panel for presentations in the Pets application.

plane resolution to 256 × 240 because we cannot enlarge video to fill a 512 × 480 screen. The video enlargement is achieved by cutting the screen resolution in half. We could leave the screen resolution at 256 × 240 all the time, but then the video would look bad when reduced to quarter-screen.

The treatment specifies that the Feeding presentation use images with text instead of audio. A block below the image window will display the text. Therefore, the presentation must disable the Full-screen button on the images window so that the text block area of the screen will always be visible. For this presentation, we should add a Next button to the control panel so the user can move ahead more quickly than the timeout for the text and image display.

Notice that there are only four scripts required for this application:

- the main menu script,
- the Species menu script,
- the audio/images presentation engine, and
- the text/images presentation engine.

Everything else is controlled by the data files no matter how large the database becomes. Once you have written the scripts for the application, the database can be filled as you collect the material. Because the structuring of data is pretty simple, you can even send out the work to people who don't know much about multimedia. That way, you may be surprised at how large an application you can build!

Estimating for Development of the Pets Application

As you gain experience with multimedia, you will become better at estimating, especially if you follow a planning regimen. My estimate for this project (based on the participants having the required experience—there is no learning time) is as follows:

- preparing data for one species: one day—assuming that the images are available as photographs, the video is on tape, and scripts for the audio and text presentations are already written. Thus, it includes digitizing images and video, and capturing and digitizing the audio.

- writing and debugging the four scripts: two to four days.
- testing and modifying the overall application: two days.

As you can see, the data preparation task is going to dominate this project. Note that the estimate does not include the writing of presentation audio text and any shooting for the images; those tasks could easily double the time per species. Since there are 34 species in the plan, the data part of the project is going to take between 34 and 68 days, while the programming and testing is a maximum of six days! This is not unusual—unless the data already exists in nearly the right format, data acquisition and preparation is most of the work.

Creating the Main Script for Pets

Using MEDIAscript OS/2, building the scripts for this application is not too difficult. We'll start with the main script first.

Nearly every application begins with setting up windows; it is good practice to think through the use of windows at the outset. The *Pets* application requires the windows shown in Table 14.4.

To begin the main script, we have to create only Window 0. We can leave the creation of Windows 1 and 2 until the Species script since they will not be used until then. In handling windows, it is always good to build them in the invisible state first, and then show the finished window all at once. That way, the user does not see whatever operations go into building the window. Therefore, we'll create Window 0 as invisible, using a Window object.

The creation of a window with a lot in it may take a few seconds at runtime, possibly more than the user expects. In these cases, it helps if you put up something like "Please wait" while that is going on. Since the main window (Window 0) has an image to load and a lot of text to draw, we will use a "Please wait" routine. We can copy one of these into our script from the MEDIAscript Library window—it uses Window 2, which we'll have to destroy once the main window is shown. Once "Please wait" is displayed, we'll proceed to create the main menu as an invisible window.

The buttons for the main menu are PM drawings, so the next operation is to use a Draw object to draw the button rectangles and text for the title and the buttons. This completes the main menu, and it can now be displayed using a Message object to tell Window 0 to show itself. Another Message object destroys the "Please wait" prompt.

Now the system waits for the user to do something. This is done with an Input object, which is set up to respond to the user clicking any of the buttons on the screen. For any of the six pet class buttons, the Input object

Number	Use	Type
0	Main menu	PM full-screen, no borders or controls
1	Species menu	DVI, and PM, full-screen size
2	Image or video display	DVI, quarter-screen, maximizable
3	Temporary, for species list	PM only
4	Temporary, for presentation control panel	PM only

Table 14.4 Windows used by Pets

has a subscript that assigns string 0 to the name of the species list file for that class, and then exits to the species menu script. The only other button is the Exit button, which ends the application. However, before it ends, we destroy all three windows used by the application. The easiest way to do that is make the Exit button tell the script to jump (using **goto**) to the **end** label, following which two Message objects destroy the windows.

The actual main menu script is shown in Figure 14.5. This script shows a MEDIAscript optional feature which allows the author to write her own description for each object. That is in the form of a comment which appears in the script listing in the AUI. In order to see the actual contents

Figure 14.5 Script for the Main menu for the Pets application.

of an object, you have to double-click on its line in the script to open it. Then the object dialog appears showing all the object details and allowing editing.

Now let's go back over some of this script and look at it in a little more detail. Several more features have been added to the script in order to deal with the case where the application returns later to the main menu. First, we will keep the main menu window throughout the application; we'll simply hide it when we go to other screens. Therefore, when we return to the main script, we shouldn't create the main window all over again—we just have to show it. The first object in the script tests a global variable called *first*; if this is zero, we skip all the setup objects and go to **label2**, which shows the window.

Another feature is that the menus all use a custom RGB color for the buttons. Rather than define this specifically every time it is needed, we added a variable object that assigns **color(0)** to hold the button color.

The creation of Window 0 has to specify that window to be full-screen size, PM type, but with no PM controls or borders. Figure 14.6 shows the dialog for the Window object which does that. However, there's more, because this window also has to define hotspot controls for all the buttons on the main menu screen. This is needed so that the buttons will become sensitive to the mouse; it is done in the Window object by positioning hotspot rectangles over each of the buttons shown in the background image. Figure 14.7 shows the Window object sample window with all the hotspot areas highlighted. When we create the Input object, we will

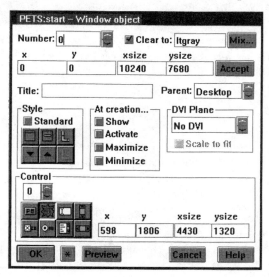

Figure 14.6 Window object for the Main menu for the Pets application.

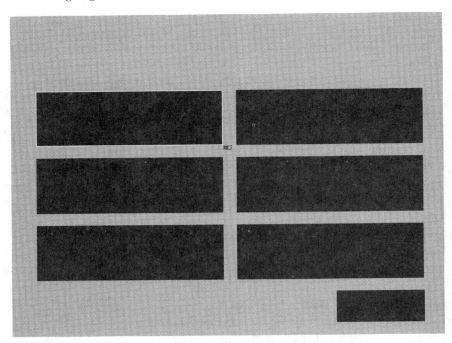

Figure 14.7 Hotspot layout of the Main menu window.

import these buttons into that object and specify actions for each of them. Figure 14.8 shows the Draw object, which draws the main menu, with the main menu showing in the background.

The remaining object in this script that we should examine more closely is the Input object. There are seven items in the Events list of the Input object, corresponding to the six class selections and the Exit button. Figure 14.9 shows the Input object dialog, with six subscript actions for the class selections and one Goto action for the Exit button.

All of the subscripts are simular; the contents of one of them (cats) is shown in Figure 14.9. There is a variable object, which sets string 0 equal to the name of the species list for the selected class—in this case it is **cats.lst.** Then a condition object performs an unconditional Exit action, passing the link name **species,** which (through the project's main files) will cause the species script to run. To set this up, we must select the Organizer window from the Project window, hook up the **start** script to the **start** icon, and hook up the **species** link of **start** to the **species** script. This is shown in Figure 14.10. The Organizer shows two columns of data for each script in the project: The left column is the name of the links in the script, and the right column is the name of the script assigned to that link. If there is no name assigned to a link it either means that link will never be used by the project; or, if it is used, the project will end. In this

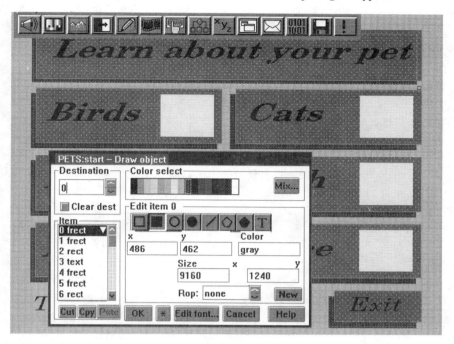

Figure 14.8 The Draw object which creates the Main menu.

project, the scripts **feeding** and **present** are called from the **species** script and their end links are never used. The first line of the Organizer

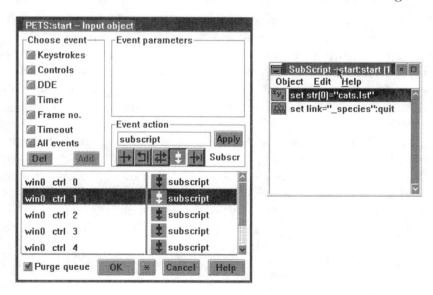

Figure 14.9 Input object for Main menu of the Pets application. The subscript to the right is for the Cats selection.

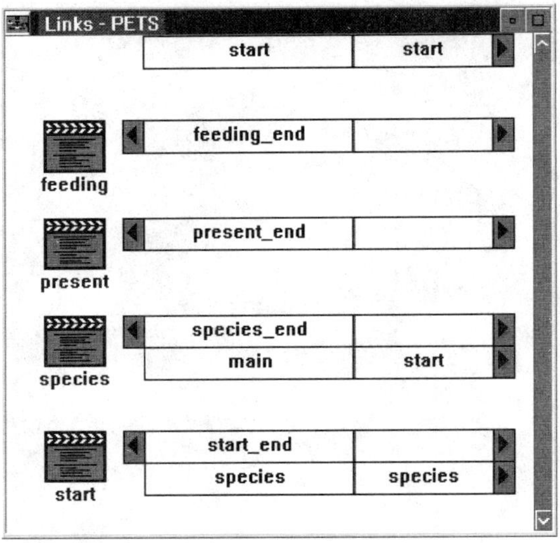

Figure 14.10 MEDIAscript OS/2 Organizer window for the Pets application.

identifies the starting script as **start**, and the lack of a script name for the **start_end** link means that the project ends when it runs to the end of the start script.

Once the user makes a selection from the main menu, we move to the Species menu, which is created by the **species** script, using the species list file whose name is in string 0. This file will be read into an array of string variables, beginning with string 2, by using a Data object with the **assign** option. However, we need to have two variables to keep track of this: One is *select*, which we already explained—it points to the current species selection—and the other is *species_count*, which tells us how many species are currently in the list. Both of these variables will be used in several scripts, and therefore they should be declared in the Project window as project variables. We also will have to add another line in the Variable objects of the **start** script to set *select* to 0 every time we go back through the main menu script.

Since the MEDIAscript string array is a global resource, it is a good idea to plan globally how the application will use it. Table 14.5 shows the use of the string array for the Pets application. The default array of strings has 100 strings, each is 80 characters long. However, the size of the array and the size of any string can be redefined dynamically in the Server if needed by an application. For this application, the default array will be adequate.

String	Use
str(0)	Name of current species list file
str(1)	Temporary buffer
str(2) – str(19) (max)	Current species list
str(20) – end of array	Current control file

Table 14.5 Use of MEDIAscript string variables in the Pets application

Creating the Species Script for the Pets Application

When the Species script is run from the main menu, the first action assigns the list of species to an array of string variables, using the **assign** option of a Data object. Then we run the sequence, which builds the Species screen while audio explains how to use the screen. A storyboard for this sequence was shown in Figure 5.2 in Chapter 5. The sequence requires preparing the initial version of the window (Window 1) in the invisible state, showing that window, and starting the audio. Then, on specific frame number cues in the audio, the other parts of the screen are added. Finally, the screen is activated for user selection. Figure 14.11 shows the actual script for all of this.

The first object is a Data object, which assigns the species names to the strings beginning with string 2. This object returns the number of strings

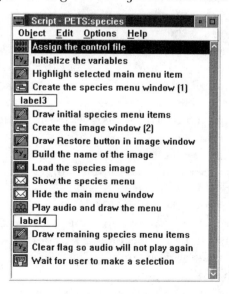

Figure 14.11 Script for Species menu of the Pets application.

assigned in the system variable *assigncnt*. Since this system variable might be used again by another Data object, we add a Variable object to save its value in the project variable *species_count*, which we created in the Project window. This Variable object also initializes some other variables, which will be used by the next object, a Draw object, to put highlighting around the main menu button that was selected. This serves to indicate the selection to the user during the several seconds it will take to build the species screen and show it.

Then we create Window 1, which will be the Species screen's main window. Window 1 is created full-screen, but in the invisible state; a Draw object then puts in the title block. The Species title in Window 1 comes from an item of the species list which starts at string 2, placed there by the **assign** operation at the start of the script. The actual item number is pointed to by the variable *select*.

Then we create Window 2, which will be the DVI 9 bpp window for displaying images or video; in order to have the proper behavior of the windows, Window 2 is made a child of Window 1. The parent-child relationship will make Window 2 show or hide whenever we show or hide Window 1. We also draw a "Restore" button in Window 2, which will let the user return to the quarter-screen mode. We load the first image for the species into Window 2.

The name of the image file to display is built using the five-letter code which is read from character position 24 of string 2. A Variable object appends the characters "0.a9" to the five-letter code and puts the result into string 1. String 1 is then used for the name in the Image object that loads the first image.

Then we show Window 1 (and 2), and start the audio. The same audio file is used for all the classes of pets, so its name "intro.avs" is hard-coded into the audio object. The audio object is specified to start the audio and immediately continue the script—this gives us the control to set up other actions on frame number cues from the audio.

All the audio cues are handled from a single Input object—it is set up for six frame number events. Each event simply causes the next part of the Species screen to be drawn; this is done by having a Draw object attached to each event as a subscript. At the end of the audio (established by a frame number event on the end frame), the buttons are all drawn and this Input object ends. We then use another Draw object to put in the remaining buttons and prompts, which indicate to the user that the menu is now active. We then start another Input object that responds to all the items in the Species menu by calling the appropriate other scripts or subscripts. This second Input object has seven choices, which are listed with their actions in Table 14.6. Notice that another project variable,

Control	Action
More species	A subscript displays species choices. When the user chooses, the species list is removed and the screen is updated.
Life Cycle	Set variable *pnum* to 1, call the audio/image presentation engine script.
In Action	A subscript runs the video for this species.
Grooming	Set variable *pnum* to 2, call the audio/image presentation engine script.
Feeding	Set variable *pnum* to 3, call the text/image presentation engine script.
Training	Set variable *pnum* to 4, call the audio/image presentation engine script.
Main Menu	Exit to the main menu script.

Table 14.6 Species menu and Input events.

pnum, is declared to tell the presentation engine what presentation number to run.

The subscript that handles the More species button is of some interest, and it is shown in Figure 14.12.

When the user clicks the More species button, we temporarily create Window 3 (PM only) to present the list of species. Window 3 is sized according to the number of species in the list, and a button is drawn for each item. Figure 14.13 shows a typical case of this window.

The first object in the More Species subscript creates Window 3 as invisible. Then a loop of Draw objects draws *species_count* number of

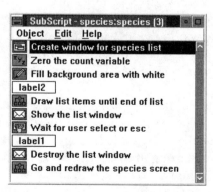

Figure 14.12 Subscript for Species menu in the *Pets* application

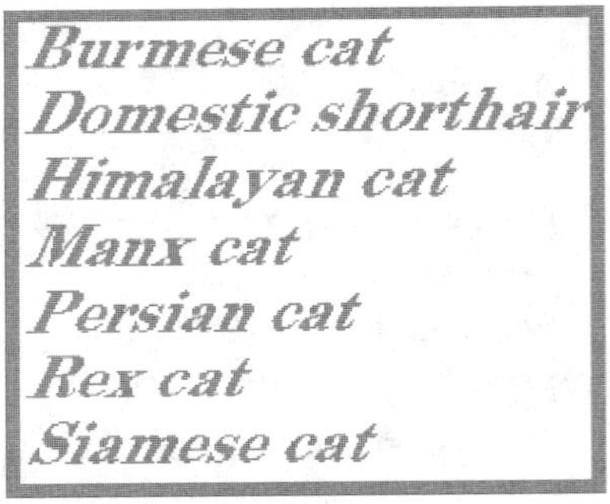

> Burmese cat
> Domestic shorthair
> Himalayan cat
> Manx cat
> Persian cat
> Rex cat
> Siamese cat

Figure 14.13 Species selection window for the Pets application.

buttons in Window 3. Window 3 is then shown. The subscript then enters an Input object that waits for user selection. If the user hits the escape key, Window 3 is destroyed, and the subscript ends. We must make sure that the user cannot continue without disposing of Window 3; therefore, the Input object responds only to a click or touch in Window 3—touching anywhere else will be ignored. If the user touches any of the list items in Window 3, a selection number is calculated and placed in the variable *select*. This is done by a Variable object. The title bar is redrawn by a Draw object using string 0, and the new image is loaded into Window 2 by using string 1. Then Window 3 is destroyed, and the subscript returns to redraw the species title, put in a new image, and restart the main Input object.

Creating the Audio/Image Presentation Script for Pets

The remaining elements of the Pets application are the two engine scripts for doing the presentations that the user can select from the Species screen. Figure 14.14 shows the script for the audio/image version of the presentation. While this presentation is setting up, we will display a title screen in the image window. This will tell the user that the selection was made. The first object of the script selects a title string based on *pnum*, as shown by the subscript in Figure 14.15. A Draw object then draws the title screen.

The next object is a Data object that reads the control file and assigns its lines to MEDIAscript string variables starting at string 20. This script extracts the species' five-letter code by using the *select* variable to index into the string array starting at string 2 (that is where the list of species begins). It also uses the variable *pnum* to know which presentation it is running—that number is used in the name of the control file, in the names of the image files, and in the name of the audio file. A Variable object performs the extraction of the names described above.

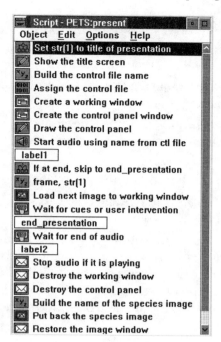

Figure 14.14 Script for the audio/image presentation engine.

We then use a Window object to create an invisible window, which will be used to preload images before we display them. Then we create Window 4 to hold the control panel and draw its contents. The control panel is made a child of the image window, and it is placed in the image window's upper left-hand corner. Finally, we start the audio, using the name that was in the first line of the control file.

We then enter a loop (marked by **label1**), in which a line is read from the control file in the string array, the image is loaded, and an Input object waits for the indicated frame number to show the image using a wipe

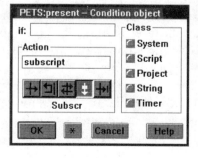 

Figure 14.15 Subscript that sets the presentation titles.

transition. The Input object also responds to user interaction with the presentation control panel. The actions for the three choices in the control panel and the Full-screen button are:

1. **Play**—resumes the audio if it was paused, and continues in the main Input object of the Species script.
2. **Pause**—pauses the audio and thus the whole presentation, since it is driven by the audio. There is a subscript with a Message object that pauses the audio.
3. **End**—stops the audio, and jumps out to **label2**.
4. **Maximize**—this causes a Message object to send Window 2 a maximize command.

When the end of the control file is reached, as indicated by having processed *assigncnt* items, the script jumps to the label **end_presentation**, where an Input object simply waits for the audio to finish playing. Then the species image in the image window is reloaded, the working window and the control panel window are destroyed, and we return to the species script.

Creating the Text/Image Presentation Script for Pets

The Feeding presentation uses a different format: It has images displayed in Window 2, but text is displayed in Window 1. It is similar to the audio/image presentation, except that the time line is determined by timeout events in an Input object instead of frame number events. The other difference is that the format of the control file is modified to also include the text that is to be displayed. The script is shown in Figure 14.16; it is pretty much self-explanatory.

This completes the description of the Pets application. Although the architecture appeared simple when we started, a lot of additional considerations cropped up as we started authoring. This is typical of a windowed environment—any application has to deal with all of the possibilities for what the user may do while the application is running. To retain the flexibility that enables an author to arrange things any way she likes, she must also face all of the possibilities created by her design.

We will not treat the other two applications in the same detail as we did with Pets. However, it is useful to look at the planning steps for each of them, and then identify the parts of the applications that introduce different issues, which we will examine in more detail.

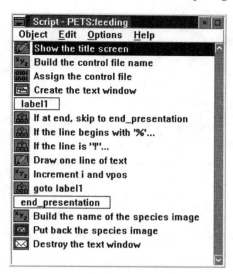

Figure 14.16 Script for Feeding presentation for the Pets application

PLANNING FOR THE CAMCORDER APPLICATION

Users for the Camcorder Application

The user for the Camcorder application is an adult with some knowledge of home video, but not necessarily any knowledge of computers.

Treatment for the Camcorder Application

A complete treatment for this application was given at the end of Chapter 3, so we won't repeat it here; refer to Chapter 3 if you need to refresh your memory.

List of Data for the Camcorder Application

This application does not have a lot of data. Table 14.7 lists the data and assets required.

Flowchart for the Camcorder Application

Figure 14.17 shows a flowchart for the Camcorder application. The application begins with the Attract video, which plays over and over until a potential customer touches the screen. When the screen is touched, a

Quantity	Asset	Comments
1	Video file	Attract video sequence (made by re-editing TV commercials)
1	Audio file	Used for product overview
15-20	Audio files	Clips to describe camcorder features
10-12	Images	Used for product overview
4	Images	Sets of images for each of the camcorder models. They are a composite of photos of the two sides and rear of the cameras
3	Text files	Camcorder specification sheets
3	Text files	Pricing information

Table 14.7 Asset files for Camcorder application

product overview presentation runs. At the end of that, the main screen comes up, shows a photo of the camera in a window, and gives the user choices to learn more about the features of the camera—its specifications, the models available, see a demonstration of the camera, or order a camera. Each of these selections runs a specific presentation. If the user does not interact for about one minute, the program returns to the Attract mode.

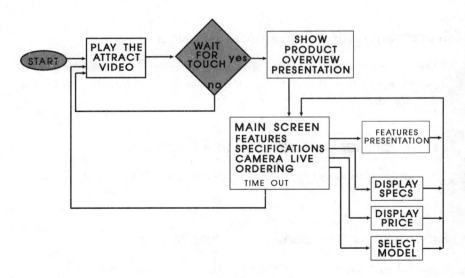

Figure 14.17 Flowchart for the Camcorder application.

Style for the Camcorder Application

Because this application will be used by the general public, a TV look will be used. All the screens are full-screen so the OS/2 desktop is never seen. The attract video and the product overview presentation will be DVI full-screen; the main screen will be full-screen PM with two DVI windows for the camera output and images. In order to get a "professional" appearance, we will use a marble textured background for the main screen. The buttons and windows will have beveled edges, the windows beveled in and the buttons beveled out.

User Interface for the Camcorder Application

A touch interface will be used. Touch buttons are used on the main screen; when presentations are running, control buttons will appear next to the presentation window for user control of pause, resume, and exit. When the user selects the Ordering button, a user-input window opens so the user can select model and options. This window will use radio buttons and check boxes.

Authoring Approach for the Camcorder Application

This application can be divided into two major parts: the attract video and the product overview presentation are one part, and the main screen is the other. However, you may want to make the product overview available from within the main screen; that will be simpler to do if the overview is in a script by itself. Let's do that for this exercise.

Within the main script, all of the routines except for the features sequences (where the user touches camcorder features in the image and gets audio prompts about what the controls do and how to demonstrate them) can be built directly in the main script routine. The features routines, of which there are four versions differing only in their data, ought to be designed with a data-driven engine. In each of these routines the user sees an image of the camera with text overlaid for the features. When the user touches a feature, an audio clip explains that feature. The user is encouraged to try it on the sample camera. Since the different camera models have different features, there must be a features list for each one, and the locations of the touch hotspots will vary. The data required for each feature is the name of the feature, the location of the touch hotspot, and the name of the audio clip.

```
Electronic Image         392      3644         eis.avs
Stabilization
Digital Zoom             136      2364       dzoom.avs
Title Memory            3752      3436       title.avs
Lux Sensitivity         3192       252        1lux.avs
5-watt Light             360       284       5watt.avs
Auto Focus               264      1004          af.avs
Remote Control           168      3180          rc.avs
```

Listing 14.4 Example of a control file for Camcorder features routine

If we assume that all the touch hotspots can be the same size, we can design the engine control file to have the coordinates of the upper left of each hot area together on a line, followed by the name of the associated audio file. When the user touches the controls image, the script logic would test the current touch location against the first value in each line of the control file. If it is closer than a certain amount to that first value, the script would then test against the second value in the line. If it is also close to that one, it means the user has touched that item and the audio file described in the third item would be played. When there is no match with one line, the next line in the control file is tested, until the end is reached. Such a control file looks like that shown in Listing 14.4.

Data List for the Camcorder Application

Table 14.8 shows the final asset and data list for the Camcorder application, with all the files named. The use of windows in this application is shown in Table 14.9.

Screen Designs for Camcorder Application

The main screen is the heart of this application. Its design was shown in Figure 8.9 in Chapter 8, but it is shown again here in Figure 14.18.

Presentation Design for Camcorder Application

The design of the Features presentations was already covered above in "Authoring Approach for the Camcorder Application."

The Ordering presentation consists of an overlay window that comes up when this item is selected in the main screen. Ordering is a PM-only

Area used	Asset
Attract video	attract.avs
Overview presentation	
Audio	overv.avs
Images	overvN.a9
Features presentations	(name is model name)
Images	name.a9
Audio files	*.avs
Data files	name.fea
Specifications	name.spc
Prices	name.pri

Table 14.8 Asset list for Camcorder application

window that contains radio buttons and check boxes from which the user can choose options that she is interested in purchasing. A price quotation window at the bottom of the screen is automatically updated whenever the user changes a selection. There also is a PM pushbutton marked "Exit," which will hide this window. If the user selects Ordering again, the Ordering window is shown, and all the selections previously made are still there. While the Ordering window is visible, a separate script called from the main script responds to user interaction. When the user hides the Ordering window, this script ends and control returns to the main script.

Number	Use	Type
0	Main screen	DVI-9, full–screen, high resolution
1	Camera monitoring	DVI-9, full–screen or quarter-screen
2	Attract video	DVI-9, full–screen, low resolution
3	Overview presentation	DVI-9, full-screen, high resolution
4	Specifications	PM–only, fixed size
5	Ordering	PM–only, fixed size

Table 14.9 Windows used by the Camcorder application

244 *Designing Interactive Multimedia*

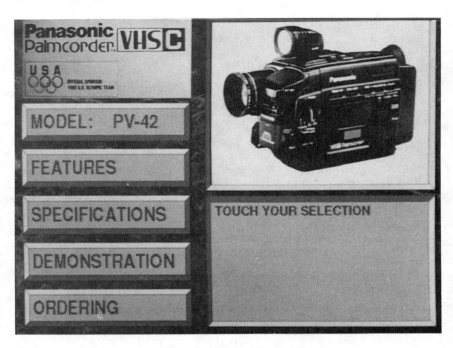

Figure 14.18 Main screen design for Camcorder application.

This means that the other items in the main window are disabled when the Ordering window is showing.

The Specifications presentation works similarly to Ordering, except that its window is simply a PM list box that contains the text of the selected camcorder specifications. The user can scroll through the text, and when she is finished, touch "Exit" to remove the Specification window and reactivate the main screen.

Estimate for the Camcorder Application

This application contains one video, about 20 audio clips, 15 images, and six data files. There are six scripts to write. An estimate for one person working on the application is shown in Table 14.10.

As explained at the start of this example, we will not go through all the details of this design. However, we will examine the details of the Controls engine script and the Specifications script, because they involve some different concepts than were in the previous example.

Item to prepare	Days	Comments
attract video	1	editing and capturing from TV commercials
audio files	2	does not include scripting
overview images	2	does not include scripting
controls images	4	does not include design
data files	1	
programming	4	
testing	2	
TOTAL	**14**	

Table 14.10 Estimate of preparation time for Camcorder application

Features Engine Script for the Camcorder Application

The Features presentation displays a composite image that shows the camcorder with text overlaid listing its features. An example of such an image is shown by Figure 14.19.

The script for the features presentations is shown in Figure 14.20. The first step of this script is to read the text file into the string array. Since there are four different data files for the four models of the camcorder, we have to build the names of the data file using a string containing the camera model name. The statement for this is

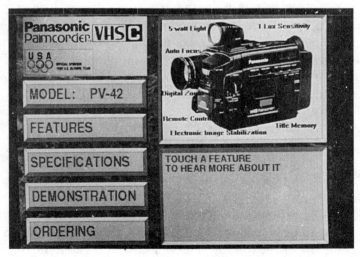

Figure 14.19 Camcorder image with feature text overlaid.

246 *Designing Interactive Multimedia*

Figure 14.20 Script for Features presentation.

```
str(10)=str(model)".fea"
```

This is MEDIAscript syntax to create the filename **name.fea** dynamically using the number in the variable *model* and a group of strings containing the model names.

The second object in the script is a Data object, which assigns the contents of the file named in string 10 to the string array beginning with string 20. The next step is to display the feature names and the camera image in the main window. A loop is set up by a Condition object and **label1**. This loop counts up to **assigncnt**—the number of strings assigned—and it displays the first 31 characters of each line at the coordinates given at location 32 and location 40 in the control line. When the loop exits, a Draw object displays the prompt "TOUCH A FEATURE FOR MORE INFORMATION" in the text window of the main screen. Then the script enters an Input object to wait for the user's next action.

The Input object responds to a touch in any of the windows or controls on the screen. For all of them except the camera image window, the script simply goes to **label3**, which erases the feature annotations from the camera image and the script ends, returning the user to the control of the main script. However, touching anywhere in the image window runs a subscript that searches the control data to see if the user touched on one of the feature items. If she did, it runs the audio file identified for that item in the control file.

Figure 14.21 shows the subscripts which implement the search of the control data. The figure is a cascade of nested dialogs starting from the top, which is the subscript invoked when the user touches in the image window.

First, a Variable object initializes the variable **scount** to zero, and uses the local variables **sx** and **sy** to hold the relative position of the user's touch within the image window. This is necessary because the control file uses relative coordinates.

Figure 14.21 Subscripts which search the features list when the user touches a feature

Next, a loop is started between **label2** and the following Condition object. The loop cycles until **scount** reaches the value in **assigncnt**, which is the number of items in the control file. The next dialog below shows the subscript in the Condition object of the loop.

For each pass through the loop, the local variables **vx** and **vy** are initialized to the coordinate values in the current item of the control list. The statements for this assignment are:

```
vx=<str(scount+20).(32)>
vy=<str(scount+20).(40)>
```

The carats cause the string to be converted to an integer value; the strings begin at character positions 32 and 40, which are the locations of the two coordinate values in each control file line. The next object in the subscript tests whether the touch location **sx,sy** is below and to the right of the start position of the current item **vx,vy**. If it is not, **scount** is incremented and the loop is recycled by going to **label2**.

If the condition statement is true, we proceed to its subscript, which is in the next dialog below. This subscript has only one Condition object, which tests whether the user's touch was within 1000 × 200 coordinates of the start location of an item. If it is not, the script falls through to recycle the loop; but if it is true, we proceed to the last subscript which starts playing the proper audio file.

In that subscript, string10 is used as a temporary buffer to hold the name of the audio file, extracted from the control string beginning at character position 48 with the statement

```
str(10)=str(scount+20).(48)
```

There is an audio stop Message object first so that any audio already playing will be interrupted. At the end of this subscript, we jump to the label **again** (in the first subscript), which causes the Input object to resume its wait for another user touch.

This example does not provide any user feedback other than the audio itself. To give visual feedback, the final subscript could include a Draw object to highlight the selected features with a rectangle. To be complete, this needs two draw objects, because any previously selected item should also be unhighlighted. That leads to the need to save the previous highlight rectangle in a rectangle variable, etc. As we have said before, the refinements to an application can get complicated.

The Specifications Presentation

This presentation lets the user scroll through the written specifications for the camera model being displayed. A Presentation Manager list box is used for that purpose; the list box is loaded from a text file. The script for the specification presentation is shown in Figure 14.22, which also shows the Window object that creates the list box.

The script begins by creating the name of the data file in a Variable object, the same as described for the Features presentation. The result is placed in string 10. Then the data file is assigned to the string array, beginning at string 20, using a Data object. Next, we create the Specifications window, Window 4, using a Window object. This is a PM-only window that contains a large list box. The reason for not creating the window first is that the list box definition requires knowledge of the number of strings to display. This is not available until we have assigned the data file to the string array; then the system variable *assigncnt* holds the value we need. The list box is created and its contents are placed when the window itself is created, so we must have everything set up before we create the window. The window is created in the visible state—this gives the fastest feedback to the user.

The user interaction with the list box (scrolling) is handled automatically by the MEDIAscript Server, and requires nothing in the script. However, we must wait for the user to touch another button in the main

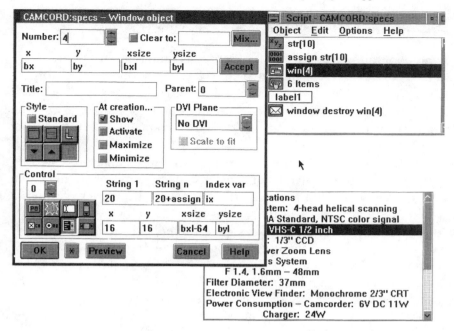

Figure 14.22 Script for Specifications presentation of the Camcorder application. The related Window object is also shown at the left.

window to end this script. This user action causes a **goto** by the Input object to the label **label4**. Following the label, we have a Message object that destroys the Specifications window, and the script ends.

This is as far as we will go with the description of the Camcorder application. As you can see from the time estimate given earlier, this application is one that a single person could reasonably do in a period of three weeks or so. Of course, as you work with a project like this one, new ideas will invariably occur and it may be somewhat of a struggle to keep the scope from growing, which, of course, will also increase the timetable.

THE SOLDERING TRAINING APPLICATION

This application was introduced in Chapter 8. We will only go through the planning steps here.

Users of the Soldering Application

The users are manufacturing workers who need to learn the techniques of hand soldering. They do not know anything about computers.

Treatment for the Soldering Application

This application teaches hand soldering techniques to new workers for an electronics manufacturing plant. Hand soldering is used for the manufacture of certain cable assemblies, and for the repair or modification on printed circuit boards. The application is part of a learning workstation that includes actual soldering equipment for performing the procedures being taught.

The application opens with a screen that shows an image of soldering equipment, and contains an entry field for the student to enter her name and employee ID. This is used by the program to keep track of who has taken the training and what the status is of each student's work. A separate file is created for each worker, using the students' ID numbers (5 digits) for a filename. If a worker uses the training station more than once, her file is appended each time.

If the student is signing in for a repeat session, she sees a screen that tells her which items in the application she has already seen and which ones she still must do. After that, she moves to the main menu of the application, which offers the following choices:

- **Introduction** is a video clip with audio that explains basic soldering theory and nomenclature. When a student has signed in for the first time, this sequence is mandatory—it is the only active item on the menu. The video plays full-screen with a control panel at the lower right that allows the student to pause, resume, or quit the video. If the student watches this video to the end, an entry is logged into the student's progress file.
- **Tools and materials** brings up a second-level menu that provides choices to see audio and image presentations on each of the standard tools used in the plant, and the materials involved. The student is expected to watch each of these presentations; as she chooses each one and runs it to the end, it is logged into her status file.
- **Wiring** is a session during which the student is expected to perform the examples using the tools at the workstation. A submenu screen provides choices of an introduction video and a series of example soldering tasks to perform. When the student is entering this section for the first time, the introduction is the only item active; again, the student's progress in logged into her file at this point. Since the student has to do the example projects, an instructor must review the results of her work and confirm in the student's file that each project has been satisfactorily performed. A special mode of the

application is available to the instructor, using a password entry scheme that is activated by a secret keystroke combination. When the instructor enters the proper password, an entry screen comes up that shows the student's status. The instructor can edit this screen; when she leaves it, the student's file is updated.
- **Repair** works just like the wiring session except that the subjects are related to repair of PC boards. It also has example projects that the student must perform and be reviewed by the instructor.

Data List for the Soldering Application

There are three major video segments in this application:

- Main introduction
- Wiring introduction
- Repair introduction

There are approximately 15 audio and image presentations. Each of these has approximately ten images and one audio file.

Flowchart for the Soldering Application

Figure 14.23 shows a flowchart for the Soldering application. As you can see, this application is quite complex and flowcharting becomes rather awkward as an application grows. You need to start breaking the flowchart into sections and use arrows and callouts to show the connections.

The flowchart indicates that there are three submenus, which have similar structure, and they are candidates for an engine script. Also, these submenus have similar presentations for which we also could write an engine script.

Style for the Soldering Application

The style for this application was described in Chapter 8 and some screens were shown in Figure 8.10. In keeping with the user characteristics, it is an entirely borderless full-screen application. The menu screens are PM-only, but most of the presentations are based on full-screen motion video or full-screen images with audio.

252 *Designing Interactive Multimedia*

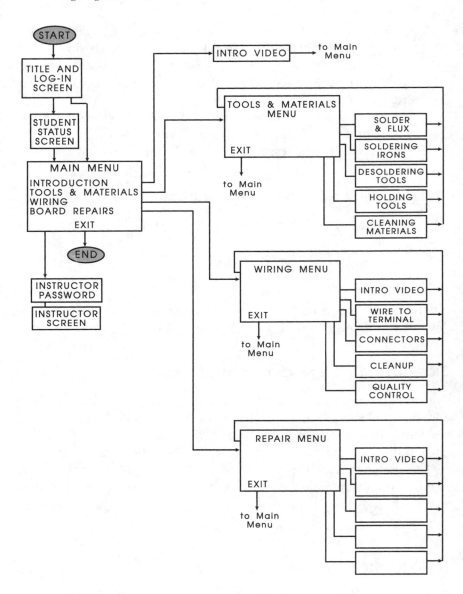

Figure 14.23 Flowchart for the Soldering application.

User Interface for the Soldering Application

The user interface is touch-based. All touch areas are rectangular buttons with text legends. Presentations and video segments have control panels for pausing, resuming, or exiting the presentation—all with text buttons rather than icons.

```
Wiring
Introduction video      wintro.avs
Wire to terminal        wterm.txt
Connectors              wconn.txt
Cleanup                 xclean.txt
Quality control         wqual.txt
```

Listing 14.5 Control file for Wiring menu

Authoring Approach for the Soldering Application

One script will be written for the initial log-in sequence and the main menu. The student status screen that is used in the initial log-in should be a separate script because it can also become the basis for the instructor screen, which has to be callable from any of the menu screens.

An engine script will be written to support the three submenus. A control file format will be designed to provide the menu item text for the submenus. For the video items in the submenus, the submenu control file can use a "video" flag, followed by the name of the video file to use—all on the same line in the control file as the menu item that invokes it. Menu items that run presentations will contain the name of another control file, which controls a presentation engine script. For example, the control file for the Wiring menu would look like that shown in Listing 14.5.

An engine script will run all the audio and image presentations that are called from the submenus. This script is controlled from text files; the first line is the name of the audio file for the presentation, and subsequent lines have three fields: the name of the image to show, the frame number to show it on, and the type of transition to use in showing it.

Data List for the Soldering Application

The only addition to the data list given above is the three control files for the submenus and the 15 control files for the presentations.

Screen Design for the Soldering Application

The screen designs are shown in Chapter 8, Figure 8.10.

Presentation Designs for the Soldering Application

We will not do the presentation design beyond what is described in the "Authoring Approach to the Soldering Application" section above.

Estimate for the Soldering Application

There are four scripts in this application: the main script, the student status screen (which also handles the instructor function), the submenu engine, and the presentation engine. The estimate is:

- 8 days to build and debug the four scripts;
- 10 days to script, plan, and shoot three videos;
- 15 days to script and produce 15 audio segments;
- 10 days to design, produce, and capture approximately 150 images; and
- 5 days for final integration and testing.

The total estimate for the Soldering training project is 48 days if one person does it all.

A significant non-multimedia complication is added to this application because of the need to keep track of each student's progress through the training. Variables have to be set up in the scripts to track the students' progress, and separate routines will be needed to save this data to disk when the students exit a session. It also adds the routines that enable the instructor to evaluate the students' results and enter data into the student files. These functions are easily programmed in MEDIAscript OS/2 using the built-in variables capability and the file I/O capability in the Data object. Most other authoring systems can also provide these features; authoring systems designed for computer-based training typically have high-level functions to set up student tracking in an application.

We will not describe any more details of the Soldering application. As you can see from the planning discussion above, it boils down to a set of only four scripts in spite of the apparent complexity of the flowchart. This is another example of the value of designing to use engine scripts. You can look at an engine script as a custom-tailored authoring module; you have set up a tool that reduces most of your detail programming to simple lists of text strings, filenames, and keywords. It is a good example of how to use a powerful authoring system like MEDIAscript OS/2 to easily build complex applications.

DISTRIBUTING YOUR APPLICATION

Except in the rare case in which the final presentation of the application is done on your own system—either in place or by taking your system to the presentation site—you have to move the application to one or more other systems. This is called *distribution*. Since a multimedia application often has many megabytes of data, distribution can become a large problem. There are six ways to distribute, based on the medium you use:

- floppy disk,
- hard disk,
- CD-ROM,
- writeable optical,
- digital tape, and
- computer network.

We will discuss each one below.

Floppy Disk Distribution

Most non-multimedia applications are distributed on floppy disk. A 3 1/2" high-density diskette holds 1.44 megabytes of data, and a 5 1/4" HD diskette holds 1.2 megabytes. In multimedia, these figures correspond to less than 10 seconds of motion video, less than 1 minute of audio, or approximately 30 full-screen compressed images—not much for any real application. For that reason, anything more than a simple business presentation will not be reasonable to distribute on floppy disks. Still, you will probably use floppies up to their limit because they are the easiest and cheapest means of distribution, and every computer has a floppy disk drive.

Hard Disk Distribution

In a situation over which you have control of all the hardware involved, hard disk drives can become a distribution medium. The simplest way to do this is to add a SCSI port to all of your machines and then get a SCSI hard drive and driver software.

SCSI is an acronym for *Small Computer Systems Interface*, which is a high-speed bus interface that is supported by a number of different kinds of hardware. Because the SCSI bus is different than the internal bus in your computers, you must use an adaptor card to convert to the SCSI bus to use SCSI hardware. SCSI is becoming more widespread now because it is the preferred interface for CD-ROM drives; thus, nearly all systems designed for multimedia will already have a SCSI interface built in.

To use hard drive distribution, first plug the SCSI distribution hard drive into your development system and copy all the application files onto a directory structure on the distribution drive. Then power off, unplug the distribution drive from the development system, and move it to the target system (also with power off). Power up the target system and copy the applications directories from the distribution drive to the system's local hard drive. You can take the distribution drive around to all of your systems and distribute as widely as you have the patience for.

Hard drives are delicate mechanisms, and care must be used in handling them outside of a machine chassis. There also are some caveats about the software for a drive that is not always installed in the machine—you will probably have to boot the target machine from a diskette to properly control the installation of the SCSI driver when you need it. However, this is not too bad because you have to power down the machine anyway to plug in the SCSI cable. This method of distribution will work in a local environment if you manage it properly.

CD-ROM Distribution

The preferred medium for large-scale distribution is the CD-ROM disc. It has a capacity of up to 680 megabytes, and it is inexpensive and reliable. CD-ROM distribution requires that you send your data out to a replication center for mastering and pressing of discs. This has an up-front cost of around $1,500 and it takes at least a week to get discs back. The discs themselves cost only about $2–$3 each, depending on quantity. However, this will prove to be economical compared to the other physical medium methods whenever you need more than 20 copies of the distribution. This is not only because of the cost of the medium itself, but because of the cost of recording the individual copies that all other media require.

An advantage of CD-ROM distribution is that your target machine does not have to copy the CD-ROM's data onto its own hard disk—it can run your application directly from the CD-ROM drive. There is a performance penalty to this, however, because of the slow seek time of CD-ROM drives, but for many applications this is acceptable. In any case, you can almost always play all your audio and video directly from the CD, but you might want to copy some of the image or data files to hard drive for best performance. If you know you will use CD-ROM for distribution, you can design the application accordingly.

CD-ROM requires that you perform a *premastering* process before you can send your data out for mastering. The premastering provides for the formatting of the directory and path structure on the CD-ROM disc in order to obtain optimum performance. Proper premastering requires special equipment that contains a large hard drive and special software that can store a digital image of the final CD format. Such systems cost from $15,000 up, an investment that may not make sense except in a large organization that does many CD-ROMs. In most large cities there are vendors who will do CD-ROM premastering as a service, and this is the way to go if you do it only occasionally.

Writeable Optical Distribution

The writeable optical technologies mentioned in Chapter 2 "Mass Storage," can be used for multimedia application distribution. They can be used as described under hard drive distribution above, or (preferred) they can be used to make multiple copies of the distribution medium. The multiple-copy approach is workable for small numbers of copies (under about ten), but beyond that quantity the cost of the medium and the labor cost of recording individual copies will add up to more than the cost of making CD-ROMs. Also, writeable optical drives are not standardized, and they are expensive—all of your target machines must have drives of the same manufacturer and type. Unless you absolutely must have quick turnaround, writeable optical for distribution is not a very good approach. The new CD-WORM drives that record discs playable on any CD-ROM drive may be another solution to the small quantity distribution problem.

Digital Tape Distribution

There are a number of digital tape drives that are low in cost and fit in the floppy disk bays of most machines. They have data capacities in the range of 40 and 150 megabytes per tape. Because the tape has serial access and is quite slow, you must copy the contents of the tape onto the target machine's hard drive. This process can take up to 20 minutes per tape.

Tape drives are not well standardized; you have to get all your drives from the same manufacturer and use the same type. This approach is workable, but not highly recommended.

Another type of digital tape just coming on the market is the DAT format, which is based on the DAT (Digital Audio Tape) drives that are on the market for home and professional audio recording. These drives have a storage capacity of several *gigabytes* (thousands of megabytes), the tapes are inexpensive, and they are reliable. However, the drives *are* expensive, and the data transfer is slow (more than an hour for 600 megabytes). Because it is a serial format, you must copy everything to the local hard drive.

DAT is a good archival format because of its tremendous data capacity. It is also being considered for large data transfers such as are needed when you send your data to a CD-ROM mastering house, or when you get PLV motion video back from a DVI compression facility. We will see more of it in the future.

Yet another digital tape format is the so-called *9-track* format, which is widely used with minicomputers. Because of the expense and size of this equipment, it is not often used with PCs. However, it is used for data transfer to a CD mastering house, and that is another reason for hiring a premastering service—they can make the 9-track tapes that are required.

Distribution by Computer Network

Many organizations have all their PCs connected by a network for exchange data, electronic mail, and programs. This is also an ideal medium for distributing multimedia application data. With a high-speed network, it is even possible to play motion video and audio over the network. However, that is a large load for a PC network, and it will limit the other uses of the network while someone is playing video. For most cases, we would recommend that multimedia data be copied to a local hard drive before use, and then play it locally without tying up the network every time video is played.

CHAPTER SUMMARY

Before diving into the detail work of building an application, a full planning process should be completed. One good set of planning steps is as follows:

- define who the users are,
- write a treatment,
- list the data to present,
- make a flowchart,
- choose the style,

- design the user interface,
- choose an authoring approach,
- finalize the data list,
- design the screens,
- design the presentations, and
- estimate time and personnel.

Three applications were planned in detail to show how these steps are used and to show different features of the application. These examples prove that careful design can reduce the amount of programming required to produce a complex application to less than ten percent of the total effort needed to create the application.

15

Where Do We Go from Here?

forecast: n. a prediction, as of weather conditions.
Webster's New World Dictionary, 1988

Forecasting the weather is a process that we are exposed to daily. It is a good example of how difficult it is to predict anything. You might think that weather forecasting would be easy: After all, today's weather in New Jersey was in Ohio yesterday; it was in Kansas the day before, etc. However, the simplistic view of west-to-east weather movement is misleading—it's actually much more complicated than that.

Forecasting the direction of digital multimedia is similar—there is a simplistic view, and then there is the much more complex real environment. The simplistic view says that because multimedia hardware and software are now on the market it is just a matter of time before multimedia is on every PC. However, the real world includes issues such as economics, standards, competition, and continued growth of technology—factors that are keeping the multimedia environment cloudy. In this chapter, I discuss these and other issues to offer you insight into what the future possibilities are for multimedia computing. Since a forecast is not fact, but rather an opinion—in this case, my opinion—I express myself in the first person in this chapter so you will have no doubt about whose opinion you are reading.

INGREDIENTS OF A FORECAST

The preceding chapters of this book exposed you to all of the skills and technologies that come into play to produce digital multimedia applications. Some of these ingredients have come from the computing world, but many originated in other industries such as television, sound recording, motion pictures, cartoon animation, and others. To understand the trends that brought us to this point, we have to examine all of the industries that are contributing to digital multimedia. This will build the background for forecasting. First, I will discuss why *volume* is important, then I will discuss each of the following items or issues:

- standards,
- IC chip technology,
- PC manufacturing,
- add-in boards,
- operating system software,
- software developers and publishers,
- new businesses,
- the television industry,
- the audio industry, and
- multimedia uses.

These items can be looked at as *wells*—wells of innovation. They are the sources of the ingredients that are building a multimedia marketplace.

The Need for Volume

Any industry that involves a mix of ingredients, as does multimedia, must reach a level of volume or quantity of use before it will truly begin paying for itself. This is like a "critical mass"; when you are below it, growth has to be forced by external input, but beyond that critical point, the industry takes off by itself. Multimedia is still below critical volume, at a stage where product development costs still exceed revenues.

The reason for a critical volume is that there must be an *infrastructure* built up to provide all the hardware, software, and services needed by the industry. The principal driver of the industry is *price*, and price depends on volume. Until the components reach pricing that appears attractive to users, sales will be limited and the potential for profits is nil. This will keep many participants from entering the market, and the infrastructure will not develop.

To get beyond this point, an industry must have pioneers who will invest in development of hardware and software while the potential return is still in the future. This takes real belief in the eventual success of the industry, and it is viewed as a big risk in the financial community. In spite of this, there are visionary people and companies who are forging ahead. IBM, Intel, Macromind, Asymetrix, Authorware, and many others are developing and marketing multimedia products. This is a necessary step.

Standards

An ingredient of success in the developing multimedia industry is *standards*, by which I mean hardware and software that works together and is marketed by many vendors. We don't have many standards today, although there are a number of industry groups working on the problem. The reason standards are so important is that users want to be sure that investments they make in hardware and software today will not be made obsolete by future developments. Industry standards deal with that problem.

However, it is difficult to create standards for a new industry in which technological development is moving rapidly. Some people feel that once a standard is set, technological development will be stifled. I don't agree with that; what happens is that technological development becomes channeled to work within the standard. The best example of this is the IBM PC "standard," which established the framework within which the entire PC industry has grown. Although at the time it was introduced many of us in the industry thought it was a step backward and would be very limiting, it has turned out to be exactly the opposite—the IBM PC standard became a *platform* upon which all kinds of innovations have been built.

We need a platform like that for multimedia—a standard that we in the industry can use to develop new products that we can assure our users will work on all multimedia machines. We're not there yet, but a number of encouraging events are pointing the way. Hardware is probably the most difficult part of the standards problem because hardware requires a large up-front investment for development, and hardware development has to come first—before software. We cannot afford to wait while potential hardware developers get together and develop standards (designing by committee); it would take forever.

What does seem reasonable is to develop a software standard that will be tolerant of different hardware—*device-independent* is the industry term for that. This is under way in the Media Control Interface (MCI) standard that has been introduced in Windows 3.1 and OS/2 2.0. MCI provides a uniform way for application programs to talk to multimedia hardware; it simply requires that new hardware be accompanied by software drivers that conform the hardware to the MCI interface. Once this is done, all application programs written to use MCI can potentially talk to new hardware—hardware that may not even have existed when the application program was written. This is a noble concept. Even though all the pieces are not yet in place, I hope it will succeed because it means that we can have our cake and eat it too—a software standard that does not limit hardware development.

There are other standards needed for multimedia at lower levels, too. The best example is the standardization of image and video compression algorithms. This has been addressed by the JPEG (Joint Photographic Expert Group) and MPEG (Motion Picture Expert Group) committees of the IEC (International Electrotechnical Commission), who have nearly completed international standards for compression. Again, this is being done in ways that will not seriously limit future developments—the standards provide frameworks within which much innovation is still possible. Hardware developers have worked closely with these committees and are now guaranteeing compatibility with the emerging standards.

IC Chip Technology

In Chapter 2 we mentioned Moore's law, the chip industry trend that leads to more and more functionality on a single chip. The increase factor of two every two years is a staggering rate; even more staggering is that this is expected to continue beyond the year 2000. What will come of that prodigious growth?

For one thing, it means that the raw cost of CPU computing power (MIPS—millions of instructions per second) will continue to drop dramatically. Many capabilities of multimedia computing depend directly on CPU power, such as animations, image manipulations, compression and decompression, etc., and these will get faster and better. Many of today's algorithms for the functions listed above are compromises between the available computing power and the speed of completing the function. With more computing power, these functions will run faster—so fast that eventually we can revise the algorithmic compromise and make the performance better, too.

Another benefit of more functionality per chip is that it becomes reasonable to go to *higher integration*—move more functionality onto a single chip. For example, a DVI multimedia system today uses an 80x86 CPU chip and two separate DVI coprocessor chips—three ICs, three packages, lots of interconnections. In the near future it will be reasonable to merge all three together onto one chip in one package. This will lower system cost, increase performance and reliability, and make the hardware smaller. The result is that more and more future PCs will have DVI Technology built right in, at a very nominal increase in cost.

Of course, the growth of IC capability also applies to RAM chips; the increase of RAM per chip up to 64 megabits is already in the wind. This will make RAM cost a trivial part of system cost, and RAM sizes of 16 megabytes or more will be commonplace. RAM limitations on performance will be a thing of the past.

The trends based on IC performance are pretty much assured, at least for the next five years or so. They are being financed by the volume of the entire IC industry and by the volume of the entire computer industry; they do not depend on any particular forecast for multimedia. You can expect that the cost/performance tradeoff will become more and more favorable to multimedia over the next two to five years.

PC Manufacturing

PCs have already become commodity products—available worldwide from hundreds of manufacturers and at very competitive prices. This is a direct result of hardware standards and the large volume of the market for PCs. However, the components for multimedia are not yet in the commodity status, for reasons that are the same, but opposite; standards are limited and the volume is small. As standards are developed and the volume increases, you will see the chip integration I mentioned above; this will make it easier for all PC manufacturers to provide multimedia in their hardware. Prices will come down, volume will increase, there will be more competition, still lower prices, still higher volume; in other words, multimedia will be off and running.

Add-In Boards

In today's PC you need add-in boards for multimedia, for both audio and video. A variety of boards is available, as indicated by the listings in Appendix A, and there will soon be more. However, as I have already said, multimedia functionality will evolve into a built-in feature of new PCs. As this happens, the use of boards in new PC products will diminish. Nevertheless, there are millions of PCs in use that are otherwise suitable for multimedia, except that they don't have audio and video. The market for add-in multimedia boards will continue for many years.

The same trends that make it possible to build multimedia into a new PC will lower the cost of add-in boards and will hasten the conversion of all existing PCs to multimedia.

Operating System Software

The trend in operating systems is to have a graphical user interface with a desktop metaphor. Windows and OS/2 are the leading examples of this. Although Windows and OS/2 have different application interfaces, and therefore the same application software will not run on both of them, they are coming closer together. OS/2 2.0 and Windows NT now give the choice of whether a window is a Windows window, an OS/2 window, or a DOS window. Applications written for any of these three environments can run and multitask in OS/2 2.0 or Windows NT.

Multimedia is now being recognized in operating systems. OS/2 2.0, Windows 3.1, and Windows NT provide a multimedia API based on the MCI concept described earlier. These interfaces primarily support audio right now, but they will soon support several video and animation systems as well. As multimedia becomes a built-in feature of new PCs, it will also become a built-in feature of operating systems.

Software Developers and Publishers

Most multimedia software today is tied to specific hardware configurations, because it was developed before the multimedia standards began emerging. That will soon change with more use of the MCI standards and with higher-level standardization of some of the delivery technologies, such as DVI Technology. The opportunity to gain a broader market of hardware platforms by use of the MCI standard will not be lost on the software developers. Reaching a broader market and thereby gaining volume is the best way for software development to become profitable.

The same factors that will lead to greater use of multimedia hardware will lead to greater software availability. This is another facet of the development of an industry.

Although major software packages will continue to be written using computer programming languages such as C, there also is a trend to greater use of authoring packages, which allow application development by people with less technical skill. A wide range of authoring software is already available for certain hardware combinations; some is directed at completely unskilled authors while others are made for full professional application development. All of these packages must keep pace with the development of standards, and I predict they will, because that assures a larger market for everyone.

New Businesses

The computer business seems to provide an ever-widening opportunity for new business. This is true for the multimedia segment as well as general computing hardware and software. Some specialty areas that are appearing and which will have impact on multimedia are:

- speech I/O,
- pen-based computing,
- artificial intelligence,
- hypermedia, and
- asset publishing.

I will briefly discuss each of these.

Speech I/O

Using the computer to simulate a human voice is an old technology, but the advances of hardware and software have improved it. However, making the computer understand human speech input is relatively new for PC platforms. This technology takes much more computing power than speech synthesis, and is still at the limits of today's PC power. The continuing advance of IC technology will soon overcome that and true speech I/O should be fully practical for PCs within about five years. There is no more natural user interface than a voice conversation between user and computer, and since multimedia is so often a part of a user interface, speech I/O will be another metaphor for the multimedia bag of tricks. Some day there will be MCI calls for speech input or output, just as with audio today.

Pen-Based Computing

Another natural interface is to write notes on a pad to communicate with a computer. This field is developing rapidly, with a number of systems already being marketed. A pen interface eliminates the need for a keyboard; the user does not need to know how to type. It will soon be an option to use a pen interface just as we use a mouse today. This also is a natural addition to multimedia.

Artificial Intelligence

AI is a much-maligned technology because it often is incorrectly defined to mean that the computer thinks like a person. That is a little too much; it is more reasonable to say that an AI computer uses a body of knowledge (a database) to solve problems. An extension of that is for an AI system to learn by experience; as it solves problems, it also can add to its database. These concepts are proving themselves in certain fields that require complex associations of data with reality, such as in medical diagnostics or troubleshooting of hardware.

AI does not have any particular tie with multimedia; to me, it is just another one of the millions of different things you can do with a computer. To that extent, if you have an AI application, it is reasonable to add a multimedia interface to it. It seems less reasonable (at this time) to want to add AI to somehow assist a multimedia application. Over time, AI is going to continue to progress and its applications will grow; however I think it will be more than five years before we will be ready for AI to be part of most multimedia applications.

Hypermedia

Hypermedia is the linking together of references in text and multimedia databases in such a way that the user can interactively explore the data. It is an important tool for multimedia that applies to many information delivery and training applications. Some authoring systems today have hypermedia capabilities; I think there will be more of these in the future.

Asset Publishing

This is one of the new business opportunities that will be attractive as digital multimedia grows. It is the offering of multimedia "clip art," audio sounds, images, icons, animations, and video clips. Many companies have libraries of such items today and many are offered in other forms to other markets. As multimedia grows, these libraries will be converted to multimedia standard formats, and products will be offered to a widening market of multimedia users.

The Television Industry

As television viewers, we probably think that the television business is pretty mature and stable. However, from a technical point of view there is still a lot of potential. I'll discuss two aspects of that here: the use of digital technology in TV broadcasting and HDTV. But first, I should discuss the consumer market, because this is where television lives, and the consumer market is a different world from the PC market.

The consumer market is made up of individuals and families who buy independently for their own use. There are more than 100 million consumers in the United States, and many more than that in the developed countries of the rest of the world. The first thing about the consumer market is that it is *large*—quantity multipliers of a million are normal.

The second thing about a consumer market is that customers have very limited financial resources compared to businesses. This causes the governing parameter for products to be *price*. Everything is driven by the price of a product; it is difficult to compete on any other basis. Consumers are looking primarily at price vs. performance; they do not care about things like technical sophistication, future growth, or customer support. This is very different from the business PC market, in which the bulk of customers are investing in the future of their business and they worry very much about being competitive in the future without their investment rapidly becoming obsolete.

Because the consumer is not interested in technical details, he is unable to make judgments between competing technical approaches. The consumer wants these decisions to be made for him; he wants somebody to set technical standards: one per product area. When there are multiple standards for a consumer product, everyone will eventually be hurt. The predominating technical approach will eventually beat the others out; at that point consumers who bought the losing approach will see their money wasted—they will not be able to participate in future growth without buying into the winning approach. This can cause a large segment of customers to be dissatisfied. Typically, the confusion and lack of confidence generated by technical competition will hold back the entire market.

The gleam in every computer marketer's eye is to have a computer product which will sell millions of copies to the consumer market. Lots of PCs have been sold into the home, but they are not consumer products—they are extensions of the office or education PC markets. These computers are the property of someone in the home who has involvement in the office or education markets; they are not purchased as consumer products to be used by anyone in the family for any purpose.

One of the problems is that PCs are still too difficult to use as a consumer product. Someone has to have a lot of skill and knowledge to set up and run the typical PC. True "plug-and-play" hasn't been achieved. But didn't we say that you can make a PC do *anything*;? It can, but only by sacrificing much of the flexibility that is the real strength of a PC.

Plug-and-play PCs are crippled in terms of general use. This approach has been tried, and it doesn't sell. A true consumer market PC is an opportunity that has still to be fulfilled. The number of unsuccessful attempts already made indicate that it isn't an easy problem.

Another difficulty with a consumer market PC is that it isn't clear what a computer should do for the consumer. Why does a consumer need a PC? Most consumers do not have enough use for the typical office tasks of word processing, graphics, spreadsheets, or databases to justify having a PC. However, one thing that consumers do want is entertainment and a computer is great for that, especially when it is interactive. But he already has television; although it is not interactive, it satisfies a lot of entertainment needs. Entertainment alone is not enough to justify spending even more money than the TV cost to have a PC in the home.

Information delivery is another possible use for a consumer PC. This is exciting to us because multimedia is great for information delivery. But how much information does the consumer want or need? He already has TV, radio, newspapers, magazines, and books to bring him information—is there room for yet another different (and expensive) medium? I don't think so—at least not yet. Maybe there will be when the present children, who are growing up with computers, begin having their own households, but that's still some years away.

The foregoing gives a picture of how and why the consumer market is different from the PC market. Multimedia is starting in the PC market, and I think it will flourish there long before it becomes a consumer product.

Television Broadcasting

Television broadcasting is analog—the signals we receive at home are analog signals, and they are displayed on an analog video display. Although there are some digital features in high-end TV receivers, such as picture-in-picture or still framing, a TV receiver uses mostly analog processing. This will change in the future, driven by the same Moore's law we have been talking about, which applies directly to digital ICs, but not so directly to analog chips. Thus, someday the ever-lowering cost of digital processing will drop below the cost of analog processing and TV sets will suddenly become digital. I won't try to guess when that may happen.

However, at the broadcasting end of TV the story is very different. Technological decisions are driven much more by performance and functionality instead of only cost considerations. TV broadcast stations are heavily digital today because digital technology frees them from the accumulated distortions of analog circuits, and digital processing can produce the striking special effects that we see all the time on TV.

The digital processing in a TV station is mostly done by special-purpose hardware, not by computers; PCs are widely used, but just for control. The reason is that until very recently, PCs could not run fast enough to do high-quality video processing in real time. That is changing—caused partly by the things we are doing in the multimedia industry. Some of today's multimedia hardware, such as DVI Technology, can do a lot of the special effects in real time. This is already leading to consideration of the use of PCs for some kinds of broadcast processing, especially video tape editing. I believe we will see broadcast TV and computer multimedia coming closer together in the future.

Computer motion video today is struggling to catch up to broadcast TV video quality; it will soon be there. But the goal may also soon move away, because the TV industry is developing new standards of much higher image quality called High Definition TV (HDTV). HDTV is completely a standards issue; there are many technical approaches, but TV broadcasting *must* have a single standard. Since central transmitters are broadcasting to millions of receivers, the signals broadcast and all the receivers must be built to the same standards for the system to work. Reaching agreement on standards for HDTV is proving to be difficult and slow, but it will be accomplished, and HDTV will begin to be distributed in the second half of the '90s. (Note that it is already being broadcast in Japan.)

HDTV will make a volume market for high-resolution displays and other hardware that we can use in computers. When HDTV goes to full-scale marketing, we can expect that there will be spin-off products (like displays) that will lower costs for computer multimedia and make higher resolutions practical.

Audio Production and the Music Industry

The audio industry is way ahead in digital technology. In fact, it has given us three of the key technologies of digital multimedia: the CD-ROM disc, MIDI, and digital audio algorithms. As multimedia grows, there will be even more cross-fertilization because the existing infrastructure for audio production and postproduction is directly applicable to multimedia. Similarly, the hardware and software developed for multimedia audio will also be used to make professional audio postproduction tools.

Uses of Multimedia

The last trend I will discuss that affects the growth of multimedia is the use of multimedia itself. In this book, I spoke of using multimedia for information delivery, training and education, selling, and entertainment. These are basic uses, but there are many other possibilities that fall between or outside of these. One of the problems at this stage of the industry development is that we can't see all the uses that will be found for the technology, so I won't try to give you a list. But believe me, new uses are there and they will emerge as the growing volume of multimedia equipment and software brings more people into the game.

NOW FOR THE FORECAST

The foregoing discussion of trends almost delivers the forecast itself. It is difficult to look at what is happening in all of the different segments of this industry and not see that an explosion of multimedia will occur. Everything appears ripe for multimedia to go to the big time in the first half of the 1990s. I'll put it in the form of a scenario:

- Multimedia standards are developed.
- Multimedia extensions are added to popular operating systems.
- Packaged multimedia PCs are offered.
- Audio and video add-in boards are available for existing systems.
- DVI Technology is available on one board.
- Various authoring systems add multimedia capabilities (this is where we are in mid-1992).
- Authored applications begin to appear for information delivery, training, and selling.
- Hardware roll-outs of corporate training systems and information kiosks occur around the world.
- Multilanguage multimedia systems are introduced.
- Intel introduces the third-generation DVI chips and the 586 CPU chip.
- Desktop users start buying multimedia systems for business presentation use.
- Multimedia PCs are introduced with all hardware integrated on the motherboard.
- Multimedia service companies begin to appear.
- Multimedia in education becomes a national priority.
- Entertainment applications on multimedia computers begin to displace dedicated video games.

The scenario could go on, but I'm sure you get the idea. This industry is pulling itself up by its bootstraps, driven by the tremendous potential of systems which:

- make information easily available to the public;
- enhance education and training to be more effective, more convenient, more fun, and lower cost;
- allow products to be demonstrated and sold at lower cost;
- provide interesting and absorbing entertainment; and
- make every business manager and educator a producer.

Digital multimedia is the future of the personal computer industry. We are not far from the time when every computer will have multimedia audio and video capabilities in the same way that every PC today has a video display. In schools, at offices, in homes, and in stores, multimedia computers will be demonstrating their value. Now is the time for everyone who wants to be on the crest of the wave to get into multimedia computing.

Bon Voyage!

Appendix A

Multimedia Hardware

This appendix lists multimedia hardware sources, grouped into categories. It is not intended to be a complete list of suppliers; rather, it gives some key multimedia hardware products to help you begin your search. Each section begins with a discussion of the considerations in choosing products for that category; this goes beyond and is more technical than the similar discussions in Chapter 2.

SYSTEMS

There are hundreds of system manufacturers, and each has several models. It is totally impractical to make any recommendations about specific systems, especially since the market is changing so fast. Instead, this section will review the considerations that should go into choosing a system for multimedia delivery or authoring.

CPU

For delivery use only, you can get along with a 386SX system, but for authoring use, we recommend that you choose at least a 386DX, and better still, a 486DX system. In either case, go for the highest clock speed that you can afford. The Intel 486DX2 "Clock Doubler" CPU, which runs internally twice as fast as the motherboard, is an attractive choice because it gives you some of the benefits of increased CPU speed without the cost of making the entire system run faster.

Bus Architecture

There are three choices for the bus architecture of a system: the ISA (Industry Standard Architecture) bus, the IBM PS/2 Micro Channel bus, and the EISA (Extended ISA) bus. All are software compatible with each other, but there are performance and price differences. The three bus architectures are not entirely compatible for add-in hardware or boards; if you want the maximum performance from the system, you must get boards that are specific to your bus architecture. The least expensive (and the most common) bus is the ISA; it is a 16-bit bus that was first introduced in the IBM PC/AT, and it is used by all low-priced IBM-compatible systems. This is where most of the "hundreds of suppliers" are.

The Micro Channel bus was introduced by IBM in the PS/2 product line. It is not offered by many other vendors. The Micro Channel is a 32-bit bus, meaning that it is inherently somewhat more expensive than the ISA bus, but it is potentially higher in performance. It also offers features such as *bus mastering*, which facilitates building systems that have multiple CPUs. However, the advanced features of Micro Channel require specialized add-in hardware, and as yet no large markets for this have developed, so there is not much hardware that uses these features. IBM is one of the pioneers in multimedia, and they have made sure their systems are competitive for multimedia—you can't go wrong with IBM!

The EISA bus resulted from a consortium of vendors who designed a high-performance bus to compete with the IBM Micro Channel. EISA is a 32-bit bus with even more features that the Micro Channel, and, more importantly, you can also use ISA boards in an EISA machine. However, EISA machines are expensive, and as with Micro Channel, there is not much of the special hardware that can take advantage of EISA's high-performance features.

Some of the newer machine designs are using what is called a *local bus*, which is a special bus that runs at CPU speed but is separate from the main system bus. It is a second bus that is closely coupled to the CPU, but is limited to certain specific uses; for example, almost all systems today use this approach for the main memory on the motherboard.

Caches

Most systems offer cache options, sometimes several different types. Cache is special memory that lets the system speed up data output to the CPU. Cache is associated either with the CPU itself, which affects all data coming to or going from the CPU, or it is associated with mass storage and thus affects only I/O from storage. There are many strategies for operating caches.

Disk cache is special memory which stores data from the most recent disk accesses. The idea is that if you make repeated accesses to the same data (which is a common thing to do in many applications), the repeats can be read from memory instead of going to the disk; this will be faster. Disk caching can be provided either by software, which uses part of the main system RAM, or (better) it can be a separate hardware high-speed memory. The latter approach may get expensive, but it offers the best performance. Some disk controller cards have caching built into them; in other cases, the cache is a motherboard function.

Disk caches may not offer as much improvement to multimedia as they do for other kinds of applications because repeated use of the same data is not so common in multimedia. For example, in playing motion video, massive amounts of data have to be transferred from storage, but each frame is only used once and then the next part of the stream is accessed. A cache will not help this kind of access.

There are various strategies or algorithms for using cache memory, which further complicate the situation. If you are considering an expensive cache option, you ought to ask for an opportunity to make some tests with your multimedia software to determine whether it will actually be an improvement for the kind of work you will be doing.

The other kind of cache memory is CPU cache. This is high-speed memory that is connected directly to the CPU chip and stores instruction blocks currently being executed and data blocks. There is 8 K of this kind of cache built into the 486DX chip. CPU cache can also be provided with high-speed memory, which is closely coupled to the CPU and managed by a *cache controller* chip. CPU caching offers significant speed-up for CPU-intensive processes, which does include many of the tasks in multimedia.

MASS STORAGE

There are probably as many manufacturers and options for mass storage as there are for systems. However, unless you are a hardware expert, you are going to have to choose from the mass storage options offered by the system manufacturer you are working with. This is because mass storage is usually tightly connected into the system; except for SCSI systems (explained below), it is difficult to interface your own mass storage.

We will concentrate on magnetic hard drives in this discussion. These are the most common—every PC has at least one hard drive. They provide read/write operation with reasonable speeds. There are also optical drives: CD-ROM (read-only), and various types of optical WORM (write-once, read many) drives, and writeable optical drives (most are magneto-optical [MO] type). Only the CD-ROM will be covered later.

The most important parameter of a mass storage unit is its *capacity*, expressed in megabytes. Single drives have capacities from 20 megabytes up to 1.2 gigabytes (1200 megabytes). Higher capacities can be obtained by using multiple drives. We have said repeatedly that you should get all the capacity you can afford, especially if you are going to author large applications. Drive prices are more or less proportional to the capacity, everything else being equal. Drive prices are also slowly dropping over time, although it is nothing like what is happening with silicon devices.

The next most important parameter is the drive's *access time*, the time for the drive to position its read/write head over the track containing the desired data. Access times are measured in milliseconds (1/1000 second), and values for current large drives range from about 10 to 20 milliseconds.

Then you should look at the *data transfer rate* for the drive. This is how fast data can be read or written by the drive, measured in megabytes per second. The data transfer must go through the system's main bus, and it depends on the interface and controller type (see below) as well as on the mechanical design of the drive itself. Transfer rate is not always specified, but it ranges from 1 to 15 megabytes per second; look for a specification of the transfer rate when the drive is actually interfaced to your desired system. Of course, you are looking for the highest numbers.

Mass storage devices require a hardware *controller* and driver software. For the main drive of the system, the driver software is usually in the ROM of the system or in ROM in the drive unit, meaning that it is built into a hardware chip and cannot be changed except by replacing the chip. The controller may either be part of the drive unit itself, on an add-in board, or built onto the system motherboard. Unless you plan to add additional drives later, it doesn't matter where the controller is.

What does matter is the type of drive interface—there are three principal ones: IDE, ESDI, and SCSI. In addition, there are various options for controllers, particularly associated with caching. The IDE (Integrated Drive Electronics) interface is the most common, but it also has the slowest data transfer rate, because it connects directly to the system bus. The ESDI (Enhanced System Drive Interface) provides greater transfer speed, but at greater expense. The SCSI (Small Computer System Interface) interface provides the most flexibility; it has good speed, and it is becoming more and more popular. SCSI is also the interface normally used with all optical drives, including CD-ROM.

The advantage of SCSI is that once you have put a SCSI interface on your system, it is like another bus, to which you can then easily add additional devices, by simply daisy-chaining them with cables. So the same interface can support your main hard drive, additional external hard drives, and CD-ROM drives.

CD-ROM DRIVES

CD-ROM drives are becoming more popular as their prices drop and their performance improves. All drives have approximately the same capacity of 680 megabytes and a data transfer rate of 150 kilobytes per second (these are standardized). The access time specification is the most important performance parameter; it varies considerably between drives and is currently the main element of competition between manufacturers. Even the best drives are slow—access times range from about 300 milliseconds to over 1 second. These numbers severely limit the performance of multimedia from CD-ROM, and you should go for the fastest access (smallest number) you can find. Access times should continue to improve as drive manufacturers give more attention to it, but it is unlikely that they will ever get down to the range of magnetic hard drives.

The maximum data transfer rate of a CD-ROM is standardized. However, some drives are interfaced in such a way that they cannot support continuous transfer at the maximum rate. That is an important requirement for multimedia motion video. You should make sure that your drive will do continuous transfer at the maximum rate.

A new type of CD-ROM drive that supports data transfer at 300 Kb/second (double the standard rate) has just come on the market. These drives also operate at the standard data rate for CD audio and other systems that require that rate. Wider availability of this new format will give a boost to motion video performance from CD-ROM.

CD-ROM drives vary in the way that they handle the CD disc itself. Most drives use a *caddy*, which is a container something like the jewel boxes that Compact Discs are shipped in. A caddy protects the disc and supports it in the drive; but unless you have a lot of caddies (they're not cheap), you are always moving discs between caddies. The other approach for disc handling uses a drawer like most audio CD players. This is simpler and cheaper, but it does not protect the discs as well, and drawer drives do not generally have the fastest access times.

Some manufacturers of CD-ROM drives are:

Hitachi Home Electronics America
Multimedia Systems Division
401 W. Artesia Blvd.
Compton, CA 90220

NEC Technologies
1255 Michael Dr.
Wood Dale, IL 60191-1094

Panasonic Communications & Systems Co.
CD-ROM Sales
Two Panasonic Way
Secaucus, NJ 07094

Sony Corp. of America
Computer Peripheral Products Co.
655 River Oaks Pkwy.
San Jose, CA 95134

Toshiba America
Information Systems—Disk Products Division
9740 Irvine Blvd.
Irvine, CA 92718

DIGITAL VIDEO BOARDS

This section covers video boards that support 16 bpp or higher. These are sometimes referred to as *true color* (24 bpp) or *high color* (16 bpp) boards. DVI boards, which meet this criterion, are covered in a separate section below. Boards that simply display analog video on the computer screen are not discussed; the boards covered here digitize analog inputs and provide full support for manipulation, storage, and display of the digital images.

Quite a few true color video boards are now appearing for use with Windows 3.x, and some are supported for OS/2 also. Many of these boards contain an accelerator or coprocessor to speed up the image manipulation and/or graphics under Windows. This is an important feature because direct CPU processing of 16 bbp or 24 bpp screens is pretty slow even with a fast 386 CPU. However, accelerators add to the cost of the board and their effectiveness depends on application programs being written a certain way. As a general statement: Make sure your intended software will support your intended board!

Most of the boards are designed for desktop publishing (DTP) use and do not necessarily have some of the features we need for multimedia. For example, in DTP you normally work with only one screen at a time, so most boards have a memory size that only holds one screen. In multimedia, you often want to have one screen in view, and at least one other screen being prepared off-screen. Many of the true color boards will not support this.

Because DTP users typically want resolution higher than 640 × 480 in order to show a full page, or maybe two pages at a time, many of the boards are designed to work at 1024 × 768 or even higher resolution. While this seems like a good feature, it is a liability for multimedia because of the extra data requirements that go along with higher resolution. This translates into larger disk files and slower loading. Another consideration of the higher resolutions is that display monitor costs go up significantly. More than 640 × 480 resolution is not worthwhile for multimedia now.

Another feature that is not uniform among these boards is what they refer to as *VGA pass-through*. This is the ability to display a standard VGA screen as well as the true color screen. This issue arises because many of the boards use NTSC-style interlaced scanning for the true color screen, which does not work for a VGA screen. With these boards you must use two monitors: one for true color, one for VGA. Some boards provide for single monitor use by mode switching, or by having a two-plane approach as is used in the DVI boards.

There is a good reason to have a mode for NTSC or PAL output: to create a presentation and record it on video tape. You must have NTSC or PAL standard output to do that; a VCR cannot record a VGA output. Thus, the ability to switch from NTSC or PAL to VGA is important (DVI boards do this, too).

The type of video input supported by the boards is another important parameter. Some boards have NTSC input only, others support NTSC and PAL or S-video, and still others support RGB. A few boards support all types (as do DVI boards). For the highest quality still images, you want RGB input; for compatibility with VCRs you also will need NTSC. Either can be obtained from the other through a converter module, such as the Truevision VID-I/O module, but this is an additional expense.

Some manufacturers of true color boards are:

Truevision, Inc.
7340 Shadeland Station
Indianapolis, IN 46256

RasterOps Corporation
2500 Walsh Ave.
Santa Clara, CA 95051

Matrox Electronic Systems, Ltd.
1055 St. Regis Blvd.
Dorval, Quebec
Canada H9P 2T4

Ventek Corporation
31336 Via Calinas, Suite 102
Westlake Village, CA 91362

Bleu Mont
4900 Jean-Talon West, Suite 220
Montreal, Quebec
Canada H4P 1W9

Hercules Computer Technology, Inc.
921 Parker St.
Berkeley, CA 94710

DIGITAL AUDIO BOARDS

The addition of audio support to Windows 3.1 has increased the number of digital audio boards available. Some of the important parameters of these boards are discussed below.

First, the number of bits per sample on the board determines the ultimate quality capability of the board. Some boards are 8 bits/sample, which is marginally acceptable for speech and simple music, but cannot in any way be called hi-fi. The other end of the range is 16 bits/sample, which is equivalent to CD-quality audio. You should also check that both the input (analog-digital conversion) and the output (digital-analog conversion) have the same number of bits per sample. The board's overall quality will be determined by whichever of these numbers is lower.

Next, consider the board's capability for sample rate. It should cover the entire range from telephone-quality rates (8 kilosamples/second) to the CD rates (44.1 kilosamples/second). The board also should have programmable input and output analog filters, which track the sample rates; this will assure minimizing of aliasing distortion.

Some audio boards contain *digital signal processor* (DSP) chips, which give them the capability to do audio compression or decompression, speech synthesis, music synthesis, and other functions. However, all of these features must be supported with special DSP software, which is normally provided by the board manufacturer.

Some audio boards also contain music synthesizer chips. This is becoming more popular because it is part of the proposed MPC specification, and MIDI synthesizers are supported by Windows 3.1. Finally, you must choose between mono or stereo operation, and you should be sure that your intended software supports your intended audio board.

Some manufacturers of audio boards are:

Sound Blaster, Sound Blaster Pro
Creative Labs, Inc.
2050 Duane Ave.
Santa Clara, CA 95054

Multisound
Turtle Beach Systems
Cyber Center, Unit 23
1600 Pennsylvania Ave.
York, PA 17404

DVI BOARDS

DVI Technology is the leading approach for full integration of audio and motion video on PCs or Macintosh computers. There are several boards available, and there is a lot of software support becoming available.

The ActionMedia II DVI boards for PCs and PS/2s are available from IBM and Intel, and The EyeQ DVI board for the Macintosh is available from New Video Corporation. Dolch Computer Systems and FAST Electronics have announced DVI boards. Contact information follows:

Dolch Computer Systems, Inc.
372 Turquiose St.
Milpitas, CA 95035

FAST Electronics
5 Commonwealth Rd.
Natick, MA 01760

Intel Corporation
Multimedia Products Operation
313 Enterprise Dr.
Plainsboro, NJ 08458

IBM Corporation
4111 Northside Pkwy.
Atlanta, GA 30327

New Video Corporation
220 Main St., Suite C
Venice, CA 90291

VIDEO CAMERAS

Video cameras range from home camcorders to broadcast cameras and cover prices from less than $1,000 to more than $100,000. Both performance and features of cameras increase with price; but in this case, what improves the most is picture performance. The lowest priced cameras are significantly lacking in picture quality compared to the needs of multimedia, particularly when it comes to still images. In the case of motion video, home cameras are not quite so limited; this is because the motion video performance of multimedia is itself limited (at present). If you are buying a camera for still images, you should at least look at mid-range cameras to get the performance you will be satisfied with.

Two features of a camera contribute the most to still image performance for digital multimedia: the type of sensor configuration and RGB output. Most low-priced cameras use a single sensor, usually a solid state CCD array. Color is obtained by some kind of multiplexing of this array using a color filter pattern over the array. This contributes to loss of resolution in most cases. Putting three separate sensors in the camera, one for each of the red, green, and blue channels, removes the single-sensor limitation. However, it increases the price substantially, often double or more; but for best quality of still images, it is worth it. Along with three sensors, the camera should have RGB separate outputs (three cables). Most three-sensor cameras have RGB outputs available; even some single-sensor cameras have it. Of course, an RGB camera must be used with a video board that has an RGB input.

There are many other camera features, such as automatic iris (desirable, although there should be a way to turn it off), automatic focusing (not too important), zoom lenses (desirable), various power management features in portable cameras (desirable), and automatic white balance (desirable, if it uses the white card method). You can make the most of the feature choices by considering the way you will use the camera; the general multimedia issues have been covered above and also in Chapter 2.

Some manufacturers of video cameras are:

Sony Corp. of America
Business and Professional Group
3 Paragon Dr.
Montvale, NJ 07645

Panasonic Broadcast and Television Systems
1 Panasonic Way
Secaucus, NJ 07094

VIDEO RECORDING EQUIPMENT

Recording equipment is available for use in the home, for professional or industrial video use, and for broadcast use. All home and professional recorders work with a composite signal, NTSC or PAL; there are some broadcast recorders that record a *component* format that separates the luminance and chrominance into two channels, and there are broadcast digital recorders that record RGB format. However, most broadcast equipment is too expensive to consider for desktop multimedia.

Home recorders are available as separate recording machines (VCRs), and as combined camera-recorder units—camcorders. There are two major formats: VHS and 8mm. These use different sizes of tapes and are totally incompatible with each other. Thus, you should choose one or the other for all of your equipment. VHS is older and more widespread; its performance is adequate for multimedia video that will be compressed with RTV, but it is not good enough to get the best from PLV compression.

8mm is a newer format that uses a smaller tape and thus, the equipment is smaller. 8mm performance is slightly better than VHS, although it still is not good enough for the best PLV. You will sometimes see better pictures from either VHS or 8mm than you see from PLV, but neither one is so good that it is transparent to PLV. The problem is that the distortions of VCRs and PLV are different, so when you use a poor VCR, the PLV tends to show *both* its own distortions and the VCR distortion.

To get beyond the problem of accumulating distortions, you should go to a better tape format. There are two formats based on the same tape sizes as VHS or 8mm, but they use better recording methods and thus get better results. These are S-VHS and Hi-8. Equipment is made in these formats for both the high end of the home market and the professional/industrial market. The difference is that professional equipment has more of the features you need for postproduction. We recommend this equipment for desktop multimedia use.

Another older format that is widely used in the professional market is the U-MATIC format, which has 3/4" tape. The equipment is larger and the tape cassettes are larger (book size). Performance is not necessarily better, however, especially with the older equipment. New S-VHS or Hi-8 equipment will outperform the old U-MATIC equipment. However, current U-MATIC equipment uses better technology and its performance is excellent for multimedia.

Some manufacturers of professional video recording equipment are:

Sony Corp. of America
Business and Professional Group
3 Paragon Dr.
Montvale, NJ 07645

Panasonic Broadcast and Television Systems
1 Panasonic Way
Secaucus, NJ 07094

IMAGE SCANNERS

Because of desktop publishing there are now many color image scanners on the market that are suitable for multimedia use. Scanners come in three forms: flatbed, slide, and handheld scanners.

Flatbed scanners are the most popular. Most of them handle up to letter- or legal-size documents and scan at resolutions up to 300 dots (pixels) per inch (dpi). Notice that the resolution of scanners is specified in terms of the input rather than the output. A 300 dpi scan of an 8 1/2" wide document will produce 2550 pixels per line—far more than any multimedia resolution we would use. However, most scanning software will handle the scaling of the scanned image to a specified output resolution, such as 512 pixels per line. The advantage of this is that for a large image going in, the scanner's resolution is so good that there is no loss from it. Also, if you have a small image such as a 3 1/2" × 5" photo, the scanner still has good enough resolution to give you excellent results.

Color flatbed scanners are either the three-pass or the one-pass type. This refers to the number of scans needed to get all three colors out. This can affect the scanning time, but scan times vary so much between machines that you can't draw any conclusion about passes. Scan times per complete color image vary from 15 seconds to more than 2 minutes for different machines.

Slide scanners are specialized machines that only handle 35mm slides. They are expensive for what they do. Some flatbed scanners have a mode where they can scan a transparency—this will also work for slides, although on a 35mm slide, the 300 dpi resolution is a little low.

Handheld scanners are inexpensive, but they are tricky to use and can typically only scan a 4" wide image. They are not recommended for desktop multimedia.

Some manufacturers of color scanner equipment are:

Chinon America, Inc.
660 Maple Ave.
Torrance, CA 90503

Epson America, Inc.
20770 Madrona Ave.
Torrance, CA 90503

Hewlett-Packard Co.
19310 Pruneridge Ave.
Cupertino, CA 95014

Howtek, Inc.
21 Park Ave.
Hudson, NH 03051

Microtek Lab Inc.
680 Knox St.
Torrance, CA 90502

AUDIO EQUIPMENT

Audio equipment (tape decks, mixers, effects processors, etc.) comes in three different levels of functionality and price: home, musician, and professional. In fact, there is practically a continuum of choices between the lowest and the highest level. We used the word *functionality* above, rather than *performance* or *quality* because equipment at all levels will give good audio quality, and the major difference between the levels is not in quality, but rather in features.

You can make acceptable recording for multimedia on a home cassette recorder, but you will have a lot of trouble using that equipment for editing or other postproduction tasks because home recorders lack the kind of control features needed to do editing. A musician-level tape deck provides some editing features, but a professional-level deck will have complete time code capability with computer control, which is the way the professionals do audio editing.

We recommend musician-level audio equipment for most desktop multimedia use. This equipment provides an excellent selection of features at attractive prices, because the musician market is very large and highly competitive. Some manufacturers are:

Yamaha Corporation of America
Digital Musical Instruments
P.O. Box 6600
Buena Park, CA 90622-6600

Roland Corporation US
7200 Dominion Circle
Los Angeles, CA 90040-3647

Fostex
(see your local music store)

(TASCAM)
TEAC America, Inc.
7733 Telegraph Rd.
Montebello, CA 90640

Appendix B

Multimedia Software

This appendix lists multimedia software sources, grouped into categories. It is not intended to be a complete list of suppliers, rather it is a list of some key multimedia software products to help you begin your search.

OPERATING SYSTEMS AND EXTENSIONS

The principal PC operating systems are MS-DOS and OS/2. Under MS-DOS there is Microsoft Windows, which is often thought of as an operating system, but it's really an extension to MS-DOS. Windows will become a stand-alone system that does not require MS-DOS when Windows NT comes out. Nevertheless, we'll talk of Windows here as if it were an operating system.

Both Windows 3.1 and OS/2 2.0 have added some functionality for multimedia; in particular, they support some audio and animation systems. They use the MCI approach, although IBM calls it MPM. However, additional extension is still needed to access DVI hardware for either of these operating systems. Intel has developed the Audio Video Kernel (AVK) driver for this purpose; AVK is available for both Windows and OS/2, but it is a low-level DVI-specific interface suitable for C programmers. A higher-level interface (but still for C programmers) to DVI hardware based on MCI is available for Windows, and a similar interface is being developed for OS/2. Application developers for Windows and OS/2 are using these interfaces. Operating system suppliers are:

MS-DOS, Windows
Microsoft Corporation
One Microsoft Way
P.O. Box 97017
Redmond, WA 98073

OS/2
IBM Corporation
1-800-342-6672

DVI drivers
Intel Corporation
Multimedia Products Operation
313 Enterprise Dr.
Plainsboro, NJ 08536

Networking software for DVI technology
ProtoComm, Inc.
Two Neshaminy Interplex
Suite 100
Trevose, PA 19047

AUTHORING PACKAGES

There are hundreds of authoring packages for different platforms and different peripheral hardware. In this section, we will list only those vendors who either have DVI support or are planning it. Many of these companies are leading participants in other authoring arenas, so this list is a good cross-section of the authoring industry. The name of a company's authoring product(s) precedes the company name and address in the listing.

Toolbook
Asymetrix Corporation
110 110th Ave., NE, Suite 700
Bellevue, WA 98004

Authorware Professional for Windows
Authorware, Inc.
275 Shoreline Dr., Fourth Floor
Redwood City, CA 94065

Authology: Multimedia, Tourguide
CEIT Systems, Inc.
12638 Beatrice St.
Los Angeles, CA 90066

Action!
Macromind • Paracomp, Inc.
600 Townsend
San Francisco, CA 94103

MEDIAscript DOS, MEDIAscript OS/2 Desktop Edition, MEDIAscript OS/2 Professional Edition
Network Technology Corporation
7401-F Fullerton Rd.
Springfield, VA 22153

Harvard Graphics, Superbase 4
Software Publishing Corporation
3165 Kifer Rd.
Santa Clara, CA 95051

PAINT OR DRAW PACKAGES

Through image file conversion, you can draw in almost any format and convert the result to any other format for use in your application. A very capable file conversion tool that runs under MS-DOS or Windows is:

Hijaak 2
Inset Systems
71 Commerce Dr.
Brookfield, CT 06804

The following are suppliers of paint or draw packages, with the names of their products listed first:

Corel Draw!
Corel Systems Corporation
1600 Carling Ave.
Ottawa, Ontario
Canada K1Z 8R7

Windows Draw, Designer
Micrografx, Inc.
1303 Arapaho Rd.
Richardson, TX 75081

Lumena
Time Arts, Inc.
1425 Corporate Center Pkwy.
Santa Rosa, CA 95407

PC Paintbrush, Publisher's Paintbrush
ZSoft, Inc.
450 Franklin Rd., Suite 100
Marietta, GA 30067

VIDEO COMPRESSION SERVICE

This is the Intel PLV Compression Service for DVI Technology motion video.

Intel Multimedia Products Operation
Compression Services
313 Enterprise Dr.
Plainsboro, NJ 08536

Glossary

access time In mass storage devices, the time from issuance of a command to read or write a specific location until reading or writing actually begins at that location.

ActionMedia II The Intel trademark for the DVI Technology delivery and capture boards, which provide DVI audio and motion video capability to PC and PS/2 computers.

A/D *See* analog to digital conversion.

additive color system A color reproduction system in which an image is reproduced by mixing appropriate amounts of red, green, and blue lights.

ADR *See* Automatic Dialog Replacement.

algorithm A group of processing steps that perform a particular operation, such as drawing a line or compressing a digital image.

aliasing In sampling, the impairment produced when the input signal contains frequency components higher than half of the sampling rate. Typically produces jagged steps on diagonal edges. *See* antialiasing.

analog Any system in which values are represented by continuous scales.

analog to digital conversion (A/D) The process of converting an analog signal into a digital bit stream. Includes the steps of sampling and quantizing.

analog video Video in which all the information representing images is in a continuous-scale electrical signal for both amplitude and time.

antialiasing The process of reducing the visibility of aliasing by using gray scale pixel values to smooth the appearance of jagged edges.

API *See* Application Programming Interface.

application A computer program written for a specific purpose.

Glossary

Application Programming Interface (API)   The means whereby an application communicates with the system software. An API is usually specified in terms of one or more computer languages, such as C or Pascal.

array   A group of data in computer memory consisting of a number of identical items placed end to end.

aspect ratio   The ratio of the width to the height of an electronic image. For broadcast television and most computer displays, the standard aspect ratio is 4:3.

asset   A data item (file) for a multimedia application. Typical assets contain audio, video, images, or text data.

Audio-Video Support System (AVSS)   In DVI Technology, the name for the format of audio and video files.

authoring   The process of creating a multimedia application.

Automatic Dialog Replacement (ADR)   a process used in audio postproduction for movies or video where the original dialog track is replaced by a new track created in a sound studio by the actor(s).

AVSS   *See* Audio-Video Support System.

balanced line   In audio production and postproduction equipment, a form of interconnecting cable that uses two signal wires to effectively cancel interfering signals.

bandwidth   Refers to the frequency range transmitted by an analog system. In video systems, specifying the highest frequency value is sufficient, since all video systems must transmit frequencies down to 30 Hz or lower.

bitmap   A region of memory or storage that contains the pixels representing an image arranged in the sequence in which they are normally scanned to display the image.

bitmap font   A special format of a text font that contains pixel values for each text character.

bits per pixel (bpp)   The number of bits used to represent the color value of each pixel in a digitized image.

bpp   *See* bits per pixel.

branching In a computer program, the act of jumping to another location in the program, instead of just continuing with the next instruction in the program.

bulleting In a list of text items, the inclusion of a highlighting character or bullet at the start of each item.

cast animation A form of animation where each frame is built by choosing and positioning *cast members* on top of a background. Also called *cel animation*.

CBT *See* Computer-Based Training.

CCD *See* Charge-Coupled Device.

CD *See* Compact Disc.

CD-I *See* Compact Disc-Interactive.

CD-ROM *See* Compact Disc-Read-Only Memory.

cel An abbreviation for *celluloid*, used in *cel animation*.

cel animation A form of animation where each frame is built by choosing and positioning objects (cels) in front of a background. Also called *cast animation*.

Central Processing Unit The unit that performs system control and computing in a personal computer. The CPU is usually a single microprocessor chip.

Charge-Coupled Device A video camera pickup device or sensor using a particular form of solidstate technology.

chroma *See* chrominance.

chrominance In an image reproduction system, the signals that represent the color components of the image, such as hue and saturation. A black-and-white image will have chrominance values of zero. Used in the NTSC television system. (Sometimes abbreviated as chroma.)

clapboard A device used in video production that consists of a slate and a hinged arm at the top. At the start of each take of a scene, the clapboard is held briefly in front of the camera; the slate contains the scene and take identification, and the hinged arm is snapped down to make a sound, which marks the audio track.

clock-doubler Refers to a particular form of microprocessor chip that runs internally twice as fast as the clock frequency provided to it.

clock frequency In a microprocessor chip (CPU), the frequency that controls all operations of the chip. Frequency is given in *megaHertz* (MHz).

CLUT *See* color lookup table.

color lookup table (CLUT) A table of color values with any bpp format, and indexed by a pixel value of smaller bpp. This allows display of a selected group of colors by a low bpp system, in which the group of colors is chosen from a much larger range (the *palette*) of colors represented by the bpp value used in the CLUT.

color scanner A device that takes hard copy images or photographs and converts them to a digital data file by moving an image sensing device across the image (scanning).

color subsampling The technique of using reduced resolution for the color difference components of a video signal compared to the luminance component. Typically, the color difference resolution is reduced by a factor of 2 or 4.

Common User Access (CUA) A user interface definition provided by IBM in order to have uniformity between all applications.

Compact Disc (CD) The 12 cm (4.75 in.) optical read-only disc used for digital audio, data, or video in different systems.

Compact Disc-Interactive (CD-I) An interactive audio/video/computer system developed by Sony and Philips for the consumer market.

Compact Disc-Read-Only Memory (CD-ROM) An adaptation of the Compact Disc for use with general digital data.

compiler A computer program that converts high-level computer language statements into executable computer instructions.

component video A color video signal system that uses more than one signal to describe a color image. Typical component systems are R,G,B; Y,I,Q; or Y,U,V.

composite video A color video signal system that contains all of the color information in one signal. Typical composite television standard signals are NTSC, PAL, and SECAM.

compression A digital process that allows data to be stored or transmitted using less than the normal number of bits. Video compression refers to techniques that reduce the number of bits required to store or transmit images.

Computer-Based Training (CBT) the use of a computer to deliver programmed one-on-one personal training.

condition In a computer language, a statement that specifies a relationship between variables or constants that will be tested by the program to determine what should happen next.

context-sensitive In computer applications, making the next action responsive to what the user has recently been doing. It is most often applied to on-line help systems, where the help information relates to what the user was trying to do at the time help was requested.

contouring In a digital system, the appearance of patterns in a digitized image because the quantization did not have enough levels.

coordinates On a computer screen, the system of numbers that specifies position relative to an origin point. Usually given in the form x,y where x is a horizontal position and y is a vertical position.

coprocessor A microprocessor chip that runs parallel to the main system CPU.

CPU *See* Central Processing Unit.

CUA *See* Common User Access.

cueing The process of positioning an audio or video tape at a specified starting point in the prerecorded material.

cyan The color obtained by mixing equal intensities of green and blue light. It is also the correct name for the subtractive primary color usually called blue.

data-driven engine A computer program that performs a process based on command data that it receives in data files, usually text.

data rate The speed of a data transfer process, normally expressed in bits per second or bytes per second. For example, the data rate of CD-ROM is 150,000 bytes per second.

DDE *See* Dynamic Data Exchange.

decibel (dB) A logarithmic unit for expression of ratios. It is based on the generic unit bel; 1 bel equals a 10:1 power ratio, decibel is 1/10 bel. Thus, 10 dB also is a 10:1 power ratio, 20 dB is a 100:1 power ratio. Since voltage ratios are the square root of power ratios, it takes 20 dB for a 10:1 voltage ratio or 40 dB for a 100:1 voltage ratio.

delta frame In a compressed video stream, a frame that is defined by identifying changes from the previous frame.

device-independent In computer graphics software, an interface specification that does not depend on the characteristics of any particular hardware.

digital A system in which values are represented by a series of binary bits.

digital video Video in which all the information representing images is in computer data form, and can be manipulated and displayed by a computer.

digitizing The process of converting an analog signal into a digital signal. With images, it refers to the processes of scanning and analog to digital conversion.

distribution For a computer application, the process of making multiple copies for use by many customers or users.

DLL *See* Dynamic Link Library.

driver A software entity that provides a software interface to a specific piece of hardware. For example, the DVI video driver provides software access to the video board hardware.

DVI Technology A hardware and software system developed by Intel and IBM to add audio and motion video capability to personal computers.

Dynamic Data Exchange (DDE) An interprocess communication technique for Windows and OS/2. Using DDE, applications can send and receive data once a communication path is established.

Dynamic Link Library (DLL) A form of computer program that contains routines or functions that may be used by a number of applications.

edit decision list In audio or video postproduction, a list of commands and values that defines a series of edits to be made in order to assemble a scene.

engine In a computer program, a program segment that performs a specified process.

executable file A file that contains instructions that can be executed by the CPU; a computer program.

file header A block of data in a file, usually at the beginning, which describes the type of data in the file and the format of the data.

filename The logical name of a computer file. For most systems, it is in the "8.3" format: up to an 8-character name, and then an optional filename extension consisting of a period and one to three alphanumeric characters.

filename extension An optional extension to a filename, consisting of a period followed by one to three alphanumeric characters.

Foley In motion picture or video postproduction, a Foley studio contains equipment that can create sound effects that are synchronized with the picture. A sound effect engineer watches the picture on a screen while performing actions in the studio that make the sounds needed to match the actions in the picture, such as walking, breaking glass, etc.

font A definition for drawing a set of text characters. It may be either in the form of a bitmap for each character or a mathematical description of how to draw each character in the specific style of the font.

frame The result of a complete scanning of one image. In motion video, the scene is scanned repeatedly, making a series of frames.

frame animation An animation technique in which a group of predetermined frames are displayed in sequence, possibly repeatedly, to create repetitive motion, such as a person walking.

frame rate In motion video or animation, the rate at which frames are displayed; normally specified as frames per second.

frame-to-frame In video compression, the process of using the information from previous frame(s) to help define the current frame.

generation In electronic recording, one record and replay process. In video production and postproduction, many generations may be required, causing concern for accumulated distortions because of the repeated recording and replay steps.

header *See* file header.

high-level language A computer language that simplifies the programming process by providing commands that generate multiple computer instructions when the language is compiled or interpreted.

hypermedia A multimedia application that lets the user point to objects, images, video, or text to navigate the application.

image processing Techniques which manipulate the pixel values of an image for some particular purpose. Examples are: brightness or contrast correction, color correction, or changing size (scaling).

integrated circuit (IC) An electronic component based on a semiconductor chip, usually made of silicon. Each IC can contain many individual circuits (sometimes millions) that are connected to perform a useful task or process.

interactivity The ability of a user to control the presentation by a multimedia system, not only for material selection, but for the way in which material is presented.

interface In computer software, a connection between two entities; for example, an Application Programming Interface (API) is the software connection between an application program and the system software of a PC. Similarly, a *user interface* is the way that a user sees, hears, and controls a computer.

interlace In scanning a video image or scene, the technique of using more than one vertical scan to reproduce a complete image. In television, 2:1 interlace is used, giving two vertical scans (fields) per frame; one field scans odd lines, and one field scans the even lines of the frame. Interlace is not desirable for computer screens because it can cause flickering of objects that have single-pixel horizontal lines in them.

interpreter A form of computer program that reads a high-level language and converts it to computer instructions that are immediately executed.

interprocess communication In a multitasking operating system, any means of passing data or commands between concurrently running applications.

Joint Photographic Expert Group (JPEG) A working party of the ISO IEC Joint Technical Committee 1, who developed standards for compression of still images, called the JPEG standard.

JPEG *See* Joint Photographic Expert Group.

justified In displaying text, the process of adjusting the spacing between words and characters in each line of text so that the left and right sides of all the lines in a paragraph align.

kernel A software module that contains one or more fundamental processes, such as the core of an operating system.

level In video or audio, the signal amplitude.

lossless In data compression, when the result of compression followed by decompression is exactly the same as the original.

lossy In data compression, when the result of compression followed by decompression is different from the original. A good lossy compression system will have its difference or errors in places where they will be difficult for the user to detect.

luminance In an image, refers to the brightness values of all the points in the image. A luminance-only reproduction is a black-and-white representation of the image.

magenta The color obtained by mixing equal intensities of red and blue light. It is also the correct name for the subtractive primary color usually called red.

mastering In optical recording, such as CD-ROM, the original optical recording process, prior to replication.

MCI *See* Media Control Interface.

Media Control Interface (MCI) In multimedia computers, a device-independent standard for communicating control information between applications and the system.

medium A means of communication or data storage.

metafile A special form of data file that contains a mixture of drawing commands and/or bitmap data, from which an appropriate driver can construct an image.

MIDI *See* Musical Instrument Digital Interface.

miking In audio recording, the process of selecting and placing microphones for optimum sound pickup.

MIPS Million Instructions Per Second.

mixer In audio postproduction, a device that allows several signals to be controllably combined into one output.

monospaced In text display, when all the characters of a font are the same width and are displayed that way.

Moore's law In the semiconductor industry, a rule of thumb that says the average number of devices that can be manufactured on one IC chip will double every two years.

Motion Picture coding Expert Group (MPEG) A working party of the ISO IEC Joint Technical Committee 1, working on algorithm standardization for compression of motion video for use in many industries.

motion video Video that displays real motion. It is accomplished by displaying a sequence of images (frames) rapidly enough so that the eye sees the image as a continuously moving picture, which usually means 24 to 30 frames per second.

MPC *See* Multimedia Personal Computer.

MPEG *See* Motion Picture coding Expert Group.

multimedia In computers, the presentation of information or training by using audio, motion video, realistic still images, and computer metaphors.

Multimedia Personal Computer (MPC) A PC that contains equipment for multimedia, such as audio, video, and CD-ROM hardware.

multitasking In a computer, a technique that allows several processes to appear to run simultaneously even though the computer has only one CPU. Multitasking is accomplished by sequentially switching the CPU between the tasks, usually many times per second.

Musical Instrument Digital Interface (MIDI) A serial digital bus standard for interfacing of digital musical instruments. MIDI is widely used in the music industry.

National Television Systems Committee (NTSC) The standardizing body that in 1953 created the color television standards for the United States. This system is called the NTSC color television system.

navigation In multimedia applications, the process whereby the user moves from one part of the application to another. Navigation is one of the objectives of the application's user interface.

nesting In computer programs, the act of performing one process "inside" of a similar process. For example, a program can call a second program; the second program is said to be nested inside the first program.

NTSC *See* National Television Systems Committee.

off-screen In multimedia computers, refers to areas of video memory that can be accessed by the CPU but are not currently being displayed on the screen.

operating system In a personal computer, the core program that provides applications with access to all of the hardware resources of the system. Typical operating systems are MS-DOS and OS/2.

oscilloscope An instrument that displays an electrical signal or waveform on a cathode-ray tube. See *waveform monitor*.

overscanned In a television receiver, the practice of scanning a little beyond the edges of the screen so that the edges of the raster are not visible.

PAL *See* Phase Alternation Line.

palette When used with color lookup tables, the range of colors from which the table colors can be selected. The number of colors in the palette is equal to 2 raised to the number of bits in a CLUT entry power.

pan In stereo audio, the process of specifying where a sound is located in the stereo field. In video, the process of moving the camera in a horizontal plane.

personal computer (PC) A software-controlled system containing general-purpose computer functions and intended for use by one user.

Phase Alternation Line (PAL) The key feature of the color television system developed in West Germany and used by many other countries in Europe. This system is called the PAL system.

pixel A single point of an image, having a single pixel value.

pixel value A number or series of numbers that represents the color and luminance of a single pixel; also color value.

platform In computers, the base architecture of a computer system. Typical computer platforms are PC AT or Macintosh.

PLV *See* Presentation-Level Video.

Point of Sale (POS) The location at which something is being sold. A POS application performs selling or information delivery in a store.

POS *See* Point of Sale.

postproduction In video or audio, the process of merging original video and audio from tape or film into a finished program. Postproduction includes editing, special effects, dubbing, titling, and many other video and audio techniques.

premastering In CD-ROM distribution, the process of preparing the data to be placed on the CD-ROM so that it optimally fits the CD-ROM format and limitations.

Presentation-Level Video (PLV) In DVI Technology, the highest-quality video compression process. PLV requires the use of a large computer for compression.

primary color In a tri-stimulus color video system, one of the three colors mixed to produce an image. In additive color systems, the primary colors are red, green, and blue. In subtractive color systems, the primaries are cyan, magenta, and yellow.

primitives In computer graphics, a set of simple functions for drawing on the screen. Typical primitives are rectangle, line, ellipse, polygon, etc.

production In video, refers to the process of creating programs. In more specific usage, production is the process of getting original video onto tape or film and ready for postproduction.

productivity In computer applications, refers to applications that assist the user in doing his or her job. Typical productivity applications are word processing, spreadsheets, planning, etc.

proportionally spaced In text display, the use of a font that has different widths for different characters, and displaying it that way. For example, an "i" is much narrower than a "w."

quantizing The process of converting an analog value into a digital value having a limited number of bits. This results in reduction of the continuous-level scale of an analog signal to a discrete number of quantizing levels represented by 2^n, where n is the number of bits.

RAM *See* Random Access Memory.

random access In digital memory or mass storage, the ability to access to any point or address without any limitation.

Random Access Memory (RAM) Usually refers to the main memory of a computer, which is solid state read/write memory.

real images Images captured from nature, usually by photography, cinematography, or television camera; also realistic images.

Real-Time Video (RTV) In DVI technology, the video compression/decompression technique that operates in real time using the DVI system itself. It provides less picture quality than PLV, but it is satisfactory for many applications.

red, green, blue RGB refers to the additive primary colors that are used in computer displays. All colors on a display are made by adding different amounts of the three primary colors according to the values specified by each pixel in the image. This is different from the *subtractive color system* used in color printing, where colored dyes are placed on white paper to control the amount of reflected light.

reference frame In DVI compressed motion video, a frame that is created without reference to any previous frame. Video playback can be started from any reference frame.

registration In video cameras or video displays, the process of causing the three color images to coincide exactly in space.

rendering In computer graphics, the process of creating an image or screen from mathematical or computer-language descriptions.

resolution The ability of an image-reproducing system to reproduce fine detail. In television, resolution is specified in lines per picture height, which is the total count of black and white lines that can be reproduced in a distance equal to the picture height.

retrieval engine A system embodying software or hardware or both for accessing indexed data from a large mass store such as a CD-ROM.

reverberation In audio, a sound which persists after an original sound has stopped, because of repeated reflections around the room.

RGB *See* red, green, blue.

riding In audio or video production, the process of constantly adjusting the level. It is not normally a recommended thing to do.

RTV *See* Real-Time Video.

sampling The process of reading the value of a signal at evenly spaced points in time.

sampling rate The clock frequency for sampling, or the number of samples per second.

sans serif A text font that does not have *serifs*.

saturation The depth of color intensity. Zero saturation is white (no color), and maximum saturation is the deepest or most intense color possible.

scaling A process for changing the size of an image.

scanner A device that performs scanning. See *color scanner*.

SCSI *See* Small Computer System Interface.

SECAM *See* Sequential Coleur Avec Memoire.

sequencer In MIDI audio systems, the computer program or hardware which collects, stores, edits, and replays a series of MIDI commands.

Sequential Coleur Avec Memoire (SECAM) French for sequential color with memory, which is the color television system developed in France and used in certain other countries.

serif In a text font, the little lines which extend at the ends of each stroke of the text characters. This paragraph is an example.

Small Computer System Interface (SCSI) An interface bus for connecting devices to a PC. Most often used to interface CD-ROM or hard disk drives.

SMPTE time code A standard for a signal recorded on video tape to uniquely identify each frame of the video signal. It is used for control of editing operations. (SMPTE stands for Society of Motion Picture and Television Engineers.)

storyboard A method of planning the content of a presentation by drawing sketches of each screen with notes about what happens in that scene.

stroke font *See* vector font.

subsampling In video compression, the process of reducing the pixel count for the color components of an image, done by discarding samples in a regular pattern.

subtractive color system Color reproduction by mixing appropriate amounts of color paints or dyes on white paper, used for color painting and printing. The color print primaries are red, blue, and yellow. Note that red as used in printing is technically a magenta color, and blue is technically a cyan color.

system bus In a computer system, the parallel data and address path connecting the CPU, memory, mass storage, and I/O devices.

Tagged Image File Format (TIFF) An image file format.

TIFF *See* Tagged Image File Format.

time code In motion video or audio, a digital code that provides time identification for each frame. The most common time code is the *SMPTE time code*.

touch screen A display monitor whose screen is sensitive to the user's touch. Touch screens are often used in kiosk applications.

transition effects Special effects that occur at the transition between different video camera shots.

treatment A narrative writeup, usually non-technical, which describes a proposed creative work such as a software application or an audio/video production segment.

tri-stimulus In color reproduction, the method that uses three primary colors or three color signals for image transmission and reproduction.

user interface The means by which a user communicates with a computer. It includes not only the devices used (mouse, keyboard, touch), but also the objects on the screen and the sounds made by the computer in response to the user.

vector font A font for text characters in which the character description is in the form of lines or equations that define the character outline. Also called stroke font or outline font. Vector fonts have the advantage that they can be scaled to any size at the time of display. Their disadvantage is that they take a lot of processing power at the time of display.

VGA *See* Video Graphics Array.

video An electronic representation of a scene, both natural (real) or computer-generated.

video compression *See* compression.

Video Graphics Array (VGA) This is the standard display type for most PCs. VGA provides many optional formats, but the most common one is 640 × 480 pixels with 16 colors.

video level The amplitude of a video signal.

viewing ratio In video displays, the ratio between the viewer's distance from the screen and the height of the display screen.

waveform monitor In television, a special *oscilloscope* that displays TV waveforms.

WORM *See* Write-Once, Read Many.

Write-Once, Read Many (WORM) An optical mass storage device that can write new data into storage but cannot change data already stored.

Bibliography

BOOKS

The following list of books is not meant to be an exhaustive bibliography of multimedia computing and related subjects. It is the list of books that was consulted in writing this book. A few remarks about some of them are below.

The Benson handbooks are in-depth technical compendia for the broadcasting and sound recording industries. They should answer almost any technical question you have.

The Bove, Pierce, and Sharp books describe three different software packages for authoring and animation.

The Kieran and the White references are books about electronic and print publishing. However, they contain valuable information that applies to multimedia screens as well.

Benson, K. Blair (ed.), *Audio Engineering Handbook.* New York: McGraw-Hill, 1988.

——— (ed.), *Television Engineering Handbook.* New York: McGraw-Hill, 1986.

Benson, K. Blair, and Fink, Donald G., *HDTV Advanced Television for the 1990s.* New York: McGraw-Hill, 1991.

Bove, Tony, and Rhodes, Cheryl, *Using Macromind Director.* Carmel, IN: Que Corporation, 1990.

Brown and Cunningham, *Programming the User Interface.* New York: Wiley, 1989.

Bunzel, Mark J., and Morris, Sandra K., *Multimedia Applications Development.* New York: McGraw-Hill, 1992.

Floyd, Steve, *The IBM Multimedia Handbook.* New York: Brady Publishing, 1991.

IBM Corporation, *Common User Access: Advanced Interface Design Guide*, Publication SC26-4582. Boca Raton, FL: IBM, 1989.

Kieran, Michael, *Desktop Publishing in Color.* New York: Bantam Books, 1991.

Laurel, Brenda, *The Art of Human-Computer Interface Design*. Reading, MA: Addison-Wesley, 1990.

Luther, Arch C., *Digital Video in the PC Environment*. Second Edition. New York: McGraw-Hill, 1991.

Microsoft Corporation, *Microsoft Windows Multimedia Authoring and Tools Guide*. Redmond, WA: Microsoft Press, 1991.

―――, *Microsoft Windows Multimedia Programmer's Workbook*. Redmond, WA: Microsoft Press, 1991.

Philips International, Inc., *Compact Disc Interactive: A Designer's Overview*. New York: McGraw-Hill, 1988.

Pierce, Joseph R., *ToolBook Companion*. Redmond, WA: Microsoft Press, 1990.

Sharp, Craig, *Using Animator*. Carmel, IN: Que Corporation, 1990.

Sherman, Chris, *The CD-ROM Handbook*. New York: McGraw-Hill, 1988.

White, Jan V., *Graphic Design for the Electronic Age*. New York: Xerox Press, 1988.

PERIODICALS

The following is a sampling of periodicals that contain information about multimedia computing or related skills. All the general computing magazines are giving space to multimedia, and there are many more than are listed here. *New Media* is a recently started magazine which is specifically about multimedia. *Keyboard* and *R*E*P* are publications about the music industry and the audio recording industry, respectively.

AV Video. Published by Knowledge Industry Publications, 701 Westchester Ave., White Plains, NY 10604.

Byte. Published monthly by McGraw-Hill, Inc., One Phoenix Mill La., Peterborough, NH 03458.

Instruction Delivery Systems. 50 Culpeper St., Warrenton, VA 22186.

Keyboard. Published monthly by Miller Freeman Publications, 600 Harrison St., San Francisco, CA 94107.

New Media. Published monthly by HyperMedia Communications, Inc., 901 Mariner's Island Blvd., Suite 365, San Mateo, CA 94404.

PC World. Published monthly by PC World Communications, Inc., 501 Second St. #600, San Francisco, CA 94107.

*R*E*P: Recording*Engineer*Producer*. Published monthly by Intertec Publishing Corporation, 9221 Quivira, Overland Park, KS 66215.

Videography. Published by P.S.N. Publications, 2 Park Ave., Suite 1820, New York, NY 10016.

Windows Magazine. Published monthly by CMP Publications, Inc., 600 Community Dr., Manhasset, NY 11030.

Index

ActionMedia II, 26
ADC, 21
ADR, 166
analog, 2
analog to digital conversion
   See ADC
animation, 95, 205
   cel, 208
   frame, 95, 205
   graphics, 209
   image transitions, 211
   panorama, 206
antialiasing, 131
API, 32
application programming interface
   See API
applications
   distribution, 255
   planning, 214
   programs, 31
artificial intelligence, 268
assets, 147
   animation, 154
   audio, 148
   data, 156
   graphics, 155
   image, 152
   motion video, 150
   text, 155
attract mode, 50
audio, 163
   ambience, 165
   capture, 149, 175
   coprocessor, 27
   editing technique, 172
   effects, 165
   effects processing, 168
   equipment, 163
   microphone technique, 170
   mixing technique, 173
   postproduction, 165
   production, 163
   recording setup, 167
   reverberation, 171
   sampling, 21
   sampling rate, 21
   setting levels, 169, 177
AUI, 83
   alert object, 97
   animation object, 95
   audio object, 91
   capture tools, 103
   condition object, 100
   coordinates, 90
   data object, 102
   draw object, 96
   file object, 103
   image object, 93
   input object, 98
   message object, 101
   object palette, 88
   objects, 87, 89
   on-line help, 85
   opening a project, 85
   Organizer, 103
   project, 84
   script window, 87
   starting up, 84
   subscript, 99
   transition object, 94
   variable object, 100
   video object, 92
   window object, 90
authoring, 4, 75
   MEDIAscript, 38
   software, 31
authoring interface
   See AUI
authoring systems, 290
   choosing, 80

Autodesk Animator, 155
automatic dialog replacement
 See ADR
AVS file format, 150

bitmap image, 152
bits per pixel
 See bpp
bpp, 19
branching, 78
building blocks, 57
bus architecture, 275
business presentations, 140

cache controller, 277
caches, 276
Camcorder application
 authoring approach, 241
 data list, 239, 242
 estimate, 244
 flowchart, 240
 presentation design, 243
 screen design, 242
 style, 142
 style design, 241
 treatment, 239
 user interface, 241
 users, 239
camcorders, 285
capture
 audio, 175
 still images, 183
 video, 200
CBT, 7
CCD, 184, 284
CD, 15
 audio, 15
 data rate, 15
 mastering process, 23
CD-ROM, 22, 194, 256, 279
 distribution, 256
CD-WORM drive, 23, 257
cel, 208
charge-coupled device
 See CCD

color
 difference, 180
 lookup table, 20
 mixing dialog, 124
 palette, 20
 scanner, 30
 scanners, 191
Common User Access
 See CUA
communication, 1
Compact Disc
 See CD
compiling, 76
compression
 frame-to-frame, 195
 image, 183
the computer look, 121
computer-based training
 See CBT
conditions, 79
context sensitive help, 85
contouring, 20
control panels, 136
controlling activity, 59
coprocessor
 audio, 27
 video, 26
CPU, 17
 cache, 277
 clock doubler, 18, 275
 clock frequency, 17
CUA, 108
cueing, 173

DAT, 258
data usage, 158
data-driven engine, 60, 220
dB, 169
DDE, 34-35, 82
decibels
 See dB
delta frame, 150
desktop publishing
 See DTP
device-independent, 82

digital, 2
digital audio boards, 282
Digital Audio Tape
 See DAT
digital tape drives, 257
digitizing, 21, 149
 audio, 175
disk cache, 276
distribution, 255
dithered colors, 124
draw programs, 152
drivers, 32
DTP, 280
DVI Technology, 26
 9 bpp format, 180
 audio algorithms, 175
 AVS files, 150
 boards, 283
 graphics, 191
 image files, 181
 images, 179
 performance, 28
 PLV, 195
 text, 191
 video compression, 27
Dynamic Data Exchange
 See DDE

edit decision list, 203
EISA bus, 276
engine programs
 data-driven, 60
Enhanced System Drive Interface
 See ESDI
ESDI, 278
executable files, 76

file
 headers, 147
 image formats, 153
Foley studio, 166
fonts, 97
 bitmap, 130
 monospaced, 131
 proportionally spaced, 131
 vector, 130
frame-to-frame compression, 195

graphics, 191
graphics assets, 155

hardware, 25
HDTV, 271
hierarchical menus, 63, 113
high color, 280
high definition television
 See HDTV
high level languages, 76
hypermedia, 11, 64, 268
hypertext, 11

IDE, 278
image file formats
 BMP, 153
 CGM, 153
 EPS, 153
 HPGL, 153
 MET, 153
 PCX, 153
 PICT, 153
 TGA, 153
 TIFF, 153
images
 capture, 184
 compression, 183
 file format conversion, 182
 processing, 190
 scanners, 286
Industry Standard Architecture bus
 See ISA bus
information delivery, 49
information retrieval, 64
Integrated Drive Electronics
 See IDE
interactive kiosk, 50
interactivity, 3

interpreter, 77
interprocess communication, 11, 34-35
ISA bus, 275

Joint Photographic Expert Group
    See JPEG
JPEG, 183, 264

kiosk, 50, 121

list box, 248
logos, 135
looping, 79
Lumena, 190
luminance, 180

Macromind Director, 154
magnetic drives
    seek time, 23
mass storage, 21, 277
    CD-ROM, 22
    CD-WORM drive, 23
    data transfer rate, 278
    WORM drive, 22
MCI, 35, 263
Media Control Interface, 263
    See MCI
MEDIAscript
    animation, 155
    AUI, 38
    DOS edition, 38
    MMS, 38
    Organizer, 230
    OS/2 desktop edition, 38
    OS/2 Professional Edition, 39
    project, 84
    Server, 38
medium, 1, 24
memory-mapping, 19
menus
    hierarchical, 63, 113

metafile, 152
Micro Channel bus, 276
microprocessor, 16
MIDI, 21, 148
MMS, 38, 81
Moore's law, 13, 24, 28, 264, 270
Motion Picture Expert Group
    See MPEG
motion video, 15, 30, 193
MPEG, 264
MS-DOS, 32
MSCDEX, 34
multimedia
    architectures, 57
    assets, 83, 147
    authoring, 30
    authoring systems, 37
    authoring workstation, 39
    building blocks, 57
    content, 53
    data demands, 14
    definition, 2
    distribution, 36
    for business presentations, 5
    for education, 6
    for entertainment, 52
    for information delivery, 8, 49
    for merchandising, 10
    for productivity applications, 10
    for sales, 10
    for selling, 44
    for teaching, 47
    for training, 6
    hardware, 16
    objectives, 41
    PC, 25
    presentations, 67
    skills, 4
    software, 30
    special hardware, 25
    typical projects, 42
    uses, 5

music synthesizers, 21
musical instrument digital interface
   See MIDI

nesting, 80
networks, 258
9 bpp, 180
NTSC, 29, 184

operating systems, 31
   kernel, 32
   multitasking, 33
   single-user, 32
optical drives, 23
   seek time, 23
Organizer, 230
OS/2, 32
outline fonts
   See fonts: vector
over-scanning, 120

paint programs, 152, 191
PAL, 29
pan controls, 167
panorama, 206
PC
   audio system, 21
   coprocessor, 24
   CPU, 16-17
   display adaptor, 17
   mass storage, 21
   RAM, 18
   system bus, 16
   video display, 19
pen-based computing, 267
Pets application
   authoring approach, 220
   data list, 217
   estimate, 226
   flowchart, 218-219
   main script, 227
   presentation design, 225
   screen design, 223
   species script, 233
   style design, 219
   treatment, 216

user interface, 220
users, 216
pixels, 15, 19
planes, 27
planning of applications, 214
point-of-sale
   See POS
points, 132
POS, 10, 44
postproduction, 165
   digital, 202
premastering, 24, 257
presentation media
   characteristics of, 6
presentations, 67
   canned, 68
   end-user interactive, 69
   linear, 59
   live speaker support, 68
   steps, 70
presenting activity, 58
Production Level Video
   See PLV

QuickTime, 36

RAM, 18
random access, 151
random access memory
   See RAM
Real time video
   See RTV
reference frame, 150
registration, 185
rendering, 130
resolution, 15, 184
RGB, 185, 284
RTV, 195, 200

sales
   using multimedia, 44
sans serif, 132
scanners, 286
screens
   background, 123
   borders, 127

design, 121
 elements, 123
 footers, 129
 headers, 128
 layout, 139
script
 sample, 104
SCSI, 255, 278
serif, 132
server, 34
 MMS, 38
simulation applications, 65
16 bpp, 15, 20
Small Computer Systems Interface
 See SCSI
software
 applications, 31
 authoring, 31
 operating systems, 31
Soldering application, 249
 authoring approach, 253
 data list, 251
 estimate, 254
 flowchart, 251
 style, 252
 treatment, 250
 user interface, 253
 users, 250
speech I/O, 267
standards, 263
still images, 30, 179
storyboard, 72
stream editing, 202
stroke fonts
 See fonts: vector
style, 119
 aural, 139
 business presentation, 140
 ingredients, 119
 selling application, 142
 text, 133
 training application, 144

teaching, 47
television broadcasting, 270

television industry, 268
the television look, 120
text, 129, 191
 assets, 155
 bold, 133
 italic, 133
 outline, 134
 shadow, 134
 styles, 133
 underline, 134
touch screen, 112
true color, 280

user task analysis, 109

variables, 78
vaved, 202
vertical roll effect, 207
VGA, 15, 19, 90, 132
video
 cameras, 184, 284
 compression, 14, 194
 postproduction, 196
 production, 196
 recording, 285
 shooting, 199
video display, 19
 adaptor, 20
 number of colors, 19
viewing ratio, 112
vimcvt, 182

windowing environments, 115
Windows, 34
 multimedia extensions, 35
word-wrapping, 134
WORM drive, 22, 36
Write Once Read Many drive
 See WORM drive

XGA, 19, 29, 90

YUV, 180